Metric Conversion Table

Inches (in.)	1/64	1/32	1/25	1/16	1/8	1/4	3/8	2/5	1/2	5/8	3/4	7/8	1	2	3	4	5	6	7	8	9	10	11	12	36	39.4
Feet (ft.)																								1	3	3¼†
Yards (yd.)																									1	1½†
Millimeters* (mm.)	0.40	0.79	1	1.59	3.18	6.35	9.53	10	12.7	15.9	19.1	22.2	25.4	50.8	76.2	101.6	127	152	178	203	229	254	279	305	914	1,000
Centimeters* (cm.)							0.95	1	1.27	1.59	1.91	2.22	2.54	5.08	7.62	10.16	12.7	15.2	17.8	20.3	22.9	25.4	27.9	30.5	91.4	100
Meters* (m.)																								.30	.91	1.00

To find the metric equivalent of quantities not in this table, add together the appropriate entries. For example, to convert 2⅝ inches to centimeters, add the figure given for the centimeter equivalent of 2 inches, 5.08, and the equivalent of ⅝ inch, 1.59, to obtain 6.67 centimeters.

* Metric values are rounded off.
† Approximate fractions.

Conversion factors

To change:	Into:	Multiply by:
Inches	Millimeters	25.4
Inches	Centimeters	2.54
Feet	Meters	0.305
Yards	Meters	0.914
Miles	Kilometers	1.609
Square inches	Square centimeters	6.45
Square feet	Square meters	0.093
Square yards	Square meters	0.836
Cubic inches	Cubic centimeters	16.4
Cubic feet	Cubic meters	0.0283
Cubic yards	Cubic meters	0.765
Pints (U.S.)	Liters	0.473 (Imp. 0.568)
Quarts (U.S.)	Liters	0.946 (Imp. 1.136)
Gallons (U.S.)	Liters	3.785 (Imp. 4.546)
Ounces	Grams	28.4
Pounds	Kilograms	0.454
Tons	Metric tons	0.907

To change:	Into:	Multiply by:
Millimeters	Inches	0.039
Centimeters	Inches	0.394
Meters	Feet	3.28
Meters	Yards	1.09
Kilometers	Miles	0.621
Square centimeters	Square inches	0.155
Square meters	Square feet	10.8
Square meters	Square yards	1.2
Cubic centimeters	Cubic inches	0.061
Cubic meters	Cubic feet	35.3
Cubic meters	Cubic yards	1.31
Liters	Pints (U.S.)	2.114 (Imp. 1.76)
Liters	Quarts (U.S.)	1.057 (Imp. 0.88)
Liters	Gallons (U.S.)	0.264 (Imp. 0.22)
Grams	Ounces	0.035
Kilograms	Pounds	2.2
Metric tons	Tons	1.1

THE FAMILY Handyman®

EASY REPAIR

THE FAMILY Handyman®
EASY REPAIR

OVER 100 SIMPLE SOLUTIONS TO THE MOST COMMON HOUSEHOLD PROBLEMS

THE READER'S DIGEST ASSOCIATION, INC.
Pleasantville, New York/Montreal

Produced by Redefinition, Inc.

The credits that appear on page 192 are hereby made a part of this copyright page.

Library of Congress Cataloging in Publication Data

The Family handyman easy repair.
         p.   cm.
    Includes index.
    ISBN 0-89577-624-3
    1. Dwellings—Maintenance and repair—Amateurs' manuals.
  2. Household appliances—Maintenance and repair—Amateurs' manuals.
  I. Reader's Digest Association.   II.   Family handyman.   III.   Title:
Easy repair.
TH4817.3.F337   1994
643'.7—dc20   94-14896

Printed in the United States of America
Third Printing, April 1997

Foreword

Although few of us would willingly give up home ownership, there are times when we're all tempted — when the house seems to have a mind of its own and it's trying to drive you crazy!

Naturally, this usually happens at the most inconvenient times, when the toilets clog just before guests arrive, or the gutters spring a leak just as the spring rains begin to fall. I'm sure similar things have happened to you.

To make nightmares like these even worse, when you call the pros they usually want big bucks to make the repair — even if the fix takes only a few minutes. The solution is to learn how to make those repairs yourself. You don't have to be an expert carpenter, plumber, or electrician to do them — or even particularly mechanically minded — when you have the basic tools and know-how.

FAMILY HANDYMAN EASY REPAIR provides that know-how. We'll walk you through dozens of repairs step by step, explaining everything as we go, so that even if your do-it-yourself license reads "rank beginner" you'll still succeed. The payback: You'll feel great about your house and save the cost of this book many times over.

EASY REPAIR is based on articles from *THE FAMILY HANDYMAN*, the leading magazine for do-it-yourself home owners. Our goal at the magazine is to give you how-to information you can really use in a style that's easy to follow. We do that by basing our articles on real repairs, accomplished by master electricians and plumbers, journeymen carpenters, and nationally recognized safety experts. We also believe that nothing teaches better than a photo or an illustration and, like the magazine, FAMILY HANDYMAN EASY REPAIR is loaded with clear, colorful how-to pictures.

The topics we've chosen reflect years of listening to our readers' suggestions, the problems they face, and the solutions that work for them. We hope the solutions you find here will work for you, too.

Ken Collier, Senior Editor
The Family Handyman

Easy Repair

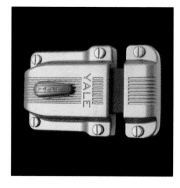

Wiring and Electricity

Roof and Eaves

Outdoor Fixes

Furniture

Home Safety

Introduction

This book could easily have been entitled *The Greatest Hits of Home Repair* because it tells you how to fix the problems that every householder bangs up against sooner or later: clogged plumbing, sticky doors and windows, drippy faucets — the inescapable dues we pay for owning a house. And as you know, it can cost a small fortune to have these things repaired by a professional.

FAMILY HANDYMAN EASY REPAIR shows you how to fix these problems yourself. None of the tasks here is a big repair job that requires special skill, fancy tools, or days of work. These are the small, nagging problems that crop up all the time, that anyone can fix — and we mean anyone.

Here, you'll find that each repair features step-by-step instructions that use none of that maddening hardware store jargon; even a beginner can understand them. You'll also find a useful list of the tools needed for each job. With rare exceptions, these won't be expensive tools, and they won't be difficult to use. In fact, most homeowners already have these tools somewhere around the house. And take look at the *Work Better, Work Safer* sections with their handy hints for getting the most out of the tools you own no matter how few or simple.

The purpose is to save you time, as well as money. Doing-it-yourself can be personally and financially rewarding, but it can also be frustrating. This book is intended to let you finish your fixing quickly and correctly — giving you time to spend some of the money you save.

These easy repairs are safe, even for the novice. Just remember to wear safety glasses whenever you're hammering or using a power tool, use extra care if you climb on the roof or use a ladder, and use an electrical tester before tackling anything involving electricity; that tool can be a one-dollar lifesaver.

If you're still not convinced that doing it yourself is the best way to make home repairs, think about this: You have nothing to lose. But chances are, with care and this book, you'll succeed.

Floors, Walls, and Ceilings

Repairing Wallpaper   12   **Patching Drywall**   13

Torn, blistered, or loose wall-paper doesn't doom you to a complete makeover. These quick and easy touch-ups may conceal the problem until you're ready to redecorate.

It can happen in any home: a doorknob, furniture movers, or an exuberant teenager breaks a hole in the drywall. But by following these simple steps, you can make your wall as good as new.

    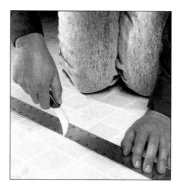

Refurbishing Plaster   **14**

The bad news is that most plaster will eventually crack. The good news: modern materials make long-lasting repairs easy.

Reviving Carpet   **18**

Spills, feet, and furniture test the best carpet. But easy maintenance will keep your carpets looking good, and these simple repairs can save expensive replacement when real damage is done.

Silencing Squeaky Floors 20

Your floor's squeaks and creaks don't need to make you groan. With a few tools, you can reinforce or tighten up the floor to limit its movement and silence your tread.

Repairing Rotted Floors   **22**

You'll need to cure the conditions that cause rot, then replace any weakened wood. This is household surgery, but most repairs can be done without professional help.

Work Better, Work Safer 24

Here is a grab-bag of tips and techniques that you can use to work smart around your home.

Repairing Wallpaper

Make blisters, tears, and open seams disappear.

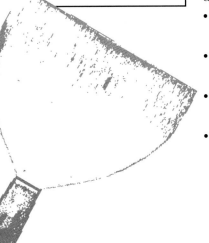

Torn, blistered, or loose areas of wallpaper got you singing the blues? Do these two quick and easy touch-ups — regluing a seam between strips and patching a torn or blistered section — and give yourself a lift.

Use ordinary premixed wallpaper paste, available at any well-stocked home center, and follow these procedures to get good adhesion:

- Apply the paste generously to the back of the paper.
- Press the paper in place to transfer paste to the wall surface.
- Peel the paper off again and wait until the paste gets slightly tacky.
- Press the wallpaper in place and gently sponge it flat.

PATCHING A DAMAGED SPOT

STEP 1 Cut a patch out of a piece of matching wallpaper at least an inch larger in each direction than the damaged area. Center it over the damaged spot, matching the wallpaper pattern on the two pieces.

STEP 2 Tape the patch in place lightly with masking tape. Cut a rectangle out of the old wallpaper beyond the damaged edges, cutting through both layers of wallpaper, old and new. Glue the patch in place.

REGLUING A LOOSE SEAM

STEP 1 Cut diagonally in one or more places with a sharp utility knife so you can peel the edges of the wallpaper back. For blisters, cut an "X" into the blister to remove the air trapped inside.

STEP 2 Apply paste to the back of the wallpaper. Push the edges of the wallpaper back into place, then peel it back again; repeat until tacky. Smooth and remove excess paste with a sponge.

Patching Drywall

You don't have to live with that hole!

WHAT YOU NEED

Utility knife or drywall saw

Hand saw

1x2 lumber

Drywall screws

Screwdriver

Drywall patch

Self-sticking fiberglass drywall tape

Joint compound

Fine-grit sandpaper

Taping knife

Repairing damaged drywall is the ultimate in low-tech house repairs. You can even substitute a utility knife for the drywall saw and a standard Phillips screwdriver for the cordless driver-drill if your tool assortment is limited.

If you encounter a 2x4 stud close to the edge of the hole in the drywall, cut the damaged drywall back to the center of the stud or secure the patch with backer boards (shown here).

Holes smaller than 2 inches across can be repaired by placing fiberglass tape across the opening, then applying two or three coats of joint compound. For damaged areas larger than 8 inches, cut the drywall back to the middle of the studs on each side of the hole, then cut and secure a patch directly to the studs.

If the hole was caused by a door, prevent future damage by installing a spring bumper on the baseboard.

REPAIRING A HOLE

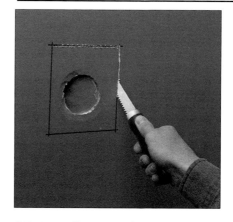

STEP 1 Cut out and remove the damaged section of drywall using a drywall saw or utility knife.

STEP 2 Slip 1x2 backer boards into the hole and secure them with 1¼-inch drywall screws.

STEP 3 Tip the patch into place, then secure it with drywall screws. Use the damaged piece of drywall as a pattern for this patch.

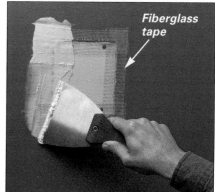

Fiberglass tape

STEP 4 Cover the seams with self-sticking fiberglass tape, then spread a thin coat of joint compound and let it dry partially. Sand and apply two more broader coats; then sand until smooth.

Refurbishing Plaster

Fix old-fashioned walls with new-fangled materials.

WHAT YOU NEED

- Premixed drywall joint compound
- Adhesive fiberglass joint tape
- 3-inch-wide putty knife
- 8-inch-wide drywall taping knife
- Utility or linoleum knife
- Plaster of Paris
- Wire mesh designed for plaster
- Bonding agent

Most plaster repairs are easy, even for first-time do-it-yourselfers. That's because plaster is a robust material that rarely needs major reconstruction, so its problems are usually minor — an occasional crack or localized softening caused by water leaks.

Consider canvassing walls that have become a mass of hairline cracks, previous patch jobs, and rough texture. It's a way of creating a clean slate for painting or wallpapering.

Plaster is messy and irritating, so use safety glasses, gloves, clothing that covers your arms and legs, and a NIOSH-approved dust mask. The fine dust is also extremely abrasive; cover floors and other surfaces, and enclose the work area to keep dust from spreading throughout your house. Also, turn off electrical circuits that run through the walls you are repairing.

FIXING CRACKS

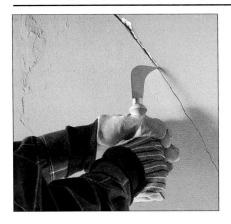

STEP 1 Hairline cracks occur in the top coat of plaster. Wider cracks that paint will not bridge should be patched. Widen and undercut the edges of the crack with a utility or linoleum knife.

STEP 2 Vacuum out the dust and chips and fill the crack flush to the surface with drywall joint compound, using a 3-inch-wide putty knife. Let the joint compound cure overnight.

STEP 3 Apply fiberglass tape, pressing firmly over the crack. The tape is self-adhesive and remains flexible to inhibit further cracking.

STEP 4 Spread drywall joint compound over the tape. After it cures, spread on a wider layer and feather out the edges until the patch is flush with the wall. Finish the wall as desired.

STEP 1 Undercut or bevel the edges of the hole so the new plaster is held in place by the old. Then brush bonding agent onto the lath and the edges of the old plaster.

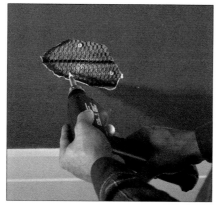

STEP 2 Cut a piece of wire mesh to size and fasten it to the existing wood lath with drywall screws. The wire mesh provides nooks and crannies for the new patch to grip.

STEP 3 Mix only enough plaster of Paris to fill one hole at a time. Fill the space with plaster, then trowel it level. Cover the seams with fiberglass tape.

STEP 4 Apply several layers of drywall joint compound to cover the tape and blend the patch with the wall. Let the compound cure; sand it smooth and flush.

Simple Tools, Simple Materials, and Simple Skills

Plaster repairs are very DIYer-friendly. You use everyday drywall tools and materials, there's no heavy lifting, and a small electric drill is the only power tool you'll need. Best of all, you can't goof up irretrievably. The worst-case scenario is that you'd have to scrape off your afternoon's labor (before it dries!) and start fresh the next day.

Here are the basic tools and supplies you will need:

- Drywall joint compound for patching. Buy premixed compound, labeled for use on joints or for "general use."

- Adhesive fiberglass joint tape for reinforcing cracks and patches.

- A pair of tools to spread and smooth the joint compound: a 3-inch-wide putty knife and an 8-inch-wide drywall taping knife.

Holes larger than 8 inches across will require a few additional supplies: plaster of Paris, a piece of wire mesh designed for plaster, and bonding agent. The bonding agent, which helps the patch cling to old plaster, is normally sold by the gallon, so if you need just a small amount, try a home-made brew of one part white glue and two parts water.

A Few Key Points

- Practice your patching techniques on an inconspicuous wall. It's better to refine your skills in the hall closet than in the living room.

- Always remove plaster down to its soundest layer before starting repairs. Sound plaster makes a solid, snappy sound when thumped with a knuckle; loose plaster makes a hollow, dull sound.

- Use drywall screws rather than nails — hammering just loosens more plaster. For the same reason, remove old plaster by cutting rather than pounding.

- Some tasks are best left to a professional. Ornamental plaster or structural repairs may warrant calling in a carpenter or plasterer — and maybe both.

Finishing Touches

- If necessary, you can texture a final coat of drywall compound to match your existing walls by dabbing it with a sponge or crumpled newspaper while it's still wet. Sand can also be added to your final coat to approximate a rough surface. Just remember: Practice, practice, practice — in the closet or on a scrap piece of drywall.

- Plaster that is water-stained but still sound should be sealed with shellac before painting to prevent the stain from bleeding through.

- Glossy paints and wallpapers reflect lots of light and highlight surface irregularities. Flat paint or matte wallpaper on your newly patched walls will put your handiwork in its best light.

- You can attach a drywall patch to sound wood lath at the edges of the repair, but it's best to cut back to the center of a joist or stud to anchor the patch.

- If more than ⅓ of a wall or ceiling needs major patching, you'll probably get faster, better-looking results by completely covering the old surface with a new layer of drywall. You'll lose the texture and feel of real plaster and you'll probably have to remove, modify, and reinstall your trim. Sometimes, however, you can carefully fit ¼-inch drywall around moldings. With severe cases, you may need to remove all the old plaster and replace it with drywall.

PATCHING LARGE AREAS

Plaster washers

STEP 1 Outline the damaged area using the precut drywall patch (used in step 3) as a template. Secure solid plaster surrounding the damaged area with plaster washers. Drill holes 2 inches apart with a carbide-tipped bit, then chip from hole to hole.

STEP 2 Cut away unsound plaster using a cold chisel and hammer. Safety goggles and a nuisance dust mask are an absolute must for the demolition portion of this project.

STEP 3 Patch with a piece of drywall of the appropriate thickness. Space the screws 6 inches apart at the edges, every 8 inches along a joist or stud.

STEP 4 Skim coat the entire surface after taping the edges with fiberglass joint tape. Work in thin layers (less than 1/16 inch) so the compound dries without cracking.

STEP 1 You can rejuvenate a ratty-looking but structurally sound plaster wall by applying a canvas lining right over firm paint or even well-attached wallpaper. Remove flaking paint or wallpaper with a putty knife and fill any holes larger than ¼ inch across.

STEP 2 Apply the special adhesive paint or coating according to the canvas lining manufacturer's instructions, using either a paint roller or a paintbrush. Work on a small area at a time.

STEP 3 Apply the canvas lining, pressing it into the wet base coat of adhesive. Apply another layer of the coating over the canvas. After drying, the lining can be painted or papered.

Plaster Washers

Plaster washers, used with 1⅝-inch drywall screws, are a great way to pull sound plaster back to wood lath, support good plaster around repairs, and draw plaster tight along a crack. The washers are perforated so joint compound adheres to them.

Anatomy of a Plaster Wall

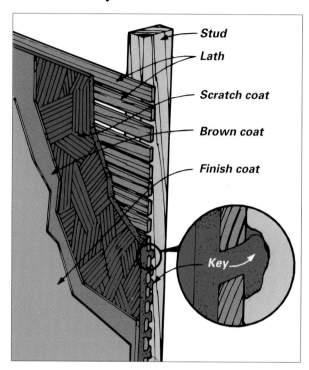

- Stud
- Lath
- Scratch coat
- Brown coat
- Finish coat
- Key

The foundation of older plaster is usually wood lath. As the first layer of wet plaster — the scratch coat — was troweled onto the wall, it was forced between these strips of lath to form the all-important "keys," which hold the plaster to the wall. After the scratch coat cured somewhat, a second, or brown, coat was applied. Finally, a finish coat was applied, which may have been textured or trowelled smooth.

Most plaster ailments are minor. But plaster that was incorrectly formulated or applied causes more serious problems. Large bulges of loose plaster can indicate failure of the scratch coat to bond, or "key," to the underlying lath. A flaky surface can indicate a finish coat that's incompatible with the brown coat underneath it. You can reattach bulges with plaster washers, and flaky finish coats can be scraped and recoated.

Wire mesh and rock lath (a special gypsum-coated material that looks a lot like drywall) have replaced wood lath in recent years, but they require similar repair techniques.

Reviving Carpet

Breathe new life into shabby carpet.

WHAT YOU NEED

Screwdriver

Steam iron

Nails

Awl

Curved upholstery needle

Fishing line

Needle-nosed pliers

Scissors

Double-faced carpet tape

Utility knife

Carpenter's square

Maintenance is the key to prolonging the life of your carpet. Avoid deep, permanent furniture dents in your carpet and pad by moving your furniture — just a couple of inches — every time you vacuum. And vacuum frequently, once a week at least.

Carpet tears occur most often at seams, where two pieces are glued or sewn together. If you're rejoining a seam that was once glued together, you'll find the old glue tough to work a needle through; use needle-nosed pliers to help push the needle.

Serious damage to a carpet may require patching. But don't despair. All it takes to patch a carpet is a carpenter's square, a sharp utility knife, double-faced tape, and about a half hour of your time.

Got a problem with stains? Consult the guide on the facing page.

REMOVING FURNITURE INDENTATIONS

STEP 1 Fluff up the carpet nap where it has been crushed by heavy furniture. Use the blade of a screwdriver or butter knife.

STEP 2 Restore the nap to its original height and texture by steaming with an iron held about ¼ inch above the surface of the carpet.

RESEWING A SEAM OR TEAR

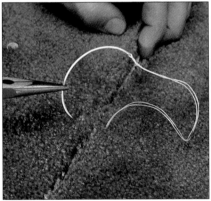

STEP 1 Pull the halves of the carpet back together and hold them in place with nails driven about 6 inches from each edge. Using an awl, bore stitch holes about ½ inch from each edge.

STEP 2 Sew the edges with an upholstery needle and fishing line. The tops of stitches run square to the tear, the undersides diagonally. Brush the carpet to hide the seam.

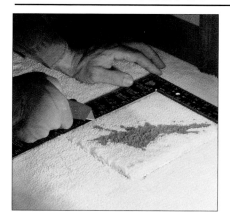

STEP 1 Cut out the damaged section of carpet. Separate the threads of the carpet so you can cut through the backing without cutting off threads along the edge. This will make it easier to blend the patch.

STEP 2 Cut a replacement patch using the damaged piece as a pattern. Use a spare piece of carpet or "borrow" from an inconspicuous place such as the back of a closet, replacing the patch with the damaged piece.

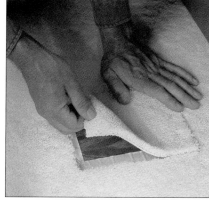

STEP 3 Apply double-faced carpet tape around the perimeter of the hole. Press the tape into position on the floor, then peel back and remove the special backing on the top of the tape.

STEP 4 Press the new patch in place. Use a rolling pin or weight it down with telephone books for a few hours. With your hand, brush the nap along the seam to blend the patch.

Carpet Stain Removal Guide

Chewing Gum
Freeze gum with ice cubes in a plastic bag; when it is hard, scrape up with a butter knife and blot with trichloroethylene (dry-cleaning fluid, available at drug and hardware stores).

Grease, Oil, Lipstick, Butter
Blot up excess with paper towels; sponge with dry-cleaning fluid; work from edges to center.

Shoe Polish, Ink, Dry Paint
Dab with paint remover; if that fails, use dry-cleaning fluid.

Coffee, Beer, Milk
Blot up excess with paper towels, scrub with diluted carpet shampoo; cover with paper towels and weight down for two to three hours.

Animal Urine
Immediately blot up excess with paper towels; soak with carbonated water; blot again; scrub with diluted carpet shampoo.

Fruit Juices, Soft Drinks
Blot up excess liquid; sponge the carpet generously with a solution of 1 teaspoon of powdered laundry detergent and 1 teaspoon of white vinegar dissolved in 1 quart of warm water.

Burns
Snip off the tips of burnt carpet threads with sharp scissors. On plush carpets, this will be less noticeable if you feather out the area by lightly snipping and tapering the nap in an ever-wider circle around the repair (right).

Silencing Squeaky Floors

Simple cures for three common floor ailments.

STEP 1 Mark squeaks while someone walks and bounces on the floor above. Listen for noises and watch for movement.

STEP 2 Install and nail bridging between floor joists to support weak points in the subfloor and lock the floor into one mass.

WHAT YOU NEED

2x4 lumber

16d nails

Hammer

Pencil

Construction adhesive

Electric drill

Coat hanger or stud finder

Drywall screws

Over time, as the wood in a house expands and contracts, nails lose their grip. Squeaking occurs when loose wood and nails rub against one another.

The ideal solution is to tighten up the floor, working from the top side (the same way the materials were originally nailed together). Unfortunately, there's often carpet, tile, or linoleum in the way. But even if you can't work from the top, you can end some squeaks by reinforcing the floor from below using nails with ribbed, spiral, or threaded shanks so they'll bite firmly into the joists.

Another option is to use "trim head" drywall screws — screws with a very small head that can be sunk below the surface of hardwood flooring. After sinking the heads, fill the holes with putty that matches the flooring. Sink existing loose nails farther into the joist with a nail set, or they'll quickly loosen again.

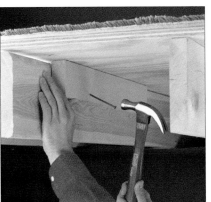

STEP 3 Coat the top edges and sides of 2x4 cleats with construction adhesive and then nail them along joists to stop the subfloor from moving and to strengthen the joists.

SILENCING SQUEAKS FROM ABOVE

STEP 1 Probe for the joist by drilling a small hole and feeling with a bent coat hanger.

STEP 2 Drill a hole, slightly larger than the shank of the screws to be installed, through the subfloor but not into the joist. Use care so the carpet fibers do not wrap around the bit.

STEP 3 Drive screws into the joists at an angle, from both directions. Sink screw heads well below the level of the carpet and pad.

SILENCING HARDWOOD FLOORING

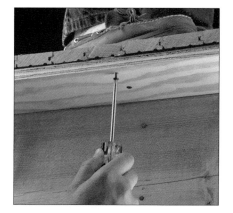

STEP 1 Drill a hole through the subfloor slightly larger than the shank of the screws to be installed. The tape on the bit acts as a depth guide to prevent drilling too deeply.

STEP 2 Squirt wood glue into the hole. Force in lots of glue so it can surround both sides of any flooring paper that was used between the wood layers.

STEP 3 Install screws from underneath while someone stands on the floor above. Space screws every 6 inches, making sure they penetrate at least $\frac{1}{2}$ inch into the hardwood flooring.

What Causes Squeaks?

Creaks are produced by boards rubbing against each other. One old-time, temporary cure is to sprinkle talcum powder between the boards (if you can get at them) to eliminate the friction and quiet the creaks. Use a squeeze-type plastic catsup bottle with a small nozzle to direct the talcum powder at the squeak.

Groans are a deeper, more ominous sound, common to older homes. As joists and beams weaken and sag, the internal stress and friction create sound. One cure is to nail additional joists (sisters) alongside the weaker ones in order to strengthen them, but in houses where generations of wire, pipe, and ductwork have been installed, this is a major job. Sometimes, it's easier to add extra support posts and beams below the joists to strengthen the groaning area. Consult a qualified contractor or construction engineer for an on-site inspection and recommendation, especially if you discover rot or termite damage.

Driving tapered shims or shingles into gaps between noisy boards or joists is another common way of silencing squeaks, creaks, and groans. Apply construction adhesive to both sides of the shim, then lightly pound it into the gap.

Repairing Rotted Floors

Rotten wood needs to be replaced now!

WHAT YOU NEED

Adjustable wrench

Screwdriver

Hammer

Chisel

Circular saw

Wood preservative

Paintbrush

Galvanized drywall screws

2x4 blocks

Nails

Sheet plywood

Drill

Pry bar

Unlike typical house ills such as broken windows, fading paint, and sagging doors, infestations of rot in floors may not be obvious until you feel a soft spot in the floor, hear a suspicious squish as you step down, or find your toilet tilting. You also might see brown stains showing up on the floor surface.

By this time the rot has already done some damage, so a cure requires eliminating the source of the moisture and replacing weakened wood.

Occasional spills and puddles won't cause trouble, but water sources that regularly wet the floor and never give it a chance to dry out will.

If rot has weakened the supporting structure of your house, call in your building inspector for advice on how you should proceed.

STEP 1   Turn off the water supply, disconnect supply lines and drains, and remove the toilet and other obstructions such as the vanity to expose the floor. Flush the toilet first and sponge out any water in the tank and bowl.

STEP 2   Probe for soft spots in the wood floor with a screwdriver, removing vinyl flooring as you go, to find the extent of the rot damage.

STEP 3   Cut through the vinyl and underlayment along the tub with your power saw, finishing the cut with a chisel at the ends. Then pull up the entire underlayment and vinyl.

STEP 4   Probe again with a screwdriver to determine the extent of rot damage to the subfloor. When cutting out the rotten sections, plan the saw cuts so they fall on the center of joists.

STEP 5 Remove the subfloor section to eliminate all soft, rotting wood. Pull nails before cutting along the joists.

STEP 6 Allow rotted areas to dry out, then apply a coat of wood preservative to damaged and discolored areas.

STEP 7 Fasten a 2x4 to the damaged joist with 3-inch galvanized drywall screws to supply a solid, flat nailing surface for the new subfloor.

STEP 8 Toenail or screw 2x4 blocks to the joists to support the edges of the subfloor and the toilet waste flange.

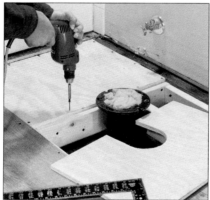

STEP 9 Fasten the new subfloor patch in place, screwing all edges, including the old floor, to joists and 2x4 blocks. Use 1½-inch screws spaced every 6 inches.

What's Under the Surface

Most floors have two layers of wood: An underlayment and a subfloor below that. The subfloor usually runs in a continuous sheet under all the walls. It can't be removed easily. The underlayment, however, is usually put in after the walls are put up, so it fits each room and is tailored to the type of floor covering being used. The underlayment, therefore, is easy to pull up and remove.

Work Better, Work Safer

Dust Catcher
Catch the dust when you drill overhead or into walls. Poke the drill bit through the bottom of a small paper cup and hold the cup rim against the wall or overhead surface while drilling.

Smooth Drywall Finish
Avoid the dust-raising job of sanding drywall seams or patches after the compound hardens. Instead, lightly smooth out the compound using wet paper towels just as it is setting up but before it hardens completely.

Wallpaper Cuts
To cut a clean edge when wallpapering an arch that doesn't have wood molding, leave about 1 inch of wallpaper untrimmed around the archway. Wait until the glue dries and trim the excess paper with a single-edged razor. You'll get a neater edge this way than if you trim the paper when it's wet.

Easy Wallpaper Stripper
If you have stubborn wallpaper that doesn't want to part with your walls, try this quick and easy stripper: Mix 2 parts very hot water with 1 part fabric softener in a paint tray and apply several coats of this brew to the wallpaper with a long-napped paint roller. Let it soak in for about 10 minutes, then scrape the paper off with a broad-bladed putty knife.

Joint Compound Keeper
Buy drywall joint compound in the economy 5-gallon container even if you have to store it for a long time. To store it so it will keep, scrape all the compound off the inner sides of the container and wipe the sides clean with a rag. Level the compound in the container, then pour in about ½ cup of water. Replace the plastic that was over the compound when you opened the container, then put the lid on tight.

Vinyl Floor Touch-up
Repair small nicks, tears, or breaks in light-colored vinyl flooring with ordinary tub and tile caulk. Just fill the depression and wipe away the excess with a damp cloth. You can even color the caulk to match by mixing in a little stain or paint.

Quick and Easy Hole Patch
To patch a baseball-sized hole in drywall, soak a piece of cloth in a solution of water-diluted taping or spackling compound. Overlap the area to be repaired by about 2 inches, smooth it out, and let it dry. Once it's dry, apply a coat of regular compound, let dry, and sand lightly to ready it for painting.

Drywall Dust Sucker
Vacuuming up drywall dust with a shop vacuum can clog the filter fast. To keep the filter cleaner longer, cut off an old T-shirt below the arms. Then wrap the lower section of fabric around the vacuum filter and secure it with two heavy-duty rubber bands. When the T-shirt filter gets clogged with dust, pull it off, shake it out, and reuse it.

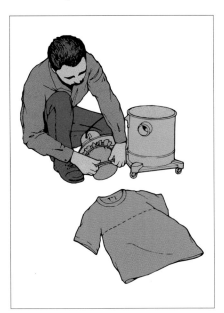

Dust filter

Removing Molding
The first step in any flooring project is removal of the quarter-round molding, usually by prying it off the baseboard molding with a small pry bar. This procedure loosens the quarter-round molding but unfortunately often damages one or both pieces of molding. To protect the molding, insert a putty knife blade between the quarter-round and the baseboard molding. Next, place a thin piece of scrap wood between the putty knife blade and the baseboard molding. Then, position the pry bar between the scrap wood protecting the baseboard molding and the putty knife blade protecting the quarter-round.

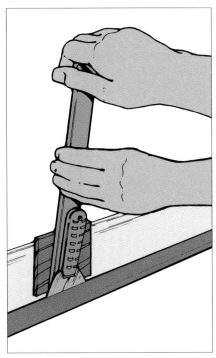

Molding technique

Water Marks on Textured Ceilings

To remove a water stain from a textured ceiling, first solve the moisture problem. If the texture is in good shape, cover the stain with pigmented shellac or a water-based stain sealer. Stain sealers typically come in pure white only and can't be tinted, so you'll need to repaint the ceiling after you've sealed the stain.

Cure for a Droopy Ceiling

If you have a sagging drywall ceiling, chances are that your ceiling joists have gotten damp and sagged over time. If you haven't seen signs of roof leakage, the problem is probably the lack of a vapor barrier in the ceiling. If you install a vapor barrier, the joists should stabilize and you can hang a new ceiling right over the old one.

First staple a 4-mil plastic sheet over the old drywall to form a vapor barrier. Then install a second layer of drywall over the vapor barrier for your new ceiling. This is an awkward job, especially for one person. You must run 1x2 furring strips across the ceiling at right angles to the joists and be sure to space them 16 inches apart on center. Screw ½-inch drywall to the furring strips, then tape and finish the joints.

There are two more critical parts to this job: getting the furring strips level and flat over the whole ceiling, and maintaining electrical safety.

Stretch mason's twine tightly across the ceiling to find the high and low spots. To get the furring strips level across the whole ceiling, you will need to put pairs of shims underneath the low spots. Screw the shims through the furring strips to hold them in place.

Any electrical boxes (for ceiling lights, for example) must be deepened so the lower edge of the box is level with the new drywall. This keeps sparks from getting to combustible materials inside the ceiling. You will need to cut power off at the box and screw on a metal box extender and/or plaster rings (available at electrical supply firms) to get the extra depth you need. If you have a plastic box, the box extender must be grounded. Consult an electrician if you have any questions.

Hanging fresh drywall

Wallpaper Remover

Rather than rent a wallpaper steamer, fill the pail of a power paint sprayer with hot water and spray it on the wallpaper just like paint. It is easy to hold the sprayer in one place to really soak stubborn areas. When the glue has softened, scrape the paper off with an ordinary wall scraper.

Keeping Stylish Records

Record paint or wallpaper identification numbers on masking tape, then stick the tape on the back of a switch plate cover in each room.

Covering Textured Walls

Instead of trying to remove the texture from textured walls, cover the texture with two thin coats of drywall joint compound. Apply it with a 10- or 12-inch-wide taping knife and let the compound dry completely between coats for about 24 hours. Light sanding is sometimes needed between coats. Apply a good primer to the walls and you're ready to paint or paper.

Getting Old Walls Smooth

In some older houses you'll find many coats of paint and large areas where the paint has peeled. To smooth the walls and not leave telltale lines where the old paint peeled, scrape off all loose paint, and then sand the edges of the scraped area with medium-grit sandpaper to feather it out. This will make the scraped areas less obvious.

Popping Drywall

The heads of drywall nails can "pop" for a number of reasons, but the most common cause is drying of the wall framing lumber. As the wood dries, it shrinks — not a lot, but enough to leave a gap between it and the drywall. The nail head fracture (pop) occurs when the house settles or if the drywall is bumped.

The best remedy is to refasten the drywall with drywall screws. They grip the drywall better than nails and reduce the chance of further popping. To insert drywall screws, drive them 1 inch above or below the existing nails. Then make sure the head of the screw is dimpled into the drywall. Finally, drive the popped nails back into the framing lumber and fill all the dimples and holes with two coats of drywall compound. Sand it smooth and repaint.

Some state building codes address this type of problem by requiring a drying-out period after the framing has been erected and before the exterior sheathing can be installed.

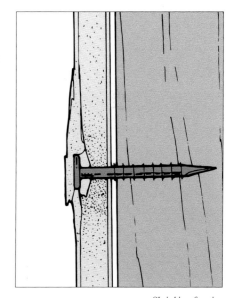

Shrinking framing

Straight, Square, Plumb, and Level

The tradespeople who built your house knew how to use a level, square, and chalk line. You should too, if you dive into projects bigger than the ones covered here. They're the assurance that your new walls, ceilings, and floors will turn out looking great.

Is It Straight?

Wood performs amazing contortions as it dries because even seasoned wood contains considerable water. So be picky when you buy your lumber. If it's too crooked, nothing built with it, on it, or next to it will fit well.

Check straightness by eye. The naked eye is as good a tool as any when it comes to judging crooked versus straight. You can detect a hump, or "crown" as it is called by carpenters, by sighting along the length of a board. A slight crown is almost inevitable, but you should reject boards where it is very noticeable.

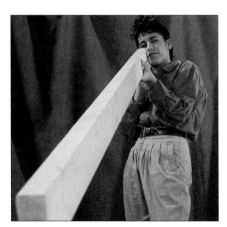

Sighting along a board

When building a wall, have all the crowns on the same side so the finished wall doesn't have a wavy surface. With floor joists, a small crown is actually desirable — just make certain you always position the crown up. A joist with a ½-inch upward crown will wind up straight if the center settles ½ inch. But a joist with a ½-inch downward crown will wind up with a full 1-inch sag after the same amount of settling.

Compare to a string line. A string pulled taut is a good way to check straightness. For instance, to see if a wall is straight, tack two spacer blocks of the same thickness at opposite ends of the wall and stretch a string between them. By measuring between the string and wall at intermediate points, you can determine how to straighten it. This is a great way to align fence and deck posts, check for sags in floors, or level the grid for a suspended ceiling.

Checking a wall with a string line

Snapping a line. Use a chalk line when you need to mark a long, straight line on a wall, ceiling, or floor. Secure the hook end, reel out the string and pull it taut, then lift the string straight up, and let it go.

Is It Square?

Cross measuring. By comparing diagonal measurements and adjusting accordingly, you can square up a wall, cabinet door, window, or any corner. The diagonal measurements will be equal when the corners are square.

Squaring with math. The secret is called the 3-4-5 rule: A triangle with sides of 3, 4, and 5 units will form a 90-degree corner. It doesn't matter whether the units are inches, feet, or light-years, or whether they are multiples like 6, 8, and 10 or 30, 40, and 50 — the corner will always be 90 degrees. The 3-4-5 technique is especially useful for large structures like walls, the framing of a deck, or fence corners.

Is It Level and Plumb?

"Level" simply means parallel to the earth's surface; "plumb" means straight up and down.

Using a level. Most levels contain three glass vials: one at each end indicating plumb and one in the middle indicating level. When the bubble is exactly centered between the two lines on the vial, your work is plumb or level — provided your level is accurate. Crowned or bowed lumber will give your level a false reading, so when

checking the corner of a wall or a door opening for plumb, take two or three readings along the length of the stud to obtain an average.

Take several readings

Using a plumb bob. The plumb bob, a string with a pointed weight on one end, is another way of establishing true vertical. A level is more convenient for truing up walls, but plumb bobs shine for transferring marks from a higher to a lower point — for example, to center a wood stove beneath a chimney or to position ceiling fans or lights. The only hard part about using a plumb bob is waiting for it to stop spinning and swaying before you can transfer your mark.

Painted-over Wallpaper

If your walls have paint over old wallpaper, you should remove the old wallcovering before applying a new layer of paper. If you simply can't get the old paper off and still want to hang new wallpaper, prep the wall with an acrylic undercoat. As you hang the new paper, be sure the seams don't line up with those in the old paper.

Using a Utility Knife

Whether you're cutting through wallpaper, drywall, or carpet, a sharp utility knife is a must. Even the most experienced do-it-yourselfer can still learn things they can do with a utility knife and its variety of razor-sharp disposable blades.

Choose the Right Knife

There are two types of utility knives: those with blades that retract into the handle and those with fixed blades.

Retractable-blade knives. One of these is a must in every home owner's toolbox (below). This kind of knife will hold different types of blades for cutting cardboard, plastics, linoleum, and shingles. It's also good for cutting ¼-inch plywood and lauan subflooring.

Retractable-blade knife

Most retractable-blade knives have a handle that comes apart for blade storage and changing. This arrangement holds the blade securely, but it's inconvenient. Better, buy a knife with flip-out blade storage and slide-in blade changing. This type of knife is not as strong but it's good for jobs that require extra-sharp blades, like cutting wallpaper and urethane foam insulation, when you want to be able to change blades fast.

Fixed-blade knives. These knives hold large special-purpose blades, many too large to retract. They're used for cutting plastics or soft materials like vinyl tile. Some professionals also prefer fixed-blade knives for ordinary use because they're extremely strong and durable, though not as safe.

Buy Extra Blades

Whatever type of utility knives you own, get lots of extra blades. You'll get better results by always using a sharp blade.

Safety First

Just because utility knives are simple hand tools, it doesn't mean they can't bite back — by slicing fingers, gouging hands, and jabbing legs. You'll avoid injury if you:
- Pull the knife toward you.
- Keep your free hand away from the line of cut.
- Stand to one side of the line of cut.
- Change blades often. A sharp blade bites in and cuts, while a dull blade skips, possibly toward you.
- When cutting ¼-inch plywood, make several passes, cutting a little deeper each time.
- Don't bend the blades or use them to open cans or pry — they're brittle and snap easily.

Clamp a straightedge

- When using a straightedge, either clamp it down or keep your hand well away from the knife.
- Wear eye protection.

Cutting Tips

Before you begin, pick the right blade for the job: either a straight blade for general use; a hooked blade for thin, flexible materials; or a scribing blade for brittle stuff.

Here are some tips for using your utility knife.
- Cut sheets of drywall and rigid foam insulation partway through on the good side with a standard blade, then snap back and pull forward to break the sheet along the cut line.
- Cut fiberglass insulation, foam rubber, and vapor barrier material such as plastic film with a single pass, using the standard straight blade.
- Cut brittle materials like ⅛-inch acrylic, ⅛-inch tempered hard-board, and plastic laminates by scratching the good side in a single firm stroke, using a scoring blade. Position the score line along the edge of your bench and press down to complete the break.
- Use a large hook blade to cut more pliable material like vinyl tile and asphalt roofing material. Cut on a firm surface.

Hook blade for vinyl

- To cut thin metal like aluminum and copper flashing, just scratch with a standard blade, then flex along the line until the metal breaks.
- To trim roof shingles or roll roofing, use a small hook blade. The blade wraps around the material and cuts as you pull it.
- Cut thicker wood such as ¼-inch plywood, lauan subflooring, wood shingles, and shims with a standard blade. Be patient — it will take several passes, each cutting a little deeper into the material.
- Change the blade whenever it starts to tear instead of cut.

Doors and Windows

Fixing Broken Screens   30

Repair those unsightly broken screens and keep the summer bugs out of your hair.

Replacing Broken Glass   31

Replacing a pane of glass is a task that most home owners can accomplish easily. It involves few tools, little time, and not much expense.

Easing Stuck Windows   32

You could replace stubborn or stuck windows, but that's costly and often unnecessary. It's faster, cheaper, and smarter to repair them yourself.

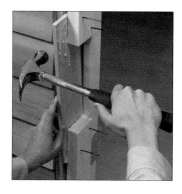

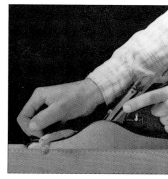

Fixing Broken Screens

It's easy to make window screens look like new.

WHAT YOU NEED

Wheeled spline roller

Awl

Screwdriver

Utility knife

Spring clamp

Screening usually is held in aluminum frames by a strip of rubber called a spline. The screen is pressed into a groove and the spline locks it in place. Replacing the screening and spline is easy with the wheeled spline roller shown here; you can find one at most hardware stores.

Two kinds of screening are available, aluminum and fiberglass. Fiberglass comes in several colors and is more flexible, a little cheaper than aluminum, and a bit easier to install. But it also tends to be more easily damaged or stretched than aluminum.

It's a good idea to replace the old spline while you're at it. You can buy it by the foot and it is inexpensive. Bring a piece of the old spline to the store to ensure a perfect match, since the material comes in several thicknesses.

REPLACING TORN SCREEN

STEP 1 Remove the old rubber spline with an awl or thin screwdriver, starting from a corner. Some screens have metal splines; remove them the same way, but be careful so you can reuse them. Lay a new square of screening on the frame and cut so it overhangs all four sides by no more than 1 inch. Clamp screening to one of the short sides of the frame.

STEP 2 Roll the new spline into the groove starting at a corner opposite the clamped side. Hold the screening taut and keep the same strand of screening aligned with the groove all the way.

STEP 3 When the spline is rolled, push it into the corners with a screwdriver. Cut off the excess screening flush with the outer edge of the spline, using a sharp utility knife.

Replacing Broken Glass

Your broken single-pane window doesn't need professional help.

Fragile, thin, and nearly invisible — glass is the weakest link in our solid houses of concrete, brick, and wood. And sooner or later one of those weak links is going to break.

It's quickest to repair windows in place (though you may elect first to remove, then repair, simple storm windows). Wear gloves and eye protection when removing the broken glass. A pair of pliers will give you even more distance from razor-sharp, jagged edges.

To make sure your new window pane seals tightly, thoroughly scrape and remove all the old putty and paint. Repaint the opening before installing the new glass to prevent future moisture damage. When you're finished glazing, let the new putty cure about a week before painting.

INSTALLING NEW GLASS

STEP 1 Soften the old putty with a heat gun or heat lamp. Remove the putty, glass, and glazing points. Gloves and a pair of pliers will help you safely remove the old glass.

STEP 2 Lay a small bead of putty (about ¼ inch in diameter) in the rabbet. Prime and paint the rabbet beforehand to help protect the window from moisture damage.

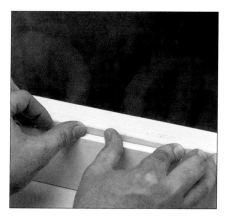

STEP 3 Press the new pane of glass firmly in place. The glass should be cut about ⅛ inch smaller than the opening in both directions.

STEP 4 Push the glazing points in place against the glass every 4 inches along the perimeter. Apply and smooth glazing compound.

Easing Stuck Windows

Opening and closing windows shouldn't be a headache.

WHAT YOU NEED

"Paint zipper" or putty knife

Utility knife

Carbon paper

Hand plane or belt sander

Pry bar

Screwdriver

Hammer

Paintbrush

Problems that affect a window's operation are simple to repair. While the work is dirty and in some cases time consuming, you need only patience and basic skills. Few specialized tools are required, and parts can be purchased from the window manufacturer or, in some cases, at hardware stores, home centers, and window repair shops.

From opening a painted-shut window to lubricating a crank, here are repairs for the problems you're most likely to encounter with double-hung windows (they move up or down within a frame) and casement windows (they're hinged to swing in or out).

DOUBLE-HUNG SASH CORD REPAIRS

STEP 1 Unscrew the stop in the jamb, or pry it out carefully using a pry bar. If metal weather stripping exists, carefully remove the nails holding it in place and save the weather stripping.

STEP 2 Pull the bottom sash out from the frame. Remove the knotted sash cord or chain from the channel in the side of the sash.

STEP 3 Unscrew or pry out the access cover in the jamb to expose the weights. The cover has a lip on one side, so it must be twisted as it is removed.

STEP 4 Pull out the weight with the broken cord far enough so you can untie the cord. Purchase new cord that is the same thickness as the old.

STEP 5 Insert new cord over the pulley. Pull the end down through the access panel, then tie it to the weight. Rest the sash on the sill and draw the cord end through the slot. Raise the weight until it touches the pulley.

STEP 6 Lower the weight about 2 inches, knot the cord, cut off the end, and place the knot in the slot. Reinstall the sash access cover, sash, and stop.

Butterflies and Springs

These tension devices can take the place of weights and cords.

Butterfly: Open the sash all the way. Push butterflies between the sash and jamb; close the window. Nail or screw the butterflies in place.

Window spring: Lower the sash. Insert the spring between the sash and jamb. Hold the spring in place with a screw.

Double-hung Window Troubleshooting

The vertical sliding window is called "double-hung" because it has two sashes that slide within one frame. The traditional system, and the one most easily repaired, operates by balancing the sash's weight against that of a weight hidden in the frame by the trim. A cord tied to the weight runs up and out of the frame via a pulley and then is attached to the side of a sash. The system holds the sash in place anywhere along the jamb. The most common problem is a window that doesn't stay up as the result of a broken cord. The step-by-step repair is shown at left.

Double-hung windows made today use a sophisticated and streamlined version of the weight-and-cord system. Others use friction, sometimes combined with a spring mechanism.

Here are some of the most common problems you'll face.

Top sash sags. Check for obstructions in the top jamb. Look for a broken sash cord and repair it. For an upper sash, you'll have to remove the parting bead as well as the stop to repair the cord.

Sashes can't be opened. Do not use force to open the window. Look for obstructions in the side jambs such as loose weather stripping or stops.

Hard-to-open or sticking sash. Check the pulleys. If any are inoperable due to paint, remove the sash and pulley. Remove paint by soaking it in paint stripper. If the pulley is bent or won't operate smoothly, replace it.

Obstructions in the jamb. If the sash is rubbing against the stop, remove the stop with a pry bar and reinstall it so the sash clears it.

If the window still binds, remove the stop and sashes. Paint buildup may be the problem. Scrape off excess paint from the stop, the parting bead, and the sash. Be sure to repaint where you've exposed bare wood. Lubricate the sash and the jamb by rubbing with paraffin wax. Reassemble the window.

Misaligned sashes. Look for debris stuck to the top or bottom of the sashes, or on the bottom sill or top jamb. If the two sashes still don't meet as they should and can't be latched, they may be warped. Remove the sashes and carefully plane them slightly. Repaint the exposed surfaces, and reassemble the window. Note: Because high humidity may be causing the windows to swell and bind, be sure to check their operation and do any necessary wood removal when humidity is low.

If repair is not possible or the window is badly warped, you may be able to replace just the sash, which will have to be custom made.

Caution: Paint on older windows may contain lead. Removing parts of windows may create paint chips; planing or sanding creates dust. Keep children and pets away, and clean up the area when finished. Wear protective goggles and mask when sanding, and vacuum up all sawdust and chips.

Casement Window Troubleshooting

Break-ins, by burglars and keyless home owners alike, account for occasional breakage of casement hinges, latches, and gears. But many more failures occur gradually as a swollen, warped, or sticking window is repeatedly forced open and shut. A little preventive maintenance — sealing or painting bare wood, along with annual cleaning and lubricating of moving parts — helps your windows last and eliminates costly repairs.

Look for paint buildup inside and out. You can make painted-shut windows operate again by breaking the paint bond between sash and frame as shown in step 1 (right). Paint that has oozed and hardened between sash and frame may need to be broken free with the gentle persuasion of a small pry bar worked between the sash and frame.

Check for binding and sticking. For a casement window to form a weather-tight seal, some resistance is normal, but the window should not need to be pushed or prodded every time it's opened or closed. Swelling, house settling, or excessively packed insulation around the window may be the cause of your sticking window. Push on a stubborn window as you crank to help it open, then close the window, noting carefully where it's binding or rubbing. You can also help locate problem areas by slipping carbon paper between the window sash and the jamb, then opening and closing the window. Binding points will show up as carbon marks on the window sash. To ease them, remove the sash and any weather stripping along the edge, then use a hand plane or belt sander to trim the window. Be sure to prime and repaint any newly exposed bare wood.

Replace stripped, corroded, or damaged gears. The entire gear and arm operator mechanism must be replaced as one unit. Step-by-step instructions begin on page 36.

Check the latch mechanism. The latch that snugs the window sash to its frame rarely malfunctions. Once paint buildup, binding, and operating mechanisms have been dealt with, the latch should do its job. If not, replacement is as easy as removing the screws and replacing the mechanism with a new one. Repair forced-entry damage. A damaged or pinched track can often be opened and restored by working a screwdriver along its length.

If your standard cranks are interfering with your blinds or curtains, you may want to replace them with compact crank handles. Examine the gears in the crank mechanism. Wind, salt water, and sand can clog, corrode, and damage operating parts. A thorough cleaning followed by a shot of silicone or other nongumming lubricant will often free up the mechanism.

STEP 1 Free up painted-shut windows by running a "paint zipper," putty knife, or utility knife between the sash and frame.

STEP 2 Slip carbon paper between the sash and frame, then open and close the window several times to determine where it's binding.

STEP 3 Level high spots that bind with a hand plane or belt sander. Removing 1/16 to 1/8 inch is enough to free most windows.

STEP 4 Tighten the crank set screw to make sure the handle isn't slipping.

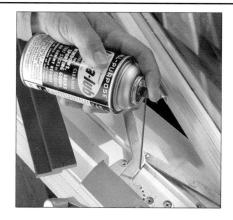

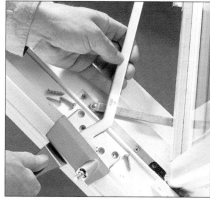

STEP 5 Lubricate moving parts with silicone or nongumming oil after cleaning. The lower wood stop may have to be pried off for access.

STEP 6 If the operator arm needs replacing, remove the screws and gear unit, then slide the roller out of the exit notch at the bottom of the track. (See page 36.)

Casement Windows

Casement windows are commonly referred to as "crankout" or "side-hinged" windows. Most are crank operated, with gears and an arm in the lower windowsill stop. The photo at right shows the types of cranks that are available.

The butterfly and disc cranks won't interfere with your blinds but are harder to turn. The long crank provides better leverage, while the other two may better match your decor.

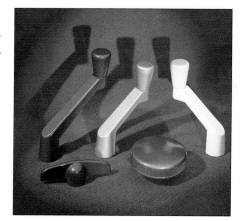

Caring for and Repairing Windows

■ Once you've repaired your windows, keep them that way with proper maintenance. Seal or paint any exposed wood on all six sides of each sash to prevent excessive expansion and contraction and deterioration from the elements. Although the paint builds up over the years and may lead to sticking and binding windows, it's easier to deal with excess paint than warped or rotted windows. Lubricate latches with a nongumming silicone spray and lubricate sashes and jambs as necessary with paraffin wax.

■ To help feed a new sash cord over the pulley of a double-hung window, cut a piece of string the length of the jamb. Tie one end of the string to the cord and the other end to a small weight (a nail bent to curve around the pulley, for example). Feed in the weight. It will drop to the bottom of the jamb where you can grab it through the access plate and pull the cord through. If your pulley has a cover, you may need to loosen the pulley cover unit to feed the cord.

■ The heat from the sun can cause the oil in new oil-based window glazing compound to be absorbed into untreated wood mullions, causing a rapid deterioration of the glazing compound. This is evidenced by shrinking, cracking, or alligatoring of the compound. To avoid this, coat the window frames with a quick-dry sealer or oil-based primer before applying the glazing compound.

■ A thin-bladed pizza cutter does a great job of loosening sticky or painted-shut window sashes. Because the blade rolls along instead of being pulled like a knife, it doesn't cut into the wood.

■ When you're puttying windows, the putty sticking to the knife makes it difficult to form a neat, smooth surface. Dip the blade in paint thinner or mineral spirits with each pass to lubricate it and keep the putty from sticking.

Curing Failed Window Cranks

Keep your casement windows working smoothly and easily.

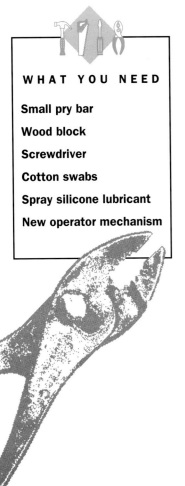

WHAT YOU NEED

Small pry bar

Wood block

Screwdriver

Cotton swabs

Spray silicone lubricant

New operator mechanism

Casement windows (side-hinged), awning windows (top-hinged), and hopper-type windows (bottom-hinged) all use the same basic mechanism; you can troubleshoot all three the same way.

First, check to make sure the window is unlatched and that a new coat of paint hasn't glued the window shut. Then try tightening the small set screw that secures the crank handle to the pivot thumb. If that doesn't help, remove the handle. If the nubs inside the handle are stripped or rounded over, replace the handle. If the thumb is stripped, replace the entire operator.

Next, check the hidden gear mechanism. Remove the operator cover and clean the gears with a cotton swab and spray silicone lubricant. If the gears are bent or severely corroded, or if some of the teeth are broken, replace the entire mechanism.

REMOVING AND REPLACING THE UNIT

STEP 1   Remove the cover from the crank using a small pry bar. Window cranks are not all alike; if your crank cover is permanently molded to the crank, go to step 2.

STEP 2   Pry and remove the stop at the bottom of the window. A small block of wood will prevent damage to the windowsill.

STEP 3   Press the crank arm down so the roller slips out of the exit notch. Remove screws securing the operator to the sill.

STEP 4   Slide the clip on the guide arm to the side and off the pivot on the sash. Remove the old operator and install the new one according to the manufacturer's instructions.

Freeing a Binding Door

Wooden doors don't have to stick.

WHAT YOU NEED

Screwdriver

Pencil

Sawhorses

Block plane or belt sander

Paintbrush

Paint

Hammer

Around many houses, doors operate with the seasons — humid summertime means sticking doors. A light sanding may be enough to free a slightly sticking door, especially one binding from seasonal humidity or paint buildup.

When doors start binding and catching year-round, however, it's time to plane them down. Use either a small block plane or a belt sander, but don't remove too much wood all at once. You may be able to trim the door while it's still on its hinges, depending on what part of the door is binding.

Before you begin your repair, tighten all the hinge screws. If you encounter a stripped screw hole, replace that screw with one 3 inches long that will bite into the stud behind the door frame.

Be certain either to paint or stain and seal the freshly exposed wood.

TRIMMING DOWN A DOOR

STEP 1 Tighten hinge screws to make certain the binding isn't caused by sagging hinges. If screw holes are stripped, replace existing screws with longer ones. If this doesn't do the trick, go to steps 2 through 4.

STEP 2 Mark the edge of the door wherever it rubs against the frame; 1/8 inch is the maximum gap needed. Open and shut the door, then watch and feel for where it's catching; the top corner is the most common area.

STEP 3 Remove the hinge pins, then place the door across a pair of sawhorses. Remove the handle and latch to plane the door in that area.

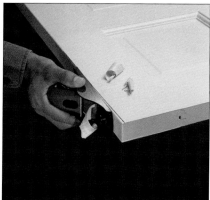

STEP 4 Plane the edge of the door, creating a slight angle or back bevel so the door will clear the frame more easily. Paint or stain the area and replace the door on its hinges.

Tuning up a Patio Door

Tips to keep this door sliding freely.

WHAT YOU NEED

Household cleaner

Sponge

Vacuum cleaner

Penetrating lubricant

Screwdriver

Cloth

Screening

Light oil

Pliers

Chisel

Wood filler

Paintbrush

Spline roller

From its massive size and weight alone, you might guess that keeping your patio door sliding smoothly would be tough. Surprisingly enough, however, it can roll on for years without needing attention. And when the door does start sticking, you need only one tool to get to the root of the problem — a screwdriver, either a Phillips or a flat blade type.

Patio door repair experts agree that the repairs shown here cover the most common problems that occur. You can use this list as an annual service check and catch potential problems before they start to cause trouble.

Occasionally in older doors, you'll encounter really big problems, like a rotting wood frame or a sagging beam overhead. These repairs aren't covered here; they often call for major surgery or a completely new door unit.

CLEANING THE TRACK AND ROLLERS

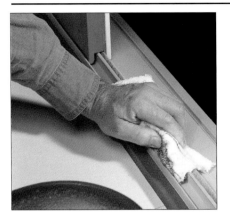

STEP 1 Wash the track and channel annually with a household cleaner. You can vacuum up dust and other debris, but you'll have to scrub to remove the grease and grime that stick to the track and clog the rollers.

STEP 2 Adjust the roller height if the door scrapes or binds against the track at the top or bottom. On wood doors, the adjusting screw is on the inside of the bottom rail. On aluminum doors, it is found on the vertical edge.

STEP 3 Remove the door and clean or replace the rollers if your door still doesn't glide smoothly. Have a friend help you, because patio doors usually weigh about 150 pounds each.

Finding Replacement Parts

The best place to begin finding replacement parts is with the door manufacturer or one of their local dealers. If you don't know who made the door, check the door hardware for a label. If that fails, contact local window repair and glass companies. They stock weather stripping and probably rollers too. Even better, they can order or tell you where to find any parts they don't stock.

STEP 1 Unscrew the latch assembly if it operates poorly. Clean and lubricate it with light oil. If that fails, or if parts have broken, you'll have to replace the assembly. To ensure getting the right type, take the old one along when buying a new latch.

STEP 2 Adjust the latch strike plate if the mechanism operates smoothly but fails to catch the plate.

Weather Stripping

Replace weather stripping when it doesn't seal the door properly. It is inexpensive, but some types might be hard to find since there are many sizes and shapes. Most types fall into two categories, the slide-in fuzzy material (A and B) and the press-in vinyl type (C). Take a sample of your old weather stripping along to find the closest match when you buy the new material.

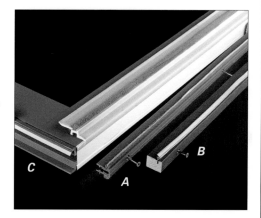

Anatomy of a Sliding Door

Shown above are the parts of a typical sliding door. This one includes both a fixed and a sliding glass panel and a sliding screen panel. Most doors are similar; differences are usually minor.

To remove a newer wood door, unscrew the top door stop (above), tilt the sliding portion inward, and lift it off its track.

If you have an older wood door or one with an aluminum frame, lift the sliding door up and swing the bottom inward. You may have to loosen the roller adjustment screw first.

Door Repair Ideas

- If you have scratches on the glass of a patio door, they can be buffed out if they are not too deep. However, this is not recommended as a DIY project. Buffing glass requires applying just the right amount of pressure, or you could shatter the glass. Leave it to a professional. Most glass company service departments can help you with this problem. Check in the yellow pages under "Glass."

- Anytime you need to inject glue, oil, or caulk into a tight space, such as around the rollers of your patio door, use a disposable irrigation syringe available at pharmacies. The tip is curved and the taper lets you snip it at different points to adjust the size of the opening.

- Keep track of screws when you disassemble parts of your door for repair. Thread the screws into the grooves in the edge of a piece of corrugated cardboard, then tape the cardboard to the disassembled items.

- Protect both the inside and outside of wood-frame exterior doors with paint or a preservative-type stain and be sure to coat the top and bottom door edges. These are critical spots because if they are left unprotected, moisture can enter the wood through the edges of the door and cause the paint to peel. Also, the door's glue joints may be loosened by moisture. Use an exterior penetrating sealer to coat the door edges. To avoid taking the door off its track or hinges, apply sealer with a small paint pad, thin enough to slip under the bottom of the door.

- Spray your sliding door tracks with aerosol furniture polish. The wax in the polish reduces friction and doesn't attract dirt.

- To make the vinyl insect screens in your doors look like new again, spray the screening with an automotive protectant. It removes the dirt and restores the color, which washing alone can't do.

- Windows in older houses may be covered with a brownish film. Rather than wasting time trying glass cleaners and acids, try polishing the glass with an automotive wax/polish. Be sure to clean the windows afterwards with a good glass cleaner to remove the wax film, especially if you're going to be painting the window frame.

FIXING A SLIDING SCREEN DOOR

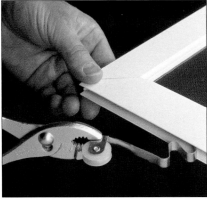

STEP 1 To replace torn screening, remove the door by lifting it up and swinging the bottom out. Pull out the vinyl spline and replace the screen.

STEP 2 Adjust the screen rollers so they operate smoothly. Replace them if they're cracked or worn. To replace, remove the adjustment screw and pull the old roller out with a pair of pliers. Push the replacement in by hand.

Major Problems

Rot often begins on the exterior of wood patio doors because rain splashes up on them from decks and patios. The best solution is prevention: Keep the exterior wood well sealed with paint. If rot begins, treat it immediately. Dig the rotted wood out with a chisel, let the rotted area dry, fill the holes with an epoxy wood filler (available at hardware stores), and seal the surface well with paint.

Restoring a Door Jamb

More than beauty is at stake.

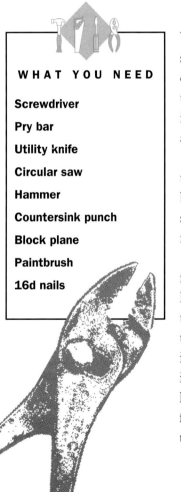

WHAT YOU NEED

Screwdriver

Pry bar

Utility knife

Circular saw

Hammer

Countersink punch

Block plane

Paintbrush

16d nails

Windy days can play havoc with the storm door if it doesn't have a check chain. If the door gets away from you in the wind and slams wide open against its automatic closer, you're likely to find a splintered jamb.

Try the simplest repair first: Refasten the closer using longer screws that reach back to the wall studs. But if those screws loosen, major surgery may be necessary in the future.

Since the door jamb will be sanded, filled, and painted, your joints don't have to be perfect. Just be sure to nail the splice securely. Fit the filler block as tightly as possible to make a solid backing. As you work, avoid damaging your inner door's weather stripping. You may have to groove your splice to fit it. When finished, install that check chain to avoid the problem in the future.

PATCHING A DAMAGED JAMB

STEP 1   Unscrew the storm door closer, remove the entire storm door, and pry off the exterior door casing.

STEP 2   Cut out the damaged section with a circular saw, making cuts perfectly square to the jamb edges.

STEP 3   Glue, insert, and nail a filler block. Its thickness must exactly fit the gap between the studs and the jamb.

STEP 4   Fit, glue, and nail the jamb block with 16d finish nails. Countersink the nail heads, plane or sand the block smooth, fill gaps, prime, and paint.

Work Better, Work Safer

Keying for Privacy

Here's a way to give yourself some extra security and privacy. When installing a separate entrance deadbolt lock, have the lock in the knob's lockset assembly master keyed. That way your master key will fit both the deadbolt and the lock in the knob, but a separate "guest key" for cleaning services, neighbors, and guests fits only the knob lock. Only you can enter when you've locked the deadbolt.

Pane Control

Replace glass panes safely and easily. Make a handle for the glass by folding over a section from the middle of a 12-inch piece of duct tape. Stick the tape in the middle of the pane (which must be clean and dry). For large panes use two handles.

Glass handle

Splinterless Door Cut

Prevent splintering when you have to cut off part of a door to allow for settling, carpet installation, or door replacement. Place ¾- or 1-inch masking tape on the end to be sawed off. Using a circular saw with a sharp blade, saw the line as marked. Then remove the tape and file smooth.

Fast Door Tune-up

To free up a door that sticks along one edge or the bottom, temporarily tape a piece of coarse sandpaper in the tight spot, then force the door back and forth across it. The sandpaper will remove enough wood or built-up paint to allow the door to swing freely again.

Neat Painting around Glass

When painting a window sash, you'll work faster and get a neater job if you let the paint flow right up against the glass. Then, before the paint dries, use a single-edged razor blade to scrape it off the glass, holding the blade at an angle. There is no need to press hard; let the blade do the work. Wipe the razor blade clean on a rag as you work.

Window Paint Scraper

It's hard to paint wooden windows without getting some paint on the glass. Scraping off the paint with a razor blade can scratch the glass, or you can slip and cut the painted wood or yourself. Instead, make a scraper by cutting a bevel on each edge of a ¾-inch x ¾-inch scrap of hardwood. It takes the paint off cleanly without marring the window. When the bevels get dull, just cut new ones.

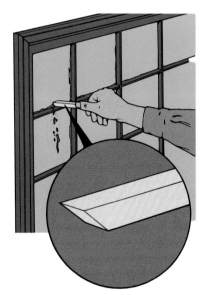

Scratchless scraper

Easy Door Keeper

What to do with a door that won't stay open? Just cut a round piece of self-adhering Velcro fastener tape and stick it on the tip of the doorstop. Line up the other piece of the fastener tape on the back of the door. It holds the door securely, yet it's easy to release.

Double-duty Door Flipper

You can speed up door painting and staining projects by driving 3-inch nails into the top and bottom of the door, then hanging it over two sawhorses. The nails act as handles for flipping the door over, and both sides can dry at the same time — without running paint.

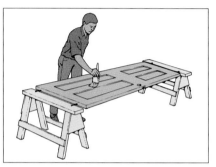

Hang nails

Doors That Won't Stay Put

If your house has settled with age, this may have caused some of your door frames to be out of plumb, making the doors swing of their own accord. There's a "quick and dirty" fix and an elaborate but longer-lasting one.

For the quick fix, remove each hinge pin (the rod that joins the two hinge leaves) and whack it with a hammer. You want the pin to be bent slightly, so the hinges are stiff enough to prevent the door from swinging by itself.

Do a permanent fix by rehanging the door so it's plumb. The first step is to take the door off its hinges. Then use a level to see in which direction the door frame is crooked: parallel with the wall, perpendicular to it, or both. Use a

6-foot level (if you have one), or a shorter level held securely against a very straight board. Place your level against the barrels (the round parts) of the hinges for checking perpendicular to the wall, and against the leaves (the flat parts) of the hinges to check parallel to the wall.

Plumbing the hinges

If the hinges are out of plumb parallel to the wall, shim under the hinge that needs it with cardboard, metal flashing, or thin strips of wood.

If the hinges are out of plumb perpendicular to the wall, one of them will have to be moved sideways. You may need to chisel out the hinge recess to enlarge it, and you may also need to remove the door stop and reposition it after you install the door. If you're moving the hinge only a small amount, the screws may insist on going back into the old holes. In this case, drill out the screw holes to $3/16$ inch, glue in pieces of dowel using five-minute epoxy glue, and trim the dowels flush. Now you should be able to get the screws to go where you want them.

Smart Trimming

When you replace or put up new door and window trim, you can save yourself a lot of grief later when it comes time to paint. Cut strips of wax paper and tape them around the untrimmed door or window so they extend an inch or two beyond the trim when it is installed. After painting, just cut off the exposed wax paper with a razor knife.

Clean trimming

Thermal Pane Window Condensation

Moisture developing between the panes of a double-glazed thermal window means that the seal around the edge has failed. Unfortunately, there is no way to repair the window. These edges are vacuum sealed at the factory. What's more, there is a moisture-absorbent desiccant in the space that separates the two panes, and once this becomes saturated, it would have to be replaced. In all, the cost of repair exceeds the cost of a new window. Applying silicone caulk to prevent this problem from happening in the first place is not a good idea, since the caulk itself can cause a chemical reaction that may cause the seal to fail even sooner.

A good replacement window will come with at least a 10-year warranty and should last 20 to 40 years. The Insulation Glass Certification Council certifies better-quality windows. Look for "IGCC approved" etched in the glass with the logo of the manufacturer. Window warranties, by the way, seem to assume you're a do-it-yourselfer: Even though the window itself may be replaced free, the owner is still stuck with the installation and finishing work.

Stop Shrinking Doors

During the heating season, you might notice your 6-panel wood interior doors shrinking to the point that you can see the unfinished edges around each of the panels. You can reduce shrinkage by making sure that all six sides of each

door are sealed. If one of the sides is left unfinished, the fluctuating moisture in the air could cause the door to shrink. Another area to check is the door's exposure to direct sunlight. During the winter, the sun's rays enter most houses at a lower angle. These rays may be falling directly on the doors during the winter, while in the summer the sun's rays enter at a much higher angle. If this is a problem, install some window blinds or shades to help prevent the sun's rays from coming in direct contact with the door.

Sagging Storm Door

To fix a sagging aluminum storm door, first check to see if the storm door frame has been installed properly and is square. To check, remove the glass panel from the door, then put it back in place. If the glass panel does not go back in easily, chances are the storm door frame is out of square.

A second area to check is the corner brace in the top of the door itself. It will sometimes bend or break, causing the door to sag. To prevent the sag, replace the bent or broken corner brace.

A last resort is to check the squareness of the exterior door frame. To do this you will probably need to remove the storm door frame completely. If the exterior door frame is not square, you will probably need to shim the hinged side of the storm door frame.

The type of hinge that is on your door (full-length or piano hinge) is harder to shim than a butt hinge. If you do try to shim the hinge, make sure that you don't cause the door to bind or rub the other frame pieces.

Painting Door Edges

Ever face this decorating conundrum? You have a door to a yellow bedroom that opens in from a blue hallway. So what color do you paint the edges of the door? There is a simple rule of thumb and it goes like this: Paint the edges the same color as the room they face. When the door is half open, the edge near the hinges will face into the hall — paint that edge blue. The other edge (the latch edge) faces into the bedroom — paint that one yellow.

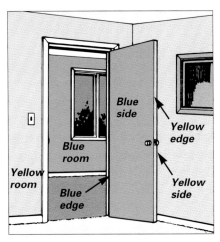

Color coordination

Plain Talk about Planes

Have you ever needed to remove just a smidgen of wood — so a drawer won't bind or a swollen door can close all the way? Often that smidgen is just too big to sand and too small to saw.

If so, the old-fashioned hand plane is just what you need. It can take the saw marks off the edge of a board, saving you lots of time sanding. It can fix a miter joint that needs just a bit of wood shaved away to fit perfectly. It can make clean beveled edges or straighten out the crooked edge of a board. Plus it'll fix those drawers and doors that won't close. But a plane can be fussy to use if you don't know how. Here's a recipe for buying, maintaining, and using one.

Buying a Plane

There are two basic planes: the bench plane and the block plane. The bench plane is about 14 to 18 inches long and is used to smooth the face or edge of a board when the board is clamped down or held in a vise. Its length makes it perfect for straightening a warped or crooked board.

The block plane is 6 to 8 inches long, with the blade set at a lower angle, making it particularly useful for slicing through end grain. It's also a convenient size for carrying in a toolbox or using with one hand.

Make sure the plane comes with an instruction manual; a good one contains lots of useful information, including blade sharpening instructions.

Adjusting for the Best Cut

Block planes are easy to adjust. Just sight down the sole of the plane to be sure the blade isn't crooked and screw the blade in and out to adjust the depth

of cut. On the bench plane you should check several adjustments before setting the cutting depth. The front edge of the chip breaker should rest tightly on the blade. If it doesn't, shavings will jam between the two pieces of metal. Honing the chip breaker flat on a stone will correct this problem. The chip breaker is usually set about $1/16$ inch from the cutting edge of the blade, on the side without the bevel. It can be set back an additional $1/16$ inch for very heavy planing. The cap iron holds everything in place. If the cap iron is too loose, the blade will chatter or won't hold a setting. If it's too tight, the blade will be hard to adjust. A partial turn of the adjusting screw on the cap iron will correct these problems.

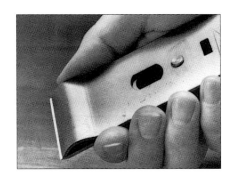

Chip breaker adjustment

Planing Tips

Begin by clamping the work firmly. Adjust the plane for a shallow depth of cut.

The first rule of planing: Plane with the grain. This will minimize tearing. An easy way to remember this is that the plane should be going "uphill" on the grain. When you plane the face of a

board, it may be hard to tell whether you are going the right way until you make the first few passes. Keep your plane set for a light cut so that torn grain is kept to a minimum.

Plane with the grain

When planing a board with knots or "wild" grain, push the plane at an angle to take a slicing cut. When you begin a cut, put more pressure on the front knob of the plane. When finishing a cut, apply more pressure on the rear handle. This will keep the plane from digging in or taking too much off of the ends. Also, you'll be more comfortable pushing with your whole upper body rather than just your arms.

When you plane the edge of a board, keep a try square handy to check that the board stays square. When planing end grain, set the plane to take a thin shaving. Plane from both ends of the piece toward the middle to avoid splintering.

Can you plane plywood edges? You bet. Just remember to plane from both ends or the plywood will splinter. Keep your blade sharp; it should produce crisp shavings. If it's making dust, it's time to resharpen it.

Blade Getting Dull?

When the plane gets hard to push and leaves the wood rough and torn, it's time to resharpen it. Take the chip breaker off and hone the blade on a sharpening stone. For a very sharp edge you must first hone the back of the blade flat and smooth, then hone the bevel. Many people like to round over the corners of the blade a tiny bit to keep the plane from gouging.

Successful Glass Cutting

Cutting glass seems like magic — a swoosh, a snap, and in just seconds you have a perfectly clean, straight edge. At least that's what you'll have once you get the knack of using a glass cutter. It's not hard. You just need practice and the right techniques; broken window glass is easy to find to practice on.

Is it worth learning? If you just need a new windowpane you might as well have the hardware store cut it, or maybe you can use one of the standard sizes available in home centers. But someday you'll want to cut a curved piece, use spare glass, or make your own picture frames, bird feeders, or stained glass, and you'll need to cut the glass yourself. And for even the simplest projects, it's always nice to perform a little bit of magic.

Caution: When cutting glass, you should always wear leather gloves and safety glasses, and avoid handling the glass by its edges.

Score, Then Run

As you probably know, cutting glass isn't cutting at all, but controlled breaking. The process has two parts: scoring a line with the glass cutter, and running the cut, which simply is breaking along the scored line and allowing the break to travel, or run, the length of the score.

Scoring the line

Getting Ready

First, clear off a hard and flat work surface. In glass cutting shops you might see tables covered with carpet, which prevents glass chips from building up, but you will have better luck with a large sheet of plywood or a clean flat workbench.

A grease pencil or felt-tip pen works well to lay out the cut. For a straight edge, select a piece of wood about ¼-inch thick (like a yard stick). A strip of masking tape on the underside will keep it from sliding around. You also need a small rag with a little light machine oil or kerosene to lubricate the cutter. Put on your safety glasses, because scoring with the glass cutter produces little chips that can fly around.

Use only a sharp cutter. A cutter with a steel wheel costs just a couple dollars, but if you anticipate cutting more than a very small amount of glass, get one with a carbide wheel, which is usually a little more expensive. The carbide wheel will stay sharp much longer.

Scoring the Line

Scoring is a knack, but one you can get with a little practice. You have to be confident, but without pushing too hard on the glass.

Lubricate the cut by putting a little oil on the cutter wheel or wiping the area of the score with an oily rag. Grip the cutter as you would a pen, not a knife, keeping it fairly straight up and down. Draw it toward you in one quick, confident, smooth motion, exerting just enough pressure to score the glass.

The best cut is a light one, almost invisible. If you see flakes along the line, you are bearing down too hard on the glass with the cutter (this is the most common error). Don't run the cutter too slowly either; a fast score cuts deeper into the glass and requires less pressure. Don't go over the line twice; it won't help the score and it will quickly dull your cutter.

Cut curves either freehand or with a curved template. When the piece you want is enclosed by waste, you can score relief lines going from your shape out to the edge of the glass. They should go to within ¹⁄₁₆ inch of the scored shape but not intersect it. They will break away, leaving your design.

Running the Cut

The principle behind running the cut is simple — stretch the score. In other words, the glass will break when the scored line is put under tension. How you accomplish this depends on the situation. You should always start the run where you ended the score, because the beginning of the score usually does not extend to the edge of the glass.

For large sheets, bend the glass over a small round object, like a pencil. The score must be on top so that it is put under tension. For small strips and pieces, you can just hold the glass on either side of the score and bend it, so the scored upper surface is stretched. For very narrow strips, you can grip the strip with a pair of pliers.

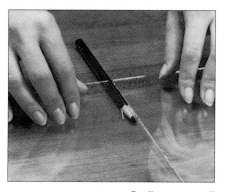
Bending over a pencil

For curves, turn the glass over onto a cushioned surface, and push down on the score with your gloved thumb or tap directly underneath the score with the ball on the end of the cutter. If there is a rough edge after you run the cut, smooth it with a sharpening stone.

Plumbing

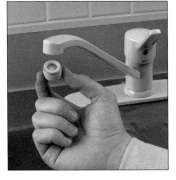

Fixing Faucets   48

Faucets work perfectly 99 percent of the time, but when they drip, it's torture. Fortunately, the fixes are fairly straightforward.

Making Faucets Flow   53

If your faucets or sink sprayer have stopped delivering like they used to, the solution may be right at your fingertips.

Unclogging Plumbing   54

In the movies, the frantic home owner floods the house before finally calling the plumber. But in real life a clogged drain doesn't have to be a catastrophe.

Adjusting a Stopper   58

Does the water in your tub drain out when the stopper is closed, or barely move at all when it's open? Adjusting the stopper assembly might be all you need to do.

Replacing a Double Drain 59

A drain that drips is not only annoying, it can ruin the inside of a cabinet or vanity. Replacing the drain assembly will solve the problem.

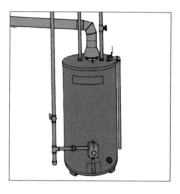

Tuning up a Toilet   **60**

Replacing worn or leaky toilet parts is a job you can easily handle regardless of how little plumbing experience you may have had.

Replacing a Toilet   **63**

A cracked bowl, a badly chipped tank, or the desire to save water are good reasons to make a simple change.

Curing a Drippy Shower   **66**

There's no need to put up with a shower head that squirts, drips, or sprays where you don't want it to.

Cleaning a Water Heater   **67**

A few quick twists of the wrist can make your water heater work more efficiently and last longer — and save you money.

Work Better, Work Safer   **68**

A cure for a dribbling faucet, a stainless steel sink saver, and some other advice to help ease your DIY days.

Fixing Faucets

Follow this guide to fix the three most common types of faucets.

WHAT YOU NEED

Pipe wrench

Adjustable wrench

Screwdriver

Pliers

Allen wrench

Replacement parts

In making any faucet repair, turn off the water at the shutoff valve before doing anything else. Your next step depends on the type of faucet.

Washer-type faucets seal with simple, round washers. When they wear out, your faucet drips at the spout. Leaks can also occur around the handle stem while the water is on. Then, the packing nut washer or the retaining nut washer needs to be replaced.

But washer-type faucets are fast giving way to cartridge valve units. A "cartridge" is a replaceable element that contains all the working parts of the faucet. Repair usually means replacing the entire cartridge.

Repair the ball-type faucet on a kitchen sink by replacing worn rubber seats and springs or worn O-rings.

REPLACING FAUCET WASHERS

STEP 1 Unscrew the retaining nut with an adjustable wrench and remove the valve stem by turning it until it releases completely.

STEP 2 Clean grit or scrape corrosion from the valve seat. If the seat is cracked or chipped, you may be able to replace it; or better, buy a new faucet.

STEP 3 Unscrew and replace the stem washer. Buy a replacement of exactly the same shape and size.

STEP 4 Replace the deteriorated retaining nut and packing nut washers to stop valve stem leaks.

Drips from the spout, or improper hot and cold mixing, indicate a worn cartridge that must be replaced. Leaks around the spout base indicate worn O-rings. Plumbing supply stores, home centers, and well-stocked hardware stores carry replacement kits for all major faucet brands.

Organization is the key to doing this job without difficulty. As you disassemble the faucet, lay out the parts in the order of removal. Then, reassembly will be a snap.

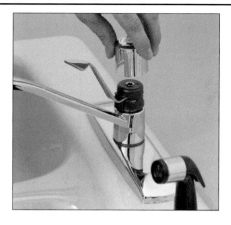

STEP 1 Pull off the handle cover to expose the handle screw. Shut off the water and turn on the faucet to relieve the pressure.

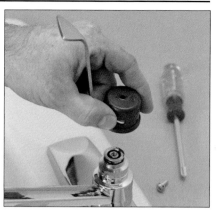

STEP 2 Remove the handle screw and lift off the handle lever and handle body assembly.

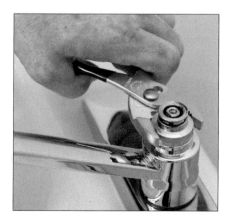

STEP 3 Unscrew the retainer pivot nut with a pair of pliers. Be careful not to scratch the spout body.

STEP 4 Remove the spout by swinging it from side to side while lifting straight up. Grip the spout by its base.

STEP 5 Lift off the spray diverter. This will be present only if your faucet has a spray accessory.

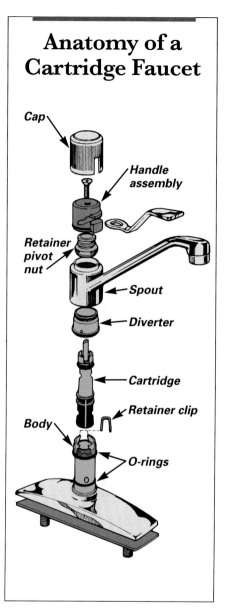

Anatomy of a Cartridge Faucet

- Cap
- Handle assembly
- Retainer pivot nut
- Spout
- Diverter
- Cartridge
- Retainer clip
- Body
- O-rings

STEP 6   Pry off the retainer clip with a screwdriver. Set it aside for rein-stallation later.

STEP 7   Place the plastic cap from the new cartridge kit over the top of the old valve and twist in both directions to release the valve.

STEP 8   Pull up firmly on the stem with pliers to remove the cartridge valve. Clean out debris.

Assembly Hint

When you insert the new cartridge valve into the faucet, orient the notched valve stem toward the sink so that the handle will mount at the proper angle. Models with knobs (usually found in bathrooms) often position the notch differently from models with handles.

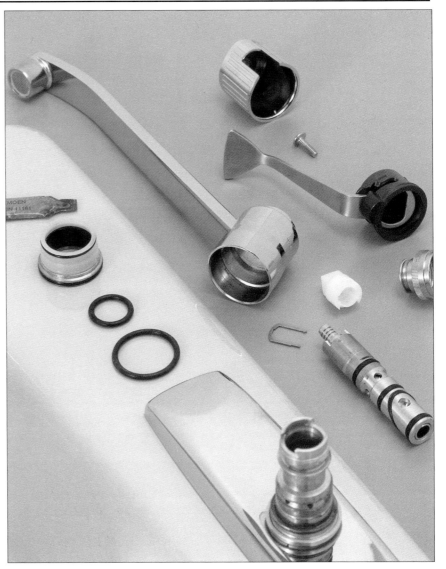

STEP 9   Lay the disassembled parts in order on a clean surface. Replace worn O-rings and the cartridge. Carefully follow the kit directions for reinsertion of the new cartridge, then reassemble the faucet.

A drippy single-arm, ball-type faucet may need new seals and O-rings eventually, but before running out to get a repair kit, try this: Following the steps shown here, disassemble the handle and cap and remove the ball assembly. Remove the rubber seals and springs from the body and slightly stretch the springs. Clean any filmy residue from all the parts, especially the ball. Lightly coat the seals and O-rings with petroleum jelly and reassemble.

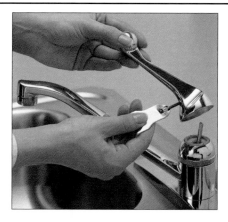

STEP 1 Drips from the spout indicate worn rubber seats and springs; leakage around the spout base means worn O-rings. To begin either repair, loosen the set screw with the Allen wrench and remove the handle.

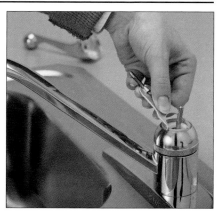

STEP 2 Loosen the adjusting ring with the special tool in the kit. This releases pressure on the ball.

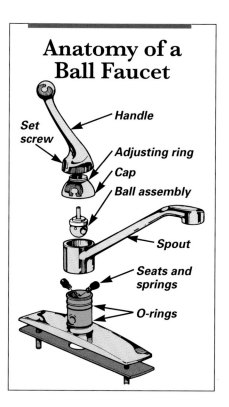

Anatomy of a Ball Faucet

- Handle
- Set screw
- Adjusting ring
- Cap
- Ball assembly
- Spout
- Seats and springs
- O-rings

STEP 3 Unscrew and remove the cap. Wrap the cap with a rag if you must use a wrench to loosen it. The adjusting ring will remain attached to the cap assembly.

STEP 4 Remove the ball assembly by grasping the protruding shaft and lifting. Lay the pieces aside in the order in which they are removed.

STEP 5 Lift out the rubber seats gently using a screwdriver and make sure you remove their springs as well. Reset the replacement parts.

STEP 6 Work the spout off by swinging it back and forth while lifting. It may be stubborn, but keep at it.

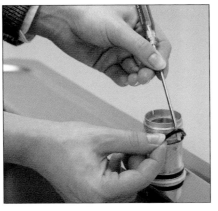

STEP 7 Replace the two rubber O-rings. Be sure to clean off all deteriorated rubber from the faucet body.

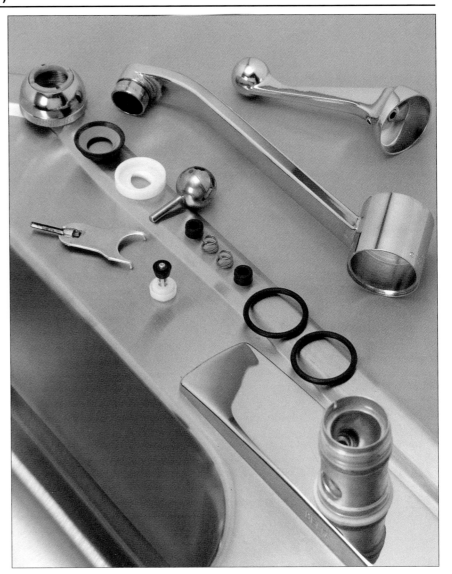

STEP 8 Lay out all the faucet parts on a clean, flat surface in the order in which you removed them. Reassemble the parts in reverse order, replacing the old parts with the new ones from the kit.

Replacing the Cap

The only tricky part of replacement is reinstalling the cap assembly. Hand tighten the cap, then tighten the adjusting ring with the special tool until no water leaks around the stem when it is in the "on" position (the shutoffs under the sink must be turned on). Don't overtighten either the cap or the adjusting ring. You should be able to move both the handle and the spout easily with just one finger. Overtightening can damage the rubber seats or cause them to wear out prematurely.

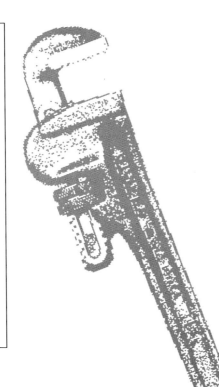

Making Faucets Flow

Simple cleaning is the only maintenance they need.

WHAT YOU NEED

Joint sealant or Teflon tape

Screwdriver

Sewing needle

Adjustable wrench

When a faucet doesn't deliver water freely, the problem may be the aerator — the small device on the end of the spout. It mixes air with the water, providing an even, splash-free flow. But it also accumulates debris (mostly iron, lime, and calcium) suspended in almost all water supplies. If a faucet's flow is slow or erratic, remove the gunk.

The kitchen sink sprayer becomes plugged in much the same way as a faucet aerator. If you can't get the sprayer head cleaned out, or if it's worn or broken, replace it. Sometimes your sprayer head is good but the hose may need replacing — also a simple task.

CLEANING THE AERATOR

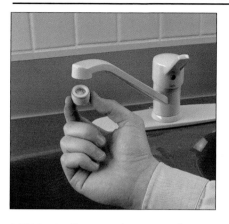

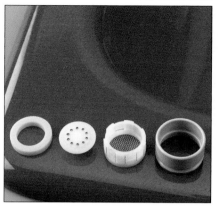

STEP 1 Remove the aerator from the faucet end by turning it clockwise. Flush away sediment and debris, using a sewing needle to clean crevices and small holes.

STEP 2 Disassemble the aerator parts if further cleaning is necessary. Lay out the parts in order so you'll remember how they go back together.

UNCLOGGING A SINK SPRAYER

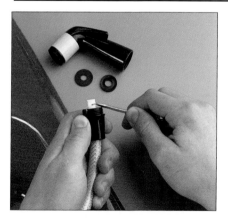

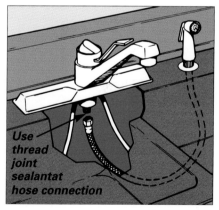

Use thread joint sealant at hose connection

STEP 1 Unscrew the sprayer head and clean deposits from the nozzle and hose connection. To remove the hose from the sprayer base, snap off the C-shaped ring with a small screwdriver.

STEP 2 To replace a sprayer hose, disconnect it from the sprayer base. Unscrew the fitting from the underside of the faucet. Use Teflon thread-sealing tape on the new connection.

Unclogging Plumbing

Try these steps before you call the plumber.

WHAT YOU NEED

Rag

Plunger

Plastic bag

C-clamp

Plumber's snake

Adjustable wrench

Bucket

Washers

Closet auger

Wax ring seal

Penetrating oil, propane
   torch, or cold chisel

Power snake

Drain tape

Leather gloves

It is as certain as the sunrise that some time, somewhere, a household drain will clog and cause its contents to back up. This is always inconvenient and often messy. Knowing how to unclog a drain remains a basic survival skill for every home owner.

The good news is that most clogs can be removed simply and safely — without resorting to caustic chemicals or professional help.

In fact, the pros almost never use chemicals. Their tools of choice are the plunger and snake.

Like a pro, try to clear clogs first using a plunger; use a steady, rhythmic motion, and be persistent. But if plunging fails, get out the snake. Instructions for using it begin on page 55.

PLUNGING KITCHEN SINKS...

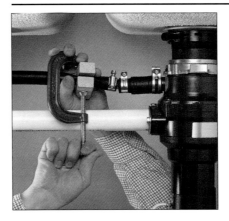

STEP 1 Clamp the hose between the dishwasher and the sink or garbage disposer so the plunger is pushing only on the clog.

STEP 2 Stop up the other side of a double kitchen sink when you plunge. A rag stuffed into a plastic bag works best. Keep some water in the sink.

BATHROOM SINKS...

AND TOILETS

Cover the overflow hole with a rag when plunging a bathroom sink so the plunger has maximum effect. Do the same on bathtubs.

A plunger with a flange is the best kind for plunging toilets because it makes a good seal. The flange folds back on itself for use on sinks and tubs.

SNAKING DRAINS...

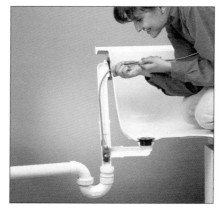

STEP 1 Remove the trap under the kitchen or bathroom sink by loosening the slip nuts. Have a bucket handy to catch water from the trap. When you reinstall the trap, use a new washer.

STEP 2 Insert the tip of the snake into the pipe until you feel it hit the clog. Twist the snake to drive the spiral tip into the clog, then pull the clog out with the snake.

TOILETS AND...

BATHTUBS

A closet auger works better in toilets than a standard snake, but it works the same way. Insert it into the toilet until it touches the clog, twist, and remove auger and clog.

Clean out the pipe and P-trap through the overflow assembly hole. Feed a snake in 6 inches at a time and rotate it.

Clean-out Tips

Removing the trap makes drain cleaning much easier. The trap is the bent section of pipe directly below the sink or tub, though some tubs have traps shaped like a drum. If the obstruction is in the trap, just push it out with a coat hanger and reinstall the assembly.

As soon as you take the trap off under your sink, buy a new slip nut gasket, taking the old one with you to the store for reference. The old gasket probably will not seal tightly a second time. If the nut's worn, replace it too. A rule of thumb: When in doubt, replace the parts now, while you have the drain disassembled.

Tubs can be tricky because the trap is hard to reach and remove. There may be a removable panel in the wall behind the tub to give you access to the trap, or, on a first-floor tub, you can reach the trap from the basement or crawl space. If you can't find the trap or get it open, check to see if the sink is also clogged. If so, that means that the problem can be reached through the sink drain. But if all else fails, get help from a plumber.

Turn off the water when removing the trap to avoid accidental floods if someone turns on the faucet before you have finished removing the clog. Perhaps the only thing worse than no water flow is an uncontrolled flood.

A plumber's snake is a flexible wire coil that slides through pipes. The spiral tip digs into obstructions to help pull them out or break them up. Fancy snakes with cranks or cases are sometimes easier to store, but they work no better than an ordinary, bent-handled model.

A closet auger is a specialized snake for toilets. The rubber sheath protects the porcelain from scratches and the bent tip helps turn the snake around the first bend.

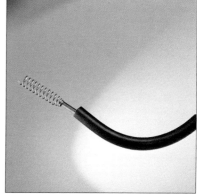

Plumber's snake

Closet auger

An Ounce of Prevention

Keep your kitchen drains flowing by periodically running hot water through them for a few minutes. This will loosen up the grease and flush it down the drain.

■ Don't put materials that harden down your drain. Do-it-yourselfers watch out: This includes materials like joint compound, spackling compound, cement, wax, latex paint, and water-based glues. If the drain is your only alternative, be sure to flush by letting the water run for 3 or 4 minutes afterward.

■ If you've plunged or snaked the toilet and it seems to flush properly, give it the "paper test" before proclaiming victory. There could be a clog that lets water through but stops solids from passing — not at all what you want.
  First, remove the tank lid and find the valve at the bottom of the tank that opens when the toilet is flushed. Get ready to close this valve if the toilet starts to back up. Then put lots of toilet paper, 20 or 30 feet, into the bowl and flush it down. If it goes down, you're all set. If not, keep plunging. You will win, eventually.

SNAKING A TOILET FROM BELOW

In extreme cases, a clogged toilet can only be cleaned by removing it and running a snake from the bottom of the fixture. Although the job is messy, it is not complicated. You will have to buy a new wax ring and slip it onto the toilet before you reinstall the toilet.

STEP 1 Shut off the water supply to the toilet, flush and drain it, and disconnect the water supply tube.

STEP 2 Remove the nuts from the bolts that secure the toilet to the floor. Using proper lifting technique, lift the toilet, rocking it to break it free from the closet flange.

STEP 3 Stuff a rag into the closet flange to block sewer gas and scrape off the old wax ring that seals the toilet to the drain pipe.

STEP 4 Snake from the underside of the toilet.

STEP 5 Replace the wax ring when you replace the toilet. Install the new wax ring so that the plastic flange faces down toward the floor.

If water is backing up out of your floor drain, there may be a block in the main drain line leaving the house caused by household wastes, tree roots, or a collapsed pipe. Find the main cleanout, a removable plug near where the main sewer pipe leaves your house. Let the water on your floor recede, then remove the plug.

When you replace the plug, use plumber's Teflon tape on the threads so it will come off easier next time.

This is one job you may want to leave to a pro. It's messy, and most home owners don't own the heavy-duty snake needed.

STEP 1 Open a rusty cleanout plug with penetrating oil, gentle heat, or a cold chisel. If these don't work, drill some holes and break the plug.

STEP 2 Use a drain tape — a long, stiff snake designed for main drain lines. Push it through with the special plier-like handle that grips the tape.

STEP 3 You can rent a power snake. Different tips are available for solid clogs and tree roots. Wear leather gloves and be careful not to let the snake wrap around your hand.

Chemical Caution

! Chemicals are hard on your pipes, they're less effective than mechanical action, and they can be dangerous if they splash.

If you use a chemical, dilute it thoroughly or let the water drain through the clog overnight before plunging or snaking. If you need to call a plumber, ALWAYS tell him if you've used chemicals first.

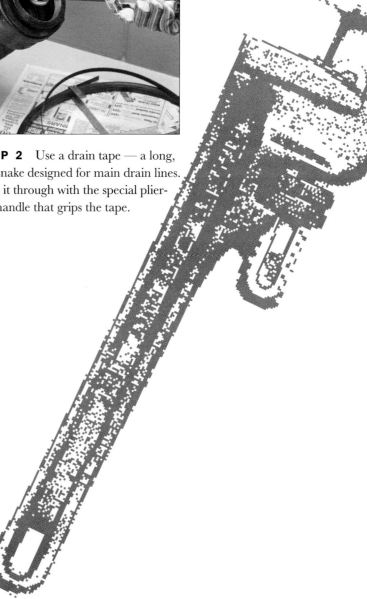

Adjusting a Stopper

Stop tub leaks or speed the draining water on its way.

WHAT YOU NEED

Screwdriver

Snake

Although the bathtub drain is a me–chanical monster, it does work — and it's adjustable as well.

The drain consists of two parts: the overflow assembly and the stopper assembly, and either or both can be adjusted. There are many different styles of drain fixtures, so yours may be a little different from the one shown here. But they all operate on the same principles.

If the tub is draining slowly, turn the striker rod in the overflow assembly to lengthen it so it pushes the stopper high-er. If the stopper leaks while water is in the tub, shorten the striker rod.

Adjust the stopper assembly by with-drawing it from the drain and adjusting the small nut and stopper up or down; lengthen the short rod to speed drain-ing, or shorten it to stop leaking.

ADJUSTING THE STRIKER. . .

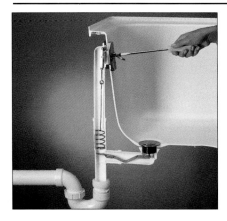

STEP 1   Remove the two screws that secure the overflow plate in place. Note how the overflow and stopper assemblies are not directly connected.

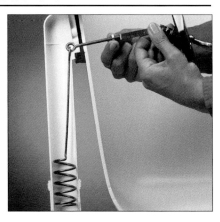

STEP 2   Adjust the length of the striker rod: longer to speed up sluggish draining, shorter to stop leaks when the bathtub is full.

AND THE STOPPER

Withdraw the stopper assembly and adjust the height of the stopper: taller to speed a sluggish drain, shorter to stop leaks.

Replacing a Double Drain

Stop annoying leaks once and for all.

WHAT YOU NEED

Pipe wrench or adjustable wrench

Bucket

Tape measure

Marking pen

Hacksaw

Any plumbing leak is annoying, but a dripping double sink drain spells double trouble. To be on the safe side, replace the whole assembly, as shown here. It's difficult to remove one section of old pipe without damaging those adjoining it — and the investment in new parts is cheap insurance against future leaks.

Plan ahead and take a Polaroid picture or make a quick sketch of the old drain to help jog your memory when you reassemble the new drain. Save the parts you remove and take them (and your sketch) to the hardware store or home center to ensure that you purchase the right parts.

If you find that a garbage disposer or dishwasher feeds into your drain, you can use one of the readily available fittings, adapters, or extensions.

Finally, remember to install all washers and firmly tighten all slip nuts.

STEP 1 Remove the old trap and drain using a pipe wrench or wide-mouthed pliers. Stubborn metal slip nuts can be loosened by tapping or heating. Keep a bucket handy to catch waste water.

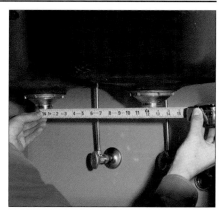

STEP 2 Save slip nuts and gaskets from the basket strainer outlets. Determine the distance from center to center of the existing strainer outlets (12 inches in this example).

STEP 3 Measure from center to center of the temporarily assembled drain; find the difference in length between it and the strainer outlet span, mark it on the waste arm, and cut.

STEP 4 Loosely assemble the entire drain. The waste arm must slope toward the trap. When all is right, hand tighten the nuts, then take ⅛ to ¼ turn with a pipe wrench.

Tuning up a Toilet

Replacing worn or leaky parts is a job you can handle.

WHAT YOU NEED

Adjustable wrench

Sponge

Bucket

Rags

Heavy-duty paper towels

Plumber's putty

16-ounce bottle of lime remover

Metal clothes hanger

The toilet uses more water than any other appliance in your house. And if it has worn or leaky parts, it can be a real water waster.

Three of the main parts of the toilet tank can be replaced. They are the fill valve (including the large float ball on older toilets); the flapper (often a small rubber ball on older toilets); and the handle (trip lever).

If your fill valve is bad, water will continue running into the tank even when the tank is full.

A leaky flapper is the culprit when the toilet continues to run but no water is leaving the tank via the overflow pipe. The flapper is made of rubber and will eventually deteriorate since it's constantly submerged in water.

A broken or sticky handle or lift arm will affect other parts in the tank, such as the flapper valve and the lift chain.

STEP 1 Flush the toilet and sponge out any water after turning off the water to the toilet. Loosen the locknut and coupling nut with an adjustable wrench.

STEP 2 Remove the old fill valve and float ball. Be careful not to chip or crack the tank.

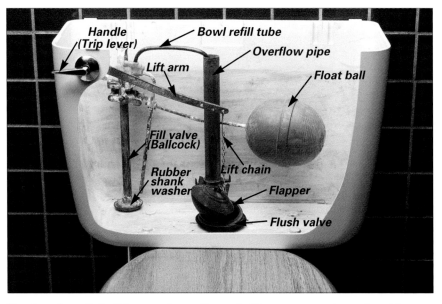

Here's a view of all of the parts in a toilet tank. These parts can be replaced by most DIYers and are available at well-stocked home centers and hardware stores.

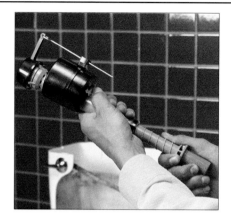

STEP 3 Adjust the new fill valve to fit by twisting the valve body. The top of the new valve should be about 1 inch below the top edge of the tank. Install the new valve.

STEP 4 Clear debris from the supply line after the valve is connected. Remove the valve's top cap, hold a cup upside down over the valve, and turn on the water to flush out the line.

STEP 5 Reconnect the top cap, connect the bowl refill tube to the overflow pipe, and adjust the float. The water level should rise to about 1 inch below the top of the overflow pipe.

REPLACING THE FLAPPER, ARM, AND CHAIN

STEP 1 Unhook the lift chain from the lift arm. Remove the flapper from the overflow pipe. If one of the ears is broken, use the retaining ring with ears that should come with the new flapper.

STEP 2 Disconnect the lift chain from the lift arm. Remove the retaining nut that secures the handle. The nut is located inside the tank. Maneuver the lift arm out through the handle hole.

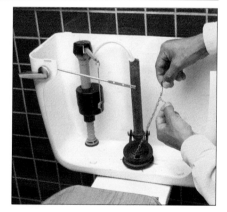

STEP 3 Install the new handle and arm and adjust the lift chain's length. Too much slack, or a chain that's too tight, will keep the new flapper from operating properly.

Tips for Toilet Maintenance

■ If you need to clean the priming jet hole in the toilet bowl, do it after pouring lime remover into the flush valve (see step 2 on page 62). This allows the lime remover to loosen the mineral buildup. Wear rubber gloves. The best way to remove the mineral buildup is with that all-purpose tool, a metal clothes hanger. Straighten the clothes hanger and gently scrape away any mineral deposits. Be careful you don't scratch or chip the bowl's porcelain finish. If you do, you'll eventually ruin the toilet bowl. Patience and persistence will produce the desired result without causing any further damage.

■ To prevent the lift chain on the flapper from getting caught underneath the flapper when it closes, cut a plastic soda straw in half and feed the chain through it. This will straighten the chain and keep it from sagging under the flapper valve.

■ An easy, inexpensive way to keep the bowl clean is to drop a large swimming pool chlorine tablet in the tank. The tablet dissolves a little with each flush and lasts for several weeks.

Solutions to a Sweating Toilet

Next time you see a puddle of water underneath the toilet on a hot and humid day, check the outside of the tank and bowl to see if "sweat" is running down the sides and onto the floor.

Of course, toilets don't actually sweat; water doesn't seep through their impervious glazed-china walls. The beads of water are condensation formed when humid air meets the cool toilet sides. Normally, the toilet would be at the same temperature as the air. But when the toilet is being used often, cool water from the underground pipes chills both the tank and bowl.

Occasional sweating does no harm, but persistent condensation will keep the floor wet, weaken the glue under the tile, cause plywood to delaminate, and encourage rot in the flooring.

Although the problem is common, the best solutions aren't that simple. You can reduce the humidity level in your house with a dehumidifier (or air conditioner), but that's expensive if your only goal is to stop condensation from forming on the toilet.

The two most-used and effective cures are:
- gluing a thin foam liner to the inside of your tank to insulate it. This works well and doesn't cost much, but it can be difficult to install. You have to remove the tank mechanisms, so you'll need a wide wrench and perhaps new rubber washers. If you need to buy a new toilet anyway, get one that includes a liner.
- connecting a hot-water line to the cold-water line through an adjustable "antisweat" valve, letting you warm the tank water during warm, humid weather. The valve costs more than a liner and requires that you run a hot-water feed line.

You will probably find the tank liner easier to install than the antisweat valve. After the initial work, it requires no maintenance and no additional expense. To install an antisweat valve you have to run a hot-water line from the nearby sink hot-water supply. Then you have to adjust the hot/cold water mix as needed. Of course, you'll pay a small energy cost to heat the water.

You can find both the tank liner and antisweat valve at most plumbing supply stores, or the store can order them for you.

There are two other very cheap, simple ways to cope with condensation:
- Insulate your tank on the outside with a tank cover. You can find one where you buy linens, matched to your towels or carpet. Launder it often to keep it sanitary and free from mildew.
- Simply lay a towel under the tank to soak up moisture if condensation occurs only a few times a year.

REPAIRING A CLOGGED TOILET BOWL

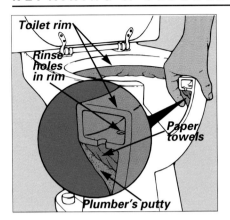

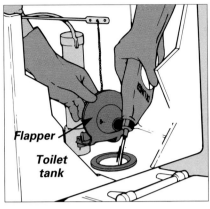

STEP 1 Turn off the water to the toilet, flush it, and soak up any remaining water in the tank. Roll wet paper towels into tubes and place them under the rim to block the rinse holes. Form a "snake" of plumber's putty and press it against the paper towels.

STEP 2 Lift the flapper and pour a 16-ounce bottle of lime remover into the hole of the flush valve. Wear rubber gloves and eye protection. Let the lime remover work — 24 hours is best, but if you can't keep the toilet out of use that long, let it work for at least 8 hours.

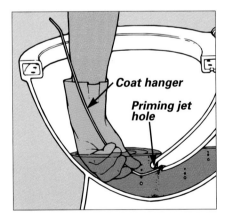

STEP 3 Wearing rubber gloves, remove and throw away the putty and paper towels. Clean the priming jet hole at the bottom of the bowl. Turn the water back on.

Replacing a Toilet

Believe it or not, you can do this job yourself.

WHAT YOU NEED

Tape measure

Adjustable wrench

⁷⁄₁₆- and ½-inch open-end or box-end wrenches

Mini hacksaw

Penetrating oil

Putty knife

Wax ring with extended collar

Plumber's putty

Flexible water-supply tube

Caulking gun

Silicone tub/tile caulk

Rags, sponge, and bucket

New toilet

Out with the old and in with the new — in a lot less time than you think.

Just about anyone can install a new toilet. It's not the most glamorous or pleasant job, but unless you run into a serious problem like a rotted floor under the toilet or a leak in the pipe in the floor, you can do it in a few hours, without advanced plumbing skills or a lot of experience.

REMOVING THE OLD

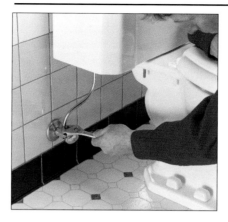

STEP 1   Shut off the water supply to the toilet, flush and sponge out the tank, and disconnect the supply tube. Be careful not to damage the shut-off valve or you'll have to replace it, too. With a plunger, force water remaining in the trap down the drain.

STEP 2   Remove the nuts from the hold-down bolts. The floor bolts nearest the wall are secured in the closet flange slots. The front hold-downs are screwed directly into the wood subfloor. Remove the closet screws and the nuts.

STEP 3   Cut off rusted or stuck nuts with a mini hacksaw.

STEP 4   Rock the old toilet to break it free from the closet flange in the floor, then lift it off. Lift carefully: Bend at the knees to avoid straining your back muscles.

Sizing the New Toilet

All toilets are not created equal — they come in different sizes. Before you can buy a new one, you need to know the distance from the finished wall to the center of the drain that's in the floor.

This distance is most often 12 inches; however, some toilets are built to fit a drain outlet centered anywhere from 10 to 14 inches from the wall. The toilets sold at most home centers fit a 12-inch space. Other sizes may need to be specially ordered.

The idea, of course, is to install a toilet that just fills the space allotted — leaving just enough room for maintenance. Extra space is all right. But if there's not enough, you could end up with a real problem on your hands.

You don't have to remove the toilet to see what size toilet you need. Measure from the wall to the middle of the bolt cap on the bowl's base, or to the floor bolt itself, which is under the cap. The floor bolts are always aligned with the center of the toilet drain in the floor.

Older toilets often have four bolts — two on each side. Newer styles have only one bolt per side. If your toilet has two bolts per side, the distance is measured from the wall to the closest bolt.

STEP 1 Scrape off the old wax ring or plumber's putty on the closet flange. Remove the old closet bolts from the slots. Put a rag in the closet flange opening to block sewer gas.

STEP 2 Place a new wax ring over the toilet's horn. Use a wax ring with an extended collar. This type helps direct the water into the drain when the toilet is flushed. Remove the rag from the drain.

STEP 3 Position the bowl over the closet flange and align the floor bolts and holes. Pack a little plumber's putty around the floor bolts to keep them vertical in the bolt slots.

STEP 4 Install tank bolts, washers, and nuts. The bolts are used to secure the tank to the bowl; the washers seal the holes in the bottom of the tank.

STEP 5 Place the tank over the back of the bowl. The spud washer should fit into the recessed opening on the bowl. The tank bolts go into the holes on the sides of the recessed area.

STEP 6 Connect a new flexible water supply tube to the shut-off valve and toilet. With a flexible tube, there's no cutting to fit.

Toilet Connections

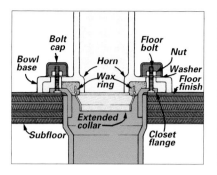

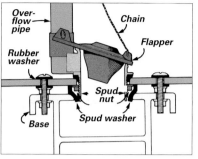

Here's how the base of the toilet fits into the drain in the bathroom floor. The view is from the front of the toilet toward the wall at floor level.

This illustrates how the tank and bowl are connected. Again, you are looking from the front of the toilet at the level of the toilet seat.

STEP 7 Apply silicone caulk where the toilet and floor meet. Before caulking, flush the toilet a few times. Check for leaks at the water supply tube, at the tank and bowl, and under the toilet.

Water-saving Toilets

Just how much water is needed to flush a toilet? Most toilets in use today consume from 5 to 7 gallons, but if you are replacing a toilet, you will find that the only models available will be so-called ultra-low-flush (ULF) toilets that use only about one quarter as much water.

Beginning on January 1, 1994, it became illegal anywhere in the United States to make or to sell a toilet that uses more than 1.6 gallons of water per flush. These toilets are designed to save water and put less strain on already overworked municipal sewer systems.

But is 1.6 gallons enough to consistently produce a good, sanitary flush? If it fails and leaves waste on the sides of the bowl or fails to clear all waste from the remaining water, naturally you'll flush a second time and perhaps a third time if necessary. Obviously, repeated flushes cancel any water-saving advantage. It is the designers' goal to come up with a ULF toilet that works right on the first flush.

There are two types of water-saving toilets currently available to home owners: the gravity ULF and pressurized ULF. The gravity model operates like a standard 5-gallon toilet does, although plumbing engineers have re-shaped it in several subtle ways.

The interior of the bowl has been modified and streamlined to make the flush as smooth as possible. You might not be able to notice any difference between it and an older toilet. With some models, however, the changes will be much more obvious; the gravity ULFs have steeper-sided bowls to increase water velocity.

Some manufacturers produce smaller tanks, although, curiously, the tanks on other models of gravity ULFs appear as large as on the old ones. Designers made those tanks taller and slimmer, raising the flush water higher and thereby increasing its flushing power.

These taller tanks also hold more than 1.6 gallons of water. Of course, that would violate the 1.6-gallon limit, except that the flush valves don't release it all, harnessing the force of only the topmost 1.6 gallons. The tank never empties completely, a clever way to increase flushing power.

Pressurized ULFs look conventional from the outside but use an air-assisted flush mechanism inside the tank. As the home water supply fills the plastic tank, the water pressure also compresses air in a closed compartment. This compressed air is used to accelerate the water in the tank whenever the flush button is pushed. The extra velocity provided by the air pressure leads to a more powerful flush.

Curing a Drippy Shower

The cause is simple — and so is the fix.

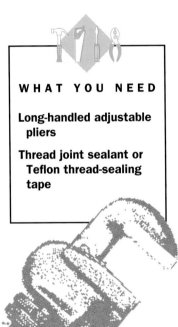

A shower head that squirts, drips, or sprays you where you don't want it takes all the joy out of a good, hot shower. There's no need to put up with that. A couple of good soaking sprays of ordinary supermarket de-limer may clean out minor clogging, but if the shower head is worn or clogged beyond hope, replace it. A new shower head — even a muscle-relaxing one with an adjustable or pulsating spray — is easy to install.

The installation is simple if you have external threads on the bottom end of the shower arm.

If you remove your old shower head and discover a ball shape at the end of the shower arm, the arm itself as well as the shower head will have to be replaced. This is a bit more work, but it's no big deal. The cutaway wall helps show how to do it.

SHOWER HEAD REPLACEMENT

STEP 1   Remove the old shower head from the shower arm. If the arm end has external threads, simply apply thread joint sealant or Teflon tape, and screw the new head in place.

STEP 2   To install a new shower head if your shower arm has a ball end, you'll also need to replace the arm, as shown in the cutaway photos below.

REPLACING THE ARM

STEP 1   Unscrew the old shower arm by sliding back the cover plate and using long-handled adjustable pliers. The wall cutaway shows how the arm unscrews from the shower supply pipe.

STEP 2   Screw the new shower arm into the supply pipe and tighten. Then mount the new shower head on the arm. Use pipe thread sealant or Teflon thread-sealing tape at both joints.

Cleaning a Water Heater

Make sure this vital appliance keeps working efficiently.

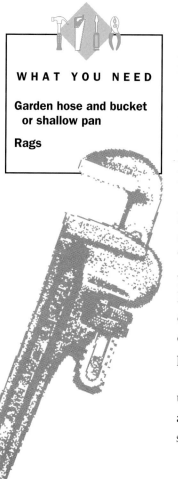

WHAT YOU NEED

Garden hose and bucket or shallow pan

Rags

Manufacturers recommend that you periodically drain some water from the bottom of the water heater tank to flush out iron, lime, and calcium particles that can settle to the bottom of the heater tank, making it less efficient. A gas water heater, with the burner at the bottom, has to heat through all of this buildup.

All water heaters have a drain valve located near the bottom of the tank, about 5 or 6 inches from the floor. These valves have external threads so you can connect an ordinary garden hose to direct the water into a floor drain. You can also drain the water directly into a small bucket or shallow pan. Be careful: The water will be hot.

Flush the tank for two to four minutes with the water flowing as forcefully as the valve will allow so that it will siphon out the sediment.

Types of Water Heater Drain Valves

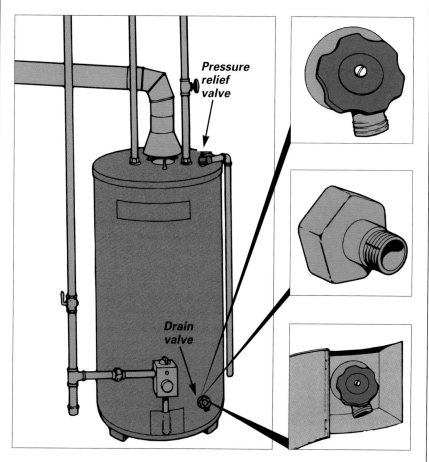

Pressure relief valve

Drain valve

Water heater drain valves come in several shapes and styles. The standard-looking drain valve (*top*) is the most common. It has a round handle that you turn counterclockwise to open the valve.

The style shown in the center doesn't look like a valve at all, but you can identify it by the external threads on the end of its central spout. This valve is usually white plastic and round or hexagonal — about 3 inches in diameter. To open, turn the outside ring by hand, counterclockwise.

A third drain valve style (*bottom*) isn't always easy to spot because it's located in a recess behind a small metal door on the water heater tank.

Work Better, Work Safer

Stubborn Valve Seat

If you have a leaky bathroom faucet, you can try to remove the worn valve seat, but you might end up rounding the square opening for the valve wrench.

If you've stripped the tool opening, use a screw extractor to get the valve seat out. This tool looks like a tapered drill bit except it has wide spirals that run in the opposite direction of a drill bit. The top of the extractor has flat sides so you can grip it with an adjustable wrench or the "T" handle used with taps. Insert the extractor into the valve seat opening and gently tap it tight. As you turn the extractor counterclockwise, it is forced tighter and tighter into the valve seat opening.

Dribbling Faucet

If the faucet in your bathtub dribbles when the shower is turned on, you may find you don't get as strong a stream of water through the shower head as you should. The first step toward solving the problem is replacing the spout. A combination tub/shower faucet has a diverter that is triggered when the but-ton on the spout is pulled up. Diverters can wear out, causing the problem.

However, if you're still experiencing the problem even after installing a new spout, it's likely you have low water pressure — a situation common in older homes.

Over time, mineral deposits collect inside water pipes, reducing the amount of water that can flow through. If there's not enough water flow, then pressure is reduced as well. The result is wimpy showers, because the diverter is unable to send all the water to the shower head.

To solve the problem of low water delivery, you may have to go so far as to replace your house's main water pipes. This is a fairly expensive undertaking, so before you start, get professional advice from at least two plumbers who can take a closer look at your situation.

Soft Touch

To protect the surface of chrome-plated metal parts when using a pair of pliers, fit the jaws of the pliers with protective leather "fingertips." Cut the fingertips from an old pair of leather gloves and slip them over the plier jaws.

Drain Line Noise Control

Muffle the noise of drain lines inside the house when you're remodeling. Wrap carpet pad scraps around the pipes and duct-tape them in place. In hard-to-reach areas, stuff the padding around the pipe. The result is blissfully quiet plumbing.

Expanding Solution

Solve the problem of loose plumbing wall pipe straps. Pull the flange away from the wall and spray aerosol insulating foam in the wall cavity. The foam will harden and hold things tightly. Tape the pipe in the desired position before using the foam. This may save you a major repair job.

Foam in place

Kinkless Bending

Bend copper tubing without kinking it by taping one end shut and filling the tube completely with sand. Make your bends carefully, then remove the sand by shaking and lightly tapping the tube. Rinse the tubing before using it.

Better Pipe Cutting

It can be awkward to cut a piece of chrome-plated pipe, such as a P-trap, with a hacksaw. If you secure the pipe in a vise, you often squash it or mar the finish. And cutting it freehand is usually sloppy. Try inserting a piece of wood closet rod or handrail that's slightly smaller than the inside diameter of the pipe. Wrap one end of the rod with double-faced tape before inserting it. The tape holds the rod in place while you cut through the pipe and wood.

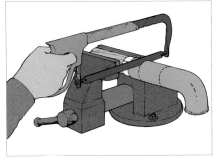

Clean pipe cutter

Vacuum a Clogged Drain

If the plunger doesn't work on a clogged drain, try your wet-dry shop vacuum. Just place the nozzle over the drain, alternately running hot water and applying the vacuum. Cover the overflow outlet in the sink or tub with a wet towel to get maximum suction. You'll be amazed how much debris the vacuum can remove.

Plastic Pipe Leak Cure

Try stopping minor leaks in plastic PVC drain fittings by tightening an ordinary stainless steel hose clamp around the hub of the fitting. It's a lot easier than cutting out the old fitting and replacing it. It may be temporary, and it's not by the book, but it works every time.

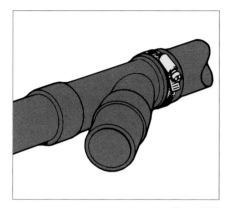

Clamp PVC

How Tight the Toilet?

Instructions for fastening a toilet tank to the bowl say, "Do not overtighten the bolts." But how do you know when you've overtightened?

Typically, you should only have to turn the tank bolts to a "firm" tightness so you get a watertight seal without the toilet tank's rocking. Wing nuts usually secure the bolts, meaning you should tighten them only by hand, not with a pliers or wrench.

Unfortunately, the problem is compounded by the great variety of systems used by manufacturers on their many models. Tanks can be fastened with two, three, or four bolts, and the rubber gaskets that are used are sometimes spongy, sometimes firm.

Keep in mind that the whole point is to avoid cracking the fragile tank.

Old Lead Joints

Planning to reroute some water pipes in your older house? Since the original copper piping was installed some time ago, you can be sure the solder contains lead. Is it safe to reuse the fittings if you resolder them with no-lead solder?

The answer is "no." First of all, small amounts of lead solder will probably remain on them, and lead leaching from lead solder into drinking water is a known health hazard. Besides the health risk, it's difficult to get the new joint to seal when you use lead-free solder over the old solder, since the two have different melting points.

It's plenty aggravating when a plumbing joint leaks, so don't increase the odds of it happening by using an old fitting. The best thing to do is cut the old fittings out and replace them with new ones. It's fine to reuse the old copper pipe, however.

Stuck Water Shut-off

When you need to turn off a water shut-off valve that hasn't been used for a long time, the packing around the valve stem may be dried or corroded. Don't force it and risk a leak around the valve stem. Put a few drops of light oil on the stem around the packing nut. Loosen the packing nut about one turn, then retighten it hand tight. Let the packing absorb the oil for a few minutes, and you should be able to turn the valve with no trouble. Tighten the packing nut until there's no water seepage around the stem.

Stainless Steel Sink Saver

Instead of replacing a scratched, stained, and etched stainless steel sink, give it a good rubdown with 220-grit, extra-fine sandpaper dampened with vegetable oil. It will come out looking like new. Make sure you move the sandpaper in the same direction as the original polishing lines.

Gurgling Sink Driving You Nuts?

Are you plagued with a bathroom sink that gurgles when the toilet is flushed? It happens, especially in older houses.

That gurgling is a sign of a serious problem with your plumbing: no venting. Chances are that your sink and toilet were not properly vented when they were installed. Here's what's going on:

When you flush the toilet, water goes down the waste pipe. As it travels, it sucks air in behind it — air that is normally supplied by vent pipes. If there is no venting, however, the water produces a suction so strong that it pulls water out of the sink trap, making a gurgling sound. Your pipes are gasping for air. Not only is it annoying, but without water in the sink trap, smelly and poisonous sewer gases can enter your house.

For a permanent solution, you should add the vent pipes, a complicated job that must be done in consultation with a licensed plumber. As an interim solution, however, you could run water in the sink after you flush the toilet to refill the sink trap.

On rare occasions, a bathroom that is properly vented will have a gurgling problem. That means the vent pipes are clogged. Call a plumber for help.

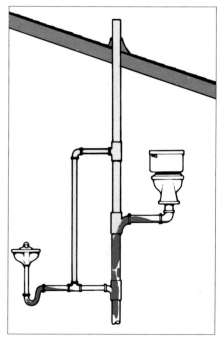

Venting problem

Cheap Lime Remover

The next time you need to remove lime deposits from faucets, fixtures, or lawn sprinklers, save some money by using plain old hydrogen peroxide from the drugstore. The peroxide softens the lime just as well as the over-the-counter lime removers but is much cheaper and probably safer.

Propane Torches

Carpenters have their circular saws, electricians their wire cutters, but for plumbers the tool that goes on every job, and that's often used from morning until night, is the propane torch.

Home owners find it a useful tool as well, for soldering copper plumbing pipe and a wide variety of other chores that require a portable source of intense heat. Here's a quick guide to propane torch techniques.

Buying a Torch

A standard torch consists of a brass nozzle and valve, which screws onto the bottle of propane. It may include accessories such as a striker, flame spreader, and soldering tip. If you will be doing a lot of plumbing work, you might look at models that have a trigger control and built-in lighter. They are convenient and economical because the gas is turned on for less time.

Torch and accessories

Basic Operation

Screw the torch head onto the propane bottle and open the valve all the way. Be careful: Don't risk a leak with flammable gas. Disconnect the torch head from the propane bottle when not in use. Light the flame with a striker or match. You should turn the flame down for certain circumstances, such as when you are soldering next to wood, but don't leave it that way for long periods because it heats up the torch tip and can damage the orifice.

Soldering Preparation

You can't solder a joint in a pipe that already has water in it, so if you are going to work on existing pipes, you will first have to drain them. Pipe can be cut with a rotating pipe cutter or a hacksaw. Remove the burr from the end of the pipe with the triangular tool attached to the pipe cutter or with a file. Then take a strip of coarse emery cloth or medium steel wool and polish the inside of the pipe fitting and the outside of the pipe. You should have bright, shiny copper on both surfaces to ensure a good, tight joint. You can also buy a metal brush to help polish the inside of fittings.

(Here's a classic plumber's trick: If you are working on a pipe where the water won't drain out readily, take some squishy white bread, form it into a ball, and push it firmly down the pipe. It will hold the water long enough to let you solder the joint, then dissolve away harmlessly.)

Doing the Soldering

Brush flux on the pipe and fitting. The first rule of soldering pipe is to heat the fitting, not the pipe. The fitting is thicker and, if it is thoroughly hot, the solder will be automatically drawn into the joint by capillary action.

Brush on flux

The second rule is to let the fitting and pipe, not the torch, melt the solder; this gets the solder into the joint, not just on the surface. Heat the the fitting until the solder melts when you touch it to the joint. Then remove the torch and flow on the solder.

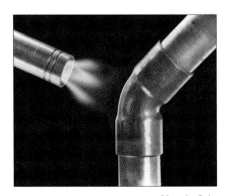
Heat the fitting

When solder starts dripping off, wipe the joint with a wet rag to clean it off and remove the excess solder. Check the joint for gaps ("holidays") and reflux and heat if you find one.

Be careful of the solder you use. Many areas of the country have banned lead from solder used for drinking-water pipes for health reasons. Check when you buy solder or when you use up an old supply. Use solder labeled "lead-free."

Here are a few more tips. If you are soldering very close to an old joint you don't want to melt, just wrap that joint with a wet rag to keep it cool. To solder pipes that are near a wall, a scrap of sheet metal will help keep the wall from burning. And, if you are soldering a threaded adapter — the kind you use for going from iron to copper pipe — keep the fitting pointed up to prevent solder from flowing over the threads and ruining the fitting.

Other Uses for Your Torch

Because the torch is a convenient source of portable heat, you can use it for a wide variety of miscellaneous chores. One is soldering sheet metal, which, because of its surface area, needs a lot of heat. Often a rusted bolt will loosen if you heat it with a torch.

If you're careful, you can use the torch to loosen floor tiles, bend vinyl flooring products, and soften other plastics. You can also strip paint with a torch, but you get less damage to the wood using a hot-air gun instead.

Working with Threaded Pipe

If your house was built more than 30 years ago, it most likely has a maze of threaded pipe twisting through the walls and basement. And the older, more remodeled your house is, the more tangled — and leaky — this maze is likely to be.

Threaded pipe, also referred to as steel or iron pipe, carries hot and cold water to sinks, fixtures, and radiators. In larger diameters it serves as drain, waste, and vent plumbing pipe. Today, copper and plastic have taken over many of threaded pipe's duties, but it continues to be used for gas piping — and lots of repairs.

Threaded pipe is relatively easy to work with. Screw-ups are simply unscrewed — there's no soldering, torches, or gluing involved. Some DIYers prefer using it for that reason.

Threaded-pipe Anatomy 101

The tapered threads, which provide an ever-tightening seal as pipe and fitting are screwed together, give threaded-pipe joints their strength.

Tapered pipe threads

"Galvanized" threaded pipe is rust resistant and is the type used for water lines. "Non-galvanized" black pipe is less expensive but is susceptible to rust and should be used only for natural gas and propane lines. Threaded pipe is referred to by its "inside diameter" (I.D.), with ½- and ¾-inch sizes being the most common in the house.

The Tool with an Iron Grip

Threaded pipe — round, smooth, and slick — seems an impossible material to grab and turn; and it would be, if not for the pipe wrench's clever design. This wrench has sharp teeth, which bite the pipe, and a spring-loaded upper jaw, which pinches the pipe as the wrench is turned. The upper jaw loosens momentarily when the handle is backed up, providing a grip-release-grip ratchet action. Center these jaws on the pipe for the best grip.

As any experienced plumber will tell you, always use two pipe wrenches — one to twist the pipe, the other to keep the adjacent fitting from turning. A "hold-back" wrench prevents damage to pipes further down the line — a real disaster if loosening or a break takes place deep inside a wall.

Avoid cheap pipe wrenches; their teeth dull quickly and lose their bite. Invest in a pair of good-quality 10- and 14-inch wrenches.

Measuring and Cutting

When you are measuring threaded pipe, you must account for the distance the pipe and its fittings overlap after they are joined. Measure the distance between the fittings, then add ½ inch per end for ¾-inch pipe or ⁷/₁₆ inch for ½-inch pipe.

You can buy or rent special tools for cutting and threading pipe at home, but they won't save you time or money. Instead, have it done at the local hardware store; most will cut pipe to length and thread it for an extra dollar or two. Bring along an old section of pipe to ensure a correct match. Nipples — short pieces of pipe threaded on both ends — are available right off the shelf at well-stocked hardware stores and home centers.

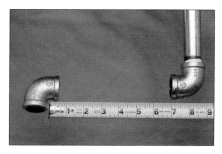

Measure the overlap

Simple Repairs and Add-ons

You can't simply unscrew a leaking section of pipe from the middle of your plumbing system — as you unscrew the joint on one end of the pipe, you tighten the joint on the other. You need to cut and remove the affected piece of pipe, then use a union and some shorter pieces for reconstructing the section. You can also add a tee or repair a section of pipe in the middle of a run.

Any time you end up having to work with threaded pipe, keep the following points in mind:

- Before you begin work, shut off the water or gas supply to the pipe.
- Always apply a pipe sealant, such as Teflon sealing tape or liquid sealant, before joining pipes and fittings. Sealants seal the threads and protect and lubricate them.
- Rusted or stubborn joints can usually be loosened with bigger pipe wrenches — ones that apply more leverage. As a last resort, use penetrating oil or heat the joint with a propane torch (watch your flame, please!). Don't hammer on pipes — this can loosen mineral deposits, clogging valves and faucets.

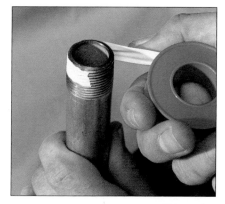

Using sealant

PVC Cutting Made Easy

The best tool for cutting PVC pipe is a regular metal tube cutter. It leaves a smooth cut that requires no further dressing other than cleaning before assembling.

Tile and Tub

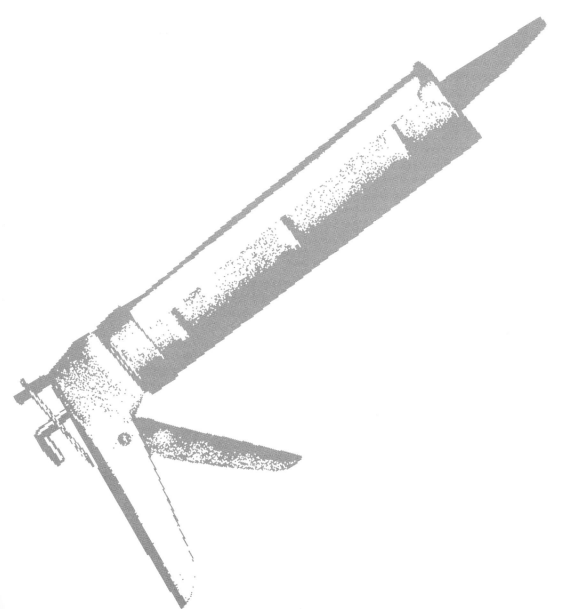

Replacing Vinyl Tile   74

You can remove and replace a cracked, chipped, or curled-up tile in no time at all.

Repairing Porcelain   75

Repair unsightly chipped porcelain the quick and easy way.

It's hard to keep a watertight joint between the bathtub and tile or the countertop and back-splash. But caulking this joint takes almost no time at all.

Grout helps protect the under-lying surface from harmful moisture. Repair or replace damaged grout now to avoid major repairs later.

Ceramic tiles can break, loosen, or chip. Luckily, replacing a tile is an easy fix.

Here are some handy hints for cutting, fixing, and even paint-ing ceramic tile, running a professional-looking bead of caulk, and buying tile, adhe-sives, and grout.

Replacing Vinyl Tile

Make your whole floor look new again.

STEP 1 Remove the damaged tile by heating and softening it with a hair dryer. Chip and remove pieces of tile, starting at the center and working toward the edges. Try to avoid damaging surrounding tiles.

STEP 2 Scrape off all of the old adhesive with a sharp paint scraper. Fill any large gouges in the floor with wood putty; after it dries, sand it smooth. Spread new adhesive with a small notched trowel.

STEP 3 Position the new tile and lower it into place. Wipe off any adhesive that works up through the seams with special adhesive remover.

STEP 4 Weigh down the new tile using scrap lumber and bricks. Leave the weights in place for 24 hours while the adhesive dries.

WHAT YOU NEED

Hair dryer

Chisel

Paint scraper

Wood putty

Vinyl tile adhesive

Replacement tile

Notched trowel

Utility knife

Carpenter's square

Adhesive remover

Scrap lumber

Bricks

The nice thing about 12 x 12-inch vinyl floor tiles is that they're easy to install. However, the completed tile floor has hundreds of little seams that can chip or curl and let water seep through to the wood or concrete beneath.

But replacing a broken tile is easy. The toughest part of this project might be finding replacement tile in the right color or pattern. You may get lucky and find an extra tile or two stored on a basement or pantry shelf. If not, check your local tile shop and home center.

After you remove the damaged tile, test fit the new tile. Trim or cut it as necessary by making multiple passes with a sharp utility knife guided by a carpenter's square or other straightedge. Spread an adhesive designated for use with vinyl tile using a notched trowel. Press the tile in place and weigh it down until the adhesive has dried.

Repairing Porcelain

Banish those unsightly scars!

WHAT YOU NEED

Emery cloth

Oil-based paint

Resin repair paste

Fingernail polish remover, xylol, or acetone

There's really no sure-fire, long-term repair for a chip in your porcelain enamel sink or bathtub. But if the chipped area is dry most of the time, a repair will withstand wear for several years.

Begin the repair by sanding the chipped area with medium-grit emery cloth to remove rust and scale and expose fresh metal and porcelain.

You can find resin filler at hardware stores or home centers. To tint it, read the label directions; you may be able to use a few drops of oil-based paint, gradually adding it until you get a close match.

Don't worry about slightly overfilling the chip or spilling over onto the porcelain surface. You can remove the excess and blend the edges with a strong solvent such as fingernail polish remover, xylol, or acetone. You can purchase these last two solvents at home centers. Ventilate the room when you use them.

APPLYING RESIN REPAIR PASTE

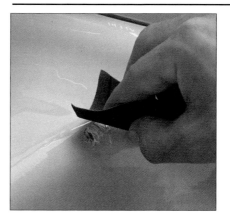

STEP 1 Sand the damaged area to remove rust and expose a fresh surface for good bonding. Be very careful not to scratch the finished porcelain surface outside the chipped area; scratches there will be permanent.

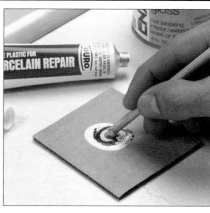

STEP 2 Mix several drops of oil-based paint with the white resin repair paste to exactly match the color of the old porcelain.

STEP 3 Cover the bottom of the hole first to avoid trapped bubbles, then add resin a bit at a time until the chip is filled to the top.

STEP 4 Smooth and blend the edges after the resin dries with a strong solvent, such as fingernail polish remover, xylol, or acetone.

Caulking Joints

Stop leaks and improve appearance.

WHAT YOU NEED

Screwdriver

Bathroom cleaner

Tub and tile caulk

Sponge

Cloth

The joint where your bathtub meets the ceramic wall tile is bad news because there's a lot of expansion and contraction along this joint, and it's not easy to keep it watertight. The problem is worse when the joint is filled with the same cement-based grout used between the tiles. Grout won't flex; instead it cracks and admits water into the drywall or plaster behind the tile or the ceiling of the room below, turning it to mush.

Repairing this joint is quick and easy. Use a latex acrylic caulk or a 100-percent silicone adhesive caulk, both of which are available at any home center. It's usually called tub caulk, or tub and tile sealer. It stays flexible for years, so it resists cracking despite expansion and contraction. Most varieties are off-white to match standard tile grout, but you may be able to find colored caulk, especially at a specialty tile store.

CAULKING BATHTUB/TILE JOINTS

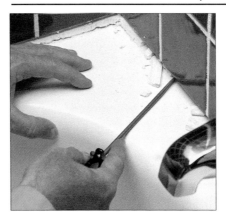

STEP 1 Pick out cracked and loose grout or caulk from the joint using a thin screwdriver that's slightly narrower than the joint. Grout that is solid can be left in place.

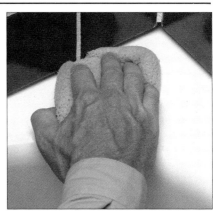

STEP 2 Clean off all debris and powder so the new caulk will adhere properly. Use the bathroom cleaner of your choice; rinse and dry thoroughly with a sponge and dry cloth.

STEP 3 Apply tub caulk in a slow, steady motion, filling the whole width and depth of the joint in one pass. You can ensure this by cutting the nozzle of the tube to the same size as the joint.

STEP 4 Smooth the caulk with a wet finger, forming a slightly concave shape. Make sure there are no gaps between the caulk and the tub or tile. Wipe away the excess before it hardens.

If you have a tile countertop and backsplash in your kitchen or bathroom, pay careful attention to maintenance. The joint formed where these two surfaces meet really gets abused. Every time you close a drawer or bump the countertop you jar the joint. And while these bumps may seem minor, over time they can — and usually do — crack the grout, which can allow water to penetrate the joint.

If the grout is not cracked, apply a bead of 100-percent silicone rubber adhesive caulk directly over the grouted joint. The caulk helps prevent the grout from cracking whenever the countertop is bumped. If the grout joint is already cracked, remove it and regrout before applying the caulk.

Notice that the caulk used in the adjacent photos looks white, but it will dry clear. (Many clear caulks are white when they come out of the tube.) A clear caulk was used here because it's very difficult to find a caulk to match the grout color. If you do find one to match, use it. If not, use clear.

STEP 1 Remove cracked or badly stained caulk and grout from the joint. Clean the area with a solution of water and phosphoric acid. (When you use phosphoric acid, be sure to follow the manufacturer's directions exactly to avoid personal injury.) You don't have to regrout — the caulk will seal the gap.

STEP 2 Apply a bead of 100-percent silicone adhesive caulk over the grouted joint between the countertop and backsplash. Use clear caulk if you can't find a color to match the grout.

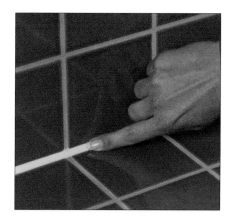

STEP 3 Dip your finger in water, then run it over the bead of caulk to smooth and shape it. Use a cloth to wipe off the excess caulk that collects on your finger.

Fixing Grout

This simple repair can brighten your whole bathroom.

WHAT YOU NEED

Grout-removing tool or grout saw

Broom or vacuum

Grout

Rubber grout float

Sponge

Clean cloth

Penetrating sealer

Caulk

Phosphoric acid

Rubber gloves

Cracked, loose, missing, or discolored grout requires immediate attention. Replace it, repair it, or clean it now.

The key to a long-lasting repair or replacement is removal of the old material. The easiest way to remove bad grout is with a grout saw. A professional-style saw has two blades that work together: One blade has conventional-looking saw teeth to break up and rake out the grout; the other blade has an almost sandpaperlike edge to clean out any remaining grout and smooth rough spots.

Then prepare the tile and apply new grout according to the directions provided at right.

The phosphoric acid used to clean the tile must be handled carefully; ventilate the area well, wear gloves and safety goggles, and follow the supplier's directions exactly, for safety's sake.

GROUTING WALL TILES

STEP 1   Cut out the old grout with a grout saw. Remove any grout that's loose or cracked. A solid grout line doesn't need to be removed.

STEP 2   Clean the tile surface with a solution of phosphoric acid and water. Wear rubber gloves. Don't let the solution get on a glass shower door — it will etch the glass.

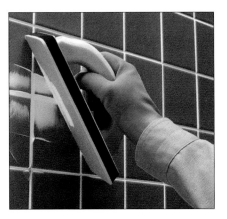

STEP 3   Spread the grout using a rubber grout float. Hold the float at a 45-degree angle to the wall and move it back and forth diagonally to spread the grout. Always use a nonsanded grout for wall tiles.

STEP 4   Apply a penetrating sealer to the grout and tiles after the grout has dried. Check the grout package for drying time. Reapply penetrating sealer annually to extend the life of the grout.

STEP 1 Remove loose and cracked grout from between the tiles with a sharp tool or grout saw. Cut down to the full depth of the tile so the new grout will grip firmly.

STEP 2 Work the new grout into the tile joints with your finger. Be sure the grout is firmly packed. Make the joints slightly concave so they blend with the existing grout lines.

STEP 3 Clean and rinse tiles with a damp sponge two or three times at 10-minute intervals. When only a haze remains, buff with a clean cloth.

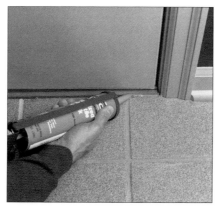

STEP 4 Run a bead of caulk where the tile meets a door threshold. Most large tile retailers and home centers carry caulks to match a wide variety of grout colors.

An Alternative: Cleaning Grout

Whether it's white, gray, or a trendy designer color, grout gets dirty. But there's no need to replace it if the grout is intact.

Most grout can be cleaned with a phosphoric acid and water solution. If the grout's really dirty, use the acid undiluted. Wear rubber gloves if you have sensitive skin. Actually, they're probably a good idea even if you don't have sensitive skin.

The best way to scrub grout is with a nylon-bristle grout brush. The long, stiff bristles let you scrub hard enough to remove dirt and mildew. Repeat scrubbing as needed.

Some Grout Tips: Mix, Match, and Seal

■ Get grout samples or a brochure from a tile store and match the color of your existing grout as closely as possible (two or more colors can be blended if necessary). Mix a small sample batch and let it dry for three days to see how the color compares to the existing grout.

■ Mix powdered grout with latex additive instead of water to make it stronger and more flexible — and longer lasting.

■ Protect all the grout lines with a sealer. Latex sealers can be applied the next day; wait two to three weeks before applying silicone-based sealers.

■ Grout is a cement product containing caustic lime. Therefore, you should always wear gloves when working with it.

Replacing Ceramic Tile

Fix minor problems now, before they become major.

Ceramic tile can last forever. But tile is brittle, and it's used in places where it gets a lot of abuse. So is it any wonder that, after all these years, there are a few tiles in your home that are cracked, chipped or loose?

Fortunately, it's an easy fix. Just cut or scrape out the old grout, then chip out the broken tile and set a new one in place as shown here. If you aren't lucky enough to have leftover tiles to replace a broken one, try to match it at a tile store. You may be able to come very close to a perfect match even if your tile is a discontinued style.

You won't need all the tools and materials at left for any one tile repair. Choose your tools according to those shown in the step-by-step instructions.

REPLACING A CRACKED TILE

STEP 1 Remove the damaged tile, starting at a grout line, then working in. Wear gloves and eye protection.

STEP 2 Break the tile into small pieces using a hammer and cold chisel. Remove the old grout but be careful not to chip surrounding tiles.

STEP 3 Scrape off the old adhesive with a cold chisel. Remove as much as possible so the new tile will adhere properly. Scraping is the best way to remove the adhesive.

STEP 4 Apply mortar or mastic to the back of the tile with a putty knife, spreading it out to the edges. Use thin-set mortar for floor tiles and premixed mastic adhesive for wall tiles.

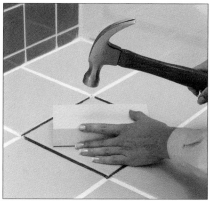

STEP 5 Set the tile firmly into place, and level with the surrounding tiles by placing a short length of wood on the tile and gently tapping the wood with a hammer.

STEP 6 Spread the grout using a rubber grout float, holding it at a 45-degree angle to the tile and working grout into the gaps from all directions.

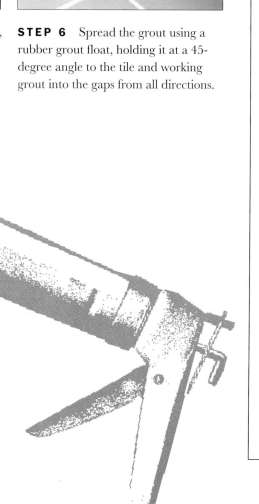

Matching Old Tile

The best place to buy tools and materials is at a specialty tile shop. Besides finding all of the stuff you'll need, you'll be able to talk with salespeople who handle tile repair questions every day. Check the yellow pages under "Tile, Ceramic" for stores in your area.

A ceramic tile specialty shop is also the best place to get help with one of the toughest ceramic tile problems: trying to match the existing tiles. Tile colors change as often as the color trends in wallpaper and paint. Even if you find tiles of nearly the same color by the same manufacturer, they still might not match because the colors can vary subtly from one batch to the next. Tile sizes change too, especially tile thickness. The odds are you won't find an exact match.

But don't despair. There are options. Consider replacing a few tiles with some of a different color and create a new pattern, which will give the room a whole new look. Another alternative is to borrow a good tile from an inconspicuous place, such as behind the toilet or the sink cabinet. If you decide to try this, you should know that removing a tile that is firmly attached without damaging it is often difficult and sometimes impossible.

If you are buying new tiles to completely refurbish a floor or wall, buy several extra — a whole box if they're not too expensive — so that you have spares of the same batch and color lot to make future repairs.

Painting Ceramic Tile

You can paint tile that is in good condition but is just the wrong color. However, ordinary paint won't stick to ceramic tile. Some paints seem to adhere fairly well at first but eventually begin to peel or chip, even in normal use. The solution involves first coating the tile with a primer formulated to anchor to slick surfaces. Using the right primer means that you don't have to sand, etch, or degloss the tiles to get a firm bond. For best results on ceramic tile, the top coat of paint should be a high-gloss alkyd compatible with the primer.

Want to remove paint from ceramic tiles? The approach that's least likely to damage the tiles is careful scraping with a razor knife. This is obviously tedious work, however.

If the amount of tile makes scraping impractical, use a water-based (not methylene chloride-based) paint stripper. You can find one at better home centers and paint stores. Test the stripper in an inconspicuous area first. Even using a stripper, the task is likely to be difficult, because you must carefully clean the old paint off the porous grout — or regrout.

Tile Tips

- When replacing tiles, remove as much of the adhesive as you can, but don't worry if you leave some of it behind. Just make sure that the surface is smooth. Once the adhesive has been scraped loose, sweep or vacuum it up.

- Don't use a heat gun or solvent to soften old adhesive. This makes the job very messy and you won't remove any more adhesive than by simply scraping.

- When you need to replace a floor tile, apply a liberal amount of mortar to the back of the tile. Be sure to spread it all the way out to the edges of the tile. Wear rubber gloves, too. Dried mortar or mastic is tough to get off of your hands.

- When you set a tile in place, check the spacing between the tiles before the adhesive has a chance to harden. Make sure the spacing matches up with all the other grout lines.

- A chipped tile doesn't cause structural problems. It's only an eyesore. Unfortunately, there's really no sure-fire way to repair chips. The easiest fix is to try to find an acrylic paint or permanent marker that matches the tile color and use it to coat the chipped area.

REPLACING A SHAPED TILE

STEP 1 A cracked tile is often one that's been shaped to fit, like this tile that's been fitted around the tub spout pipe. First remove the spout from the pipe by hand.

STEP 2 Cut out the grout around the broken tile with a grout saw. You can also scrape the grout out with an ordinary pointed can opener. Be careful not to chip adjacent tiles.

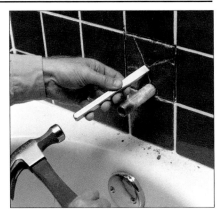

STEP 3 Crack the tile in an X pattern, from each corner, by tapping lightly with a hammer and cold chisel. Then break out the tile with the chisel, working from the center toward the edges. Wear protective goggles.

STEP 4 Apply waterproof adhesive to the new tile after shaping it with a tile nipper. Press the tile in place so it's flush with the surrounding tiles. Remove excess adhesive with a thin screwdriver.

STEP 5 Grout the joints with the same color grout as the surrounding joints. Smooth it to match using your finger, and then wipe away the excess grout with a damp sponge.

REPLACING A SOAP DISH

Some soap dishes, especially those made more than 10 years ago, are part of the tile pattern, and are installed like other tiles. To replace one of these, follow the steps in "Replacing a Cracked Tile," on page 80. To replace a soap dish mounted on the surface, follow these steps.

STEP 1   Mount a soap dish using 100-percent silicone rubber adhesive caulk on the entire back of the dish. Be sure to fill the holes in the back of the dish with caulk, too.

STEP 2   Position the soap dish on the wall and secure it with duct tape. Place one strip of tape horizontally and another vertically. Leave the tape in place overnight, then remove it.

About Buying Tile, Grout, Caulk, and Adhesive...

When you walk into the tile department of a large home center, or into a store that specializes in ceramic floor and wall tiles, you may at first feel overwhelmed by the number of tile and tile-related products that exist — not to mention the selection of brands within each type. Here's a guide to some of what's out there.

Tile

The type of ceramic tile most often chosen for home use is *glazed*; that is, it has a hard baked-on glass finish that may be either glossy, matte, or textured. Glazing serves to seal the porous ceramic against moisture and staining and makes the tiles easy to keep clean. A smooth gloss finish also makes tiles slick when they're wet, so be careful where you use them.

Unglazed tiles, on the other hand, are just fired clay. They come only in the natural colors and textures of clays and absorb moisture easily.

Tiles come in various shapes according to their use. *Field tiles* are the square tiles with four rough edges that are used on most surfaces. Other shapes are made for special uses, such as *trim tiles*, with one or more smooth, finished sides for corners and borders; *bull-nosed tiles*, with one rounded side for use on the top edge of a backsplash; and *sink caps*, with one side shaped to fit over the front edge of a countertop.

Grout

Grout is a type of water-based cement similar in composition to the mortar you see between bricks. Rather than acting as an adhesive, though, grout keeps water and dirt from working its way into the spaces between tiles.

Grout comes in different textures and colors, so it can also lend a decorative touch. You can buy it either premixed, which is quick and handy for touch-ups, or in a powder form that has to be mixed with water.

Caulk

Caulk makes waterproof joints between two tiled surfaces or between a tile surface and another one such as a bathtub or sink. Caulk is much more flexible than grout and doesn't tend to crack as quickly. Silicone caulk is long-lasting, and it comes in a few colors and in a mildew-resistant formula.

Adhesive

This is the stuff you use to stick the tiles to the subsurface. There are any number of types, depending on whether you are laying floor or wall tile, what the subsurface is made of, and the amount of moisture the tiles will be subject to. Ask your tile dealer to recommend the best type for your project.

Work Better, Work Safer

Neat Caulking

When you want a neat, uniform bead of caulking — for example, where wall tile meets the bathtub — use masking tape to keep the surrounding area clean. That way you won't mess up the bead when you clean up. Position the masking tape so that your finger will plow the excess caulk onto the tape when you form the bead.

Soap It

Before smoothing a bead of caulk, wet your finger with dishwashing liquid. You'll get a crisp, even caulk line.

Ice It

Run the bead of caulk from the caulking gun, then form the edge of an ice cube to the bead shape that you want by melting it with your hand. Then run the ice cube along the joint to form a perfect bead.

High-shine Shower Enclosure

Apply a coat of car polish to your ceramic tile or fiberglass shower enclosure. You'll get a brilliant shine, and cleaning will be a cinch — water rolls right off the walls before mold or mildew can start. Never put car wax or polish on the floor of the tub or shower, however — you would be asking for a very nasty fall.

Stick It

Determine exactly how wide you want the bead of caulk to be, then clip the corners of a paint-stirring stick to this width. Put masking tape down to accommodate this width, then caulk. Smooth the caulk with the stick.

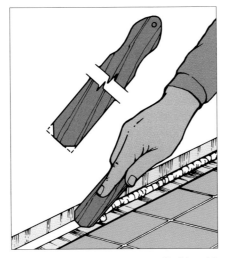

Caulking stick

Caulk Rescue

If you leave the tip of your caulking tube uncovered and the caulk hardens behind the opening, here's the best way to get it flowing again: Cut the tip back so the hole is slightly larger. Then drive a screw into the plug of hardened caulk and use the screw to pull the plug out. A screw with coarse threads, such as a drywall or deck screw, works best.

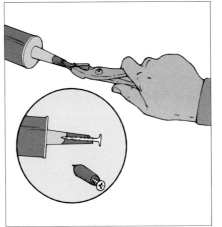

Plug puller

Removing Adhesive

When you remove an old shower enclosure, you may find that taking off the door, wall tracks, and adhesive is relatively easy. The track that is affixed to the tub may be another story.

First try to determine what type of adhesive is used to hold this track in place. If the adhesive is very hard, it is possibly an epoxy resin. Epoxy resins are just about impossible to remove from surfaces such as bathtubs and attempts to do so usually result in serious damage to the tub surface. To check the hardness, try to push your fingernail into the adhesive. If you can leave a mark in the adhesive, it is probably not an epoxy resin.

If you have a soft adhesive, you should try to pry up the track. Be very careful not to damage the tub surface. You may also try heating the track with a paint stripping gun. By heating the track, you will avoid a concentrated heat buildup on the tub surface. If your tub is fiberglass, do not use heat. This will damage the tub, probably beyond repair. Again, be extremely careful so you don't damage the finish of the tub.

Start at one end of the track and try to loosen it about 6 to 8 inches. If you are able to do this, you can probably pry off the rest of the track. Also, check to see if there are any bolts or other metal fasteners holding the track in place and remove them.

Slippery Tile

Glazed ceramic tile gets very slippery when it's wet, especially on a surface such as the floor of a shower. Here are two suggestions: (1) Apply peel-and-stick appliques to the surface. These vinyl appliques, available at department and discount stores, have a nonskid finish that gives your feet some grip; or (2) have the tile treated with an acid-based chemical solution, which will etch it. Because the acid is a dangerous chemical to work with, most manufacturers recommend that it be applied by a professional tile contractor.

Sealing Tile for Easy Cleaning

Unglazed ceramic tile makes beautiful floors but it can be difficult to clean. The tiles seem to attract dirt. To make them easier to maintain, you can apply an acrylic sealer. This should seal the surface, thus preventing dirt from being trapped in the pores of the tile and grout. However, you should note that any substance that's applied to a tile may alter the slip-resistant properties of the tile's surface.

You can find a variety of acrylic sealers at your local tile store, distributor, or home center. Some products are guaranteed not to affect tiles or grout color; they may also have built-in slip-resistant properties.

Ceramic Tile Cutter

If you have just a few ceramic tiles to cut, there's no need to buy or rent a tile cutter. Just score the glazed side of the tile with an ordinary glass cutter against a straightedge. Then place a pencil or pencil sized dowel under the tile directly below the scored line and snap it by pressing the two sides of the tile with the heels of your hands.

Ceramic Tile Fix

You can repair small nicks or chips in ceramic tile with appliance touch-up paint. The paint dries to a very hard finish and adheres well to smooth surfaces. It's available in white, almond, green, yellow, and black. White and almond can be tinted with paint to match other tile colors.

Caulk Cap

Seal off your partially used caulking tube with a plastic electrical connector twisted onto the end. The connector makes it easy to seal and later to reopen the tube.

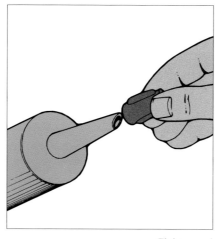

Twist-on seal

Stains on Cultured Marble

For a dark stain, soak a clean, white cotton cloth with hydrogen peroxide and leave it on the stain overnight. Rinse with cold water in the morning.

For light-colored stains, which are generally caused by hard water, use a mixture of $\frac{1}{2}$ cup ammonia, $\frac{1}{4}$ cup vinegar, and $\frac{1}{4}$ cup baking soda in $\frac{1}{2}$ gallon of hot water. Mix this in a 2-gallon bucket, because the vinegar and baking soda will foam up. Apply it with a clean sponge. Let the solution stand for five minutes, then rinse well. Test in a small area first before doing a large area such as a shower floor, and be sure to wear rubber gloves.

If these solutions don't help, you'll probably have to have the surface refinished. A professional refinisher can be found by looking in the yellow pages under "Bathtub & Sink, Repair and Refinishing."

Removing Grout Residue

Removing grout residue from terra cotta tiles can be difficult. The Tile Council of America recommends that you treat a small area at a time by scrubbing with a foaming cleanser and a stiff-bristled nylon brush, then rinse thoroughly. Use a sealer made for low-porosity tile to finish the floor.

Slate Floor Cleanup

To clean dingy finishes and paint splatters off a slate floor, you'll have to experiment a bit; unfortunately, this is a tough problem. Experiment in an inconspicuous spot.

First try to remove the paint splatters with a putty knife. If they're just on the surface and haven't penetrated the slate, they should just scrape off. Look for products to remove dried paint at paint stores.

Removing a dingy finish or paint that has penetrated the slate is tougher. Sometimes slate is sealed with floor wax or a penetrating sealer that is actually absorbed into the slate. If the slate is sealed with floor wax, your best bet is a commercial floor wax remover.

For removing stubborn sealers and paint splatters, first try washing the surface with trisodium phosphate (or laun-

dry detergent if TSP isn't available) until the water is clear. Let the floor dry overnight. If that doesn't work, try a water-based paint stripper. Strippers can discolor the slate, so be sure to test a small area first. For safety, use plenty of cross ventilation.

When the floor is as clean as you can get it, apply a paste wax with carnauba, or a penetrating tile and brick sealer. Both products can be found at home centers or hardware stores. Penetrating sealers can be reapplied from time to time to give the slate a new look. Just clean the slate and put on another coat of sealer. Waxes are less convenient because the wax buildup has to be removed periodically, but some people like the soft sheen of wax better.

Tight-fitting Tub

When you remodel a bathroom, how do you get the old tub out and a new one in when the tub is the same width as the room?

If you don't want to save the old tub and use it somewhere else, you can just break it up with a sledgehammer and take it out in pieces. This is a handy approach for a heavy cast iron tub — or if you have stress to work off. Remember to wear eye protection and remove mirrors and other breakables from the walls.

If you want to take the old tub out in one piece, you'll need to tip one end up, lift the tub out, then turn it on its side. A standard tub measuring 14 x 30 x 60 inches will fit through a door on its side.

Strip a Painted Tub?

How can you remove paint from the surface of a tub without permanently damaging the tub?

Paint stripper ought to do the trick. However, it's possible that when you get the paint off, you'll find the original surface is damaged, which may be why the former owners decided to paint it in the first place. If that's the case, it's possible your tub can be repaired and refinished. The tub will need to be chemically etched by a professional and then coated several times with a color of your choice. Heat is applied to bond and set the finish. All of the work can be done on site.

Buying Tile, Adhesives, and Grout

When you're shopping for tile, go to a tile shop rather than a hardware store or home center. Tile shops have a tremendous variety of tiles, they'll usually lend you tile-cutting tools, and they're more likely to have knowledgeable salespeople who can answer your installation questions.

Tiles with mesh backing

When you visit a tile shop, you'll be blown away by the choices: unglazed quarry tiles, little mosaic tiles, superhard porcelain tiles, marble tiles, handpainted decorative tiles, and rustic handmade tiles. The different types are installed in similar but not identical ways. Ask a salesperson at your tile shop for details. Here are some buying, design, and installation tips.

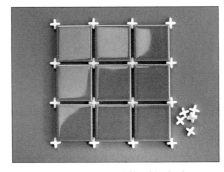

Tile with plastic spacers

- Floor tiles differ from wall tiles — they're harder and have less glaze. You can use floor tiles on a wall, but wall tiles are too slippery and fragile for use on floors.
- Tiles often have a wear rating listed either on the back side or in the manufacturer's specification sheet; a tile that is rated "3" or greater is acceptable for floors.
- Glazed tiles can be used for a floor but avoid glossy ones; they're slippery and show every little scratch or ding. It's better to select a matte or textured tile. A porcelain tile is colored all the way through, has a slight texture, and is durable.

- For kitchen counters and backsplashes, pick a hard tile — vitreous or porcelain — with a durable surface and stick with a size that's in scale with your kitchen. A too-small tile makes a kitchen look dizzyingly busy (all those grout lines!) and a too-large tile makes it look disconnected. The tile should integrate cabinets, walls, and appliances, not compete with them.
- Don't use floor tiles that are the same size as the wall tiles — it's hard to get grout lines to line up where the wall meets the floor.
- Tiles 4 inches square or larger are usually sold singly; tiles 3 inches or smaller are typically sold in 1-square-foot sheets with the tiles attached to a thin mesh. If you're a first-time tiler, buy the sheet form if possible for easier installation.
- Don't limit yourself to small tiles — especially on the floor. Large tiles look impressive, they're very quick to install, and there are fewer grout lines to mess with. A relatively large entryway would look good with 8x8-inch tiles; a smaller space might look better finished in 6-inch-square tile.
- Tiles need spaces between them for the grout. Some tiles have little lugs on the edges to keep them the right distance apart; others need plastic spacers. These are available in different widths; wall tiles usually have $1/16$-inch spaces and floor tiles $3/16$- to $1/4$-inch spaces, depending on how big the tiles are.

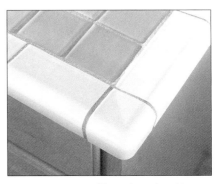

V-cap edge and outside corner

Check on the availability of trim tiles. These are the tiles with smooth edges that you use to finish off the edge of a tiled surface. Bull-nosed tiles have one smooth edge and are usually widely available; double bull-nosed tiles (two smooth edges) may have to be specially ordered. Check this out before you decide on a tile.

In addition, you need to get V-cap tiles for the edges. Countertop tiles often have a matching V-cap; or you can choose V-caps in a contrasting color. Specially formed V-caps are available for outside corners.

You need to buy thresholds for doorways. Forget about the old-fashioned marble ones, which require a wet saw, and buy Corian thresholds instead. You can cut them with a hacksaw.

When you go shopping, take along a measured drawing of each surface you want to tile. The tile shop salesperson can tell you which trim tiles you'll need and help you estimate quantities. Don't worry about ordering more than you need; most tile shops will allow you to return unused tile, and it's a smart idea to keep some tiles and grout for any later repairs.

You may want to consider using accent tiles and contrasting borders. If this is your first tiling project, though, use simple patterns and border designs to keep the project manageable; the tiles used as accents should be compatible in size and finish with the primary tile you choose.

There are few design rules when it comes to tile. Here are some hints:

- Dark-colored grout with light tiles (or vice versa) tends to emphasize the geometry of the tile.
- Dark colors make a room look smaller, while light colors tend to open up a space and make it feel larger.
- The tile selected can make a room feel formal or casual; in an entryway, it can establish the visual tone for the entire house.

Adhesives

There are two basic tile adhesives: latex-modified thin-set and organic mastic. Latex-modified thin-set is a cement product, rather like mortar, with a latex additive for increased flexibility and strength. It's the best general-purpose adhesive: waterproof, gap-filling, and strong under heavy traffic, and it has little odor. It's the hands-down choice for shower enclosures and floors that get wet, such as bathrooms and laundry rooms.

Thin-set comes as a powder that you mix with a latex additive. The mixture must be wet enough to stick to the tiles but not so wet that it oozes up between the tiles as you push them down. Do a quick experiment before starting to tile: Spread a gob of adhesive on a scrap of plywood, push down a couple of tiles, and make sure they stick without adhesive coming up between them.

Organic mastic is your other adhesive choice: It's slightly cheaper, pre-mixed, and gives you plenty of time to work. However, it isn't waterproof, so don't use it for floors or shower walls. Also, it can't fill gaps larger than $1/4$ inch and it has a strong odor.

Grout comes in two forms, sanded and unsanded. Use sanded grout for grout lines larger than $1/8$ inch; otherwise use unsanded. Like thin-set, grout is a powder that you mix with a latex additive. Grout comes in different colors so you can make the grout lines less visible by matching the grout to the tiles or more visible by choosing a contrasting color. White grout on a floor will get dirty unless you use a penetrating alkaline sealer after installation; reapply it as needed.

Special Tools

You're in luck in this department — most specialized tiling tools can be borrowed from a tile shop or rented. Here are the tools you'll need:

- A notched trowel for applying adhesive. The size of the notches determines how much adhesive goes on. Different-sized tiles require different-sized trowels. Ask your tile supplier which trowel to use with your tile. If you put cement board on the floor, you'll need a $1/4$-inch square-notched trowel for that adhesive.
- A grout float is a trowel-like tool with a hard rubber edge that you use to spread grout and push it firmly down into the grout spaces.

Tile cutter

- A tile cutter is used for cutting straight lines in tile. It has a hardened wheel that scores the glazed surface of the tile. When you push down on the handle, the cutter clamps the tile on either side of the score line and then snaps it neatly in two. Most tile shops will lend you a tile cutter if you're buying tile. If the snapped edge is a bit on the rough side, you can smooth it with a coarse sharpening stone.
- Tile nippers are special pliers with hardened jaws for breaking off bits of tile. They're especially good for curved cuts, like around plumbing pipes. As the name implies, you nip gradually away at the tile with them. It's rather crude but fast and effective. The trick is not to take too much off at a time and use the corner of the jaws for more control.

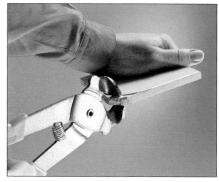

Tile nippers

- For smoother cuts, use a rod saw for curved cuts or a wet saw for straight cuts. The rod saw is simply a round carbide blade that fits into a regular hacksaw frame. It cuts slowly, but you can use it to make nice, smooth curves if you need to, especially in softer wall tiles.

The wet saw is a diamond-toothed saw with a water cooling system; you can rent one by the day. It'll make very smooth, straight cuts and is especially good for L-shaped cuts and notches. It's also very safe — it will cut tile, but will not injure flesh.

Caution: When you cut tile, sharp pieces will go flying. Please, wear your safety glasses.

You'll also need a handful of normal carpenter's tools for tiling, such as a level, chalk line, and a framing square.

Wiring and Electricity

Installing a GFCI   90

Your household electrical system is normally safe. Here is a gadget that can make kitchens, bathrooms, and basements even less accident prone.

Replacing a Bad Switch   93

A wall switch that's on the fritz doesn't have to mean there's an electrician in your future — fix it yourself!

Adding Outlets 94

Short of outlets? Here's how to tap into the existing power supply to add more.

Rekindling a Lamp 97

If a new light bulb doesn't make a dead lamp glow, here are a couple more things you might check.

Replacing Plugs 98

A damaged plug can make a small appliance dangerous. Replacing a bad plug takes only minutes.

Work Better, Work Safer 100

Here's a hot tip for stripping wires, some advice on using circuit testers, and plenty of techniques for doing electrical repairs safely.

Installing a GFCI

An ingenious life-saver.

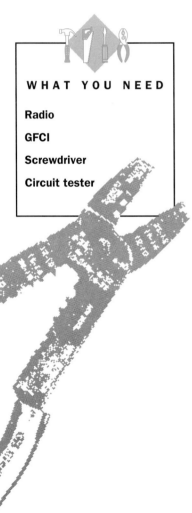

WHAT YOU NEED
Radio
GFCI
Screwdriver
Circuit tester

Our electrical systems, even old ones, usually do a good job of keeping electricity well contained.

Yet electrical accidents do occur. The Consumer Product Safety Commission reports that several thousand injuries and about 1,000 deaths occur each year from shocks and fires caused by common electrical appliances in our homes.

Many of these electrical accidents could be easily prevented by an inexpensive safety feature that you can install yourself: the ground fault circuit interrupter, otherwise known as a GFCI.

On this page are three steps to take to prepare for the installation. On the next two pages you'll find more information about GFCIs and a guide to installing and testing one in your home.

STEP 1 Plug a radio into the receptacle you want to replace with a GFCI and turn up the volume so you can hear it at the electrical panel.

Modern electrical panel

Circuit breaker switch

STEP 2A Shut off the power to the receptacle by flipping circuit breaker switches, as shown above, or…

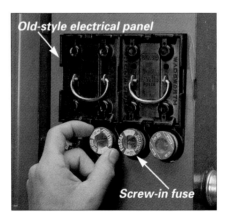

Old-style electrical panel

Screw-in fuse

STEP 2B …unscrewing fuses at the main electrical panel (as shown here) until the radio stops playing.

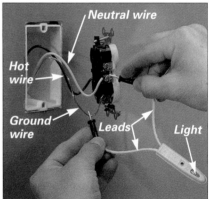

Neutral wire

Hot wire

Ground wire

Leads

Light

STEP 3 Unscrew the receptacle and pull it from its box; check for live wires with a circuit tester (see page 102). If neither is live, remove the receptacle.

What is a GFCI?

You've probably seen a receptacle-type GFCI (short for "ground fault circuit interrupter") in a kitchen or bathroom. It's the outlet with the tiny test and reset buttons. A GFCI is basically a supersensitive switch that can detect leaks of electrical current — the kind that cause deadly shocks or fires. When the GFCI detects a problem, it instantly shuts off electrical power to everything plugged into it.

Both the National and the Canadian Electrical Codes began requiring GFCIs in certain locations in 1971, for both new and remodeled construction. The 1994 Codes require them specially in bathrooms, outdoor locations and within a certain distance of pools, spas, hot tubs, and whirlpools; and in several other locations. The NEC requires them also in garages, unfinished basements, crawl spaces, and within 6 feet of the kitchen sink.

Since code requirements for GFCIs are relatively recent, your house probably won't have them in all of these key locations. But you can easily make your electrical system safer by installing them yourself.

■ Extended Protection

You can use a GFCI receptacle to protect other receptacles without having to install a GFCI at each location. This is the purpose of the "load" terminals on the GFCI. When you run the hot and neutral wires of a non-GFCI receptacle to the hot and neutral load terminals of a GFCI, you'll power that non-GFCI receptacle through the GFCI and gain protection for it, too.

Using the load side of the GFCI saves the expense of buying one for every new receptacle in a garage or unfinished basement. But make sure you don't exceed the load permitted on any one circuit. A common rule of thumb is not to exceed 8 to 10 outlets (a combination of lights and receptacles) on a 15-amp circuit. Check with your inspector to learn your local requirements.

■ GFCI Exceptions

A single plug-in receptacle dedicated to a large stationary appliance, like the washer or dryer in a basement or a laundry room, doesn't normally need GFCI protection for two reasons. First, you shouldn't be using this receptacle to power hand-held electrical devices, extension cords, or anything else. And second, appliances with large motors can momentarily disrupt the current balance and trip the sensitive GFCI. These nuisance shutdowns can be troublesome. The exact locations that require a GFCI are not always clear, so ask your local electrical inspector for advice on these exceptions.

IS YOUR OUTLET BOX BIG ENOUGH?

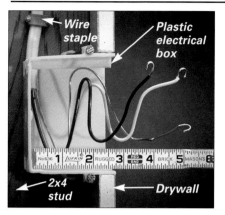

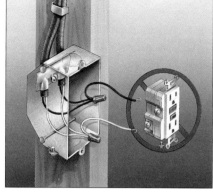

Figure 1 Count the wires, measure the box, and make the calculation below to ensure the box is large enough. The volume of a plastic box is stamped on the inside.

Figure 2 The 3- by 2-inch by 2¼-inch metal box shown here is too small to hold the GFCI and all the wires in this installation.

Because a GFCI is larger than a normal outlet, the size of the electrical box where you plan to put it is important. The electrical code requires a certain volume for each wire, so count the wires that come into the box (Figures 1 and 2 above). (Note: All ground wires together count as one.) With the wires counted, add one additional wire to account for the space taken up by all clamps included in the box (plastic boxes might not have any). The GFCI itself counts for two wires, so add this to the total.

The space a wire needs depends on its size. Most of the wires serving receptacles in your home are No. 14, requiring 2 cubic inches per wire, and occasionally No. 12, requiring 2¼ cubic inches per wire. To find the wire size, use the wire gauge on a wire stripping tool or compare the wires to spare wire that has the size stamped into or printed on its plastic insulation.

Multiply your total wire count by the volume for each wire (most wires in a box are the same size; if not, overestimate the space needed by multiplying by the volume for the larger wires) to get the total space required for everything to fit. If your box isn't big enough, you have to install a larger one.

Note: The method for determining the proper box size to meet the Canadian Code is very different. Canadian readers should consult local authorities.

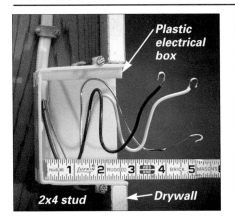

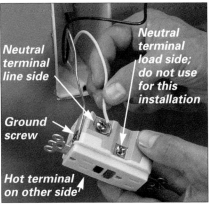

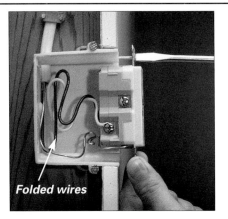

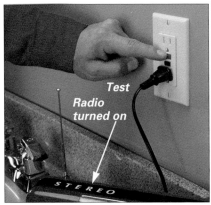

STEP 1 Calculate the volume of the box you need by measuring the depth, width, and height and multiplying these three dimensions. Compare the result with the space needed by the GFCI and its wires (see page 91).

STEP 2 Once you know the box is suitable, connect the ground wire to the green ground screw, the white wire to the neutral (silver) screw, and the black wire to the hot (brass) screw on the side of the GFCI labeled "line."

STEP 3 Fold the wires so they compress like an accordion into the box and screw the GFCI to the box. Screw on the cover plate.

STEP 4 Turn the circuit back on at the main panel and test the GFCI by following the step-by-step instructions in "Testing a GFCI" below left.

TESTING A GFCI

Test the GFCI by pushing the reset button to make sure the GFCI is switched on, then plug in the radio. While the radio is playing, push the test button. The radio should shut off. Push the reset button and the radio should start again.

If the radio continues to play after you push the test button, turn off the circuit at the main panel and check your connections. You might have incorrectly connected the wires to the load side of the GFCI rather than to the line side. If the wires are correct and the GFCI still doesn't work properly, the GFCI itself is faulty. You'll need to exchange it for a new one.

If the radio doesn't come on at all, turn off the power and check your wiring to make sure all the electrical connections are tight. If you can't find a wiring problem and the receptacle still doesn't work, either the GFCI is bad or, more likely, you have an electrical leak (either a short circuit or a fault) in your system that causes the GFCI to remain off. Call in a licensed electrician to figure out the problem.

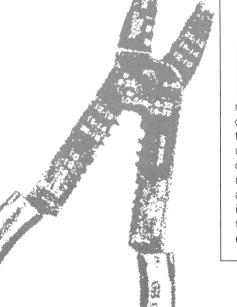

Electrical Safety

! Manufacturers warn you not to connect GFCIs to aluminum wires. Aluminum wires are gray, rather than dark orange like copper. Scrape the corrosion off a wire if you're unsure. (Make sure the circuit is dead first.) Those of you with aluminum wiring will have to contact a specially certified electrician to install GFCIs. Ask your local electrical inspector how to find these electricians.

Replacing a Bad Switch

Restore power — safely.

WHAT YOU NEED

Circuit tester

Screwdriver

Wire stripper

It's an easy enough job to replace a worn-out electrical switch, but you do need to be careful. It's not easy to tell whether a line to a faulty switch is live or not, but it's wise to assume it is "hot" until proven otherwise.

If you know which circuit breaker or fuse shuts off the power to the switch, or if you can easily shut off the main power switch to the whole house, you have no problem. If not, you'll have to use a circuit tester, which you should be able to find at hardware stores (see step 1). Make sure that the tester itself is in working order by checking it out in a live receptacle.

After you're sure the power to the switch is off, replace the switch. If you're replacing a three-way switch, or if the wiring arrangement is different from what is shown here, hook up the new switch the same way as the old one.

SWITCHING A SWITCH

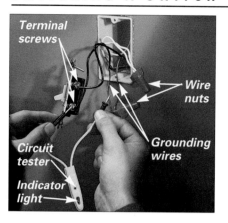

Terminal screws · Wire nuts · Grounding wires · Circuit tester · Indicator light

STEP 1 Remove the switch cover and screws holding the switch in the box. Carefully pull the switch out, keeping your fingers away from the terminal screws. Use a circuit tester to ensure the power is off (see page 94).

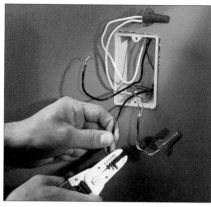

STEP 2 Cut the bare copper leads off the black wires if they are badly nicked or frayed and strip off a new lead with a wire stripper.

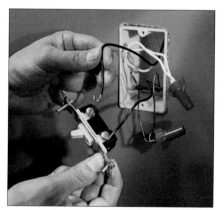

STEP 3 Bend the copper leads into hooks using the tip of the wire stripper. Attach the hooks to the terminal screws in a clockwise direction so the screws will keep the hooks tight as you turn.

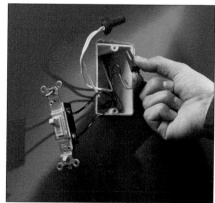

STEP 4 Fold the wires into the box, beginning with the ground wires; they must be at the back so they won't touch the terminal screws and cause a short circuit. Replace the switch and cover.

Adding Outlets

Install a convenient new outlet almost anywhere.

WHAT YOU NEED

Voltage tester

Box support

Electrical cable

Needle-nosed pliers

Screwdriver

Electrician's tape

Nut

String

Wire nuts

Wire strippers

Hammer

Single outlet

Double outlet

Diagonal cutters

3-penny box nails

Adding an electrical outlet can conjure up some unpleasant thoughts: cutting through house framing, running cable, even calling in an electrician. But these pages show you how to add new outlets easily and, most important, how to tap safely into the power supply at an existing switch or outlet.

Don't overload existing circuits — count the number of outlets and fixtures on the circuit you plan to add to. The rule of thumb is to have no more than a combination of eight outlets and fixtures on a 15-amp circuit, and no more than 10 on a 20-amp one.

Before working on any electrical circuit, be sure to turn off the power to the circuit. Remove the fuse or switch off the circuit breaker at the main service panel. Then, to be sure it's safe, go back to the switch or outlet and test each wire with a circuit tester.

Before You Start

■ Determining Whether There's Power

Not all electrical switch wiring is the same. To power an outlet from a wall switch, there must be a power source cable into the switch box.

To determine whether you can tie into a switch, count the number of wires in the switch box. Three wires — a black wire connected to one switch terminal, a white or gray one connected to the other switch terminal, and a bare copper or green one connected to the metal box — means there's no power source to tap into.

However, if there are six or more wires (two or more separate cables) in the box, you can tap in. The wire designation is usually two black wires — one is the hot (power source cable) and the other is the switch leg back to the fixture; two white or gray wires — one is neutral from the power source cable and the other is neutral for the fixture; and two bare copper or green wires — one is the ground for the fixture and the other is the ground from the power source cable that's attached to the box.

■ Finding the Hot Wire

Once you've determined that the switch has a power source and that the box is grounded, you need to identify the hot wire.

Pull the switch out of the box. With the power to the switch turned on, touch the main probe of the voltage tester to one of the switch terminal screws (right). Touch the other probe to the metal box; if it's a fiberglass box, touch it to the ground wire. If the tester shows a continuity reading but no voltage, the attached wire is the switch leg to the fixture. If the wire is hot, you'll get a voltage reading on the tester. Remember which one is the hot wire and turn off the power. Now, mark the hot wire with masking tape.

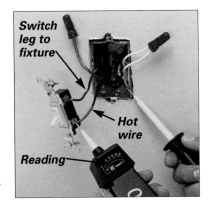

Switch leg to fixture

Hot wire

Reading

■ Testing for Ground

To determine whether the existing box is grounded, the power to the box must be on. Touch the main probe of a voltage tester to one of the switch terminal screws while the switch is turned on. If it's a metal box, touch the other probe to the box. If the box is fiberglass, touch the probe to the ground wire. If no readings register on the tester, the outlet is not grounded.

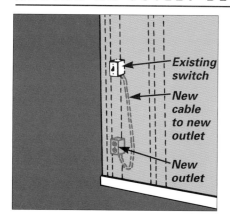

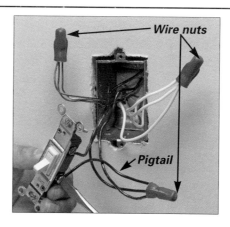

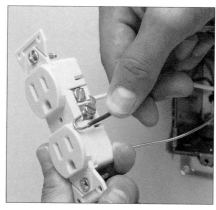

This diagram shows the proper location of the new electrical outlet and wiring relative to the existing switch. Refer to "Before You Start" (facing page) to determine whether you can add another outlet.

STEP 1   Remove a knockout in the switch box. Tie a nut to a piece of string and feed it down to the new opening. Attach the cable to the string and pull it up through the knockout.

STEP 2   Connect corresponding colored wires with wire nuts. Cut a 6-inch piece of black wire (called a pigtail) to attach the hot wire to the hot switch screw terminal.

STEP 3   Strip off ¾ inch of insulation. Attach the wires to the outlet: ground to ground; neutral to silver or terminal stamped "white"; hot to brass.

ADDING A COMMON WALL OUTLET

Use a stud finder to determine the space between the studs. Trace the new box location and cut the hole. Next, cut a 4-foot piece of cable. This is enough for a 2-foot loop in the wall and 12 inches at each box. Run the cable through a knockout in the old box, feed it into the new box, and strip off 12 inches of sheathing. Insert the box in the wall; secure it with box supports. Clamp the cable to the box. Connect the new wires to the correct wires in the old box with wire nuts. Attach the new outlet to the new wires.

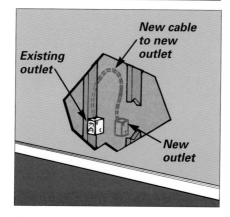

This diagram shows the addition of a new electrical box to an old one. Note the loop of cable connecting the boxes.

Grounding

The National Electrical Code (NEC) requires that all new switches and outlets be grounded. To ground the box you must run a new ground wire to a known electrical ground, such as another grounded box or the main fuse or circuit box. Running a ground wire to an existing box can be a complicated job; you should find an already grounded outlet or switch to tap into.

CONVERTING A SINGLE TO A DOUBLE

Here's how you can double the number of receptacles at one location. This installation method is recommended when the existing box is fiberglass. Metal boxes are very hard to remove without causing extensive damage to the wall.

Remove the receptacle and any wire nuts from the existing outlet. If this outlet is at the beginning or in the middle of a run of outlets, you'll have two separate cables. One cable is the power source into the box, the other carries power on to the next box. If this outlet's at the end of a run, there will only be one cable, a power source, into the box.

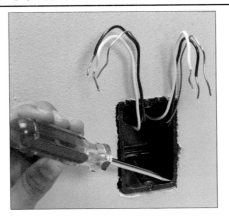

STEP 1 Disconnect the existing outlet and break out the backs and sides of the existing box.

STEP 2 Use needle-nosed pliers to remove the box pieces. Pry out the nails that hold the box to the stud with diagonal cutters.

STEP 3 Secure the new metal double-gang box to the stud with two 3-penny box nails. Drill ⅛-inch pilot holes for the nails.

STEP 4 Connect the outlets with wires, each with a ¾-inch loop at one end, a 1-inch U-shaped loop near the middle, and a ⅝-inch straight end. (See "How to Gang Two Outlets" at right.)

STEP 5 Attach the corresponding wires from the ganged outlets to the existing wires in the box. Use wire nuts to secure the connections.

How to Gang Two Outlets

Here's how to wire 2 outlets for one box: Take a 12-inch section of the cable and strip away the sheathing. This will leave you with three 12-inch wires. Strip the insulated wires as follows: Remove ¾ inch of insulation on one end and form a loop; next, measure in 3½ inches and strip away the next inch of insulation; at the other end of the wire, strip off ⅝ inch of insulation. This end will connect to the existing wire.

Attach the loop end of the hot wire (black) to the brass screw on one of the outlets. Make a U-shaped curve in the 1-inch stripped section and attach it to the brass screw on the second outlet. Connect the neutral wire (white) to the silver or stamped terminal using the same method. The ground wire is attached the same way.

At the box, connect the black outlet wire to the black wires, the white outlet wires to the white, and the outlet ground wire to the box's ground wires. Secure each connection with the correct size wire nuts.

Rekindling a Lamp

Turn darkness to light in four easy steps.

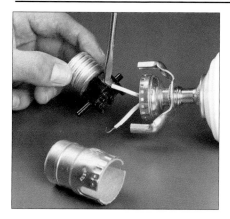

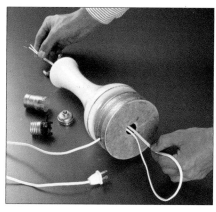

STEP 1   Disconnect the wires from the old socket/switch after you have unplugged the lamp and removed the shade, bulb, and harp. To remove the outer shell, press on the sleeve bottom with your thumb. This releases the small tabs that snap into the cap.

STEP 2   Replace a bad cord by pulling it out of the lamp body and base. Most lamps are held together by a hollow threaded rod through which the cord passes. The cap screws onto the top of this threaded rod.

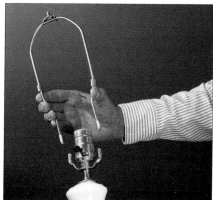

STEP 3   Install the new cap and tighten the set screw (if there is one). Then, connect the wires to the new socket/switch and replace the outer shell and sleeve.

STEP 4   Replace the harp by squeezing the ends into the wing clips. Buy a new harp if the old one is badly bent. Screw in a new bulb and give your lamp a test run.

WHAT YOU NEED

Screwdriver

The technique for fixing a dead lamp is no dark secret. Instead, it's cheap and simple. You can buy almost any replacement part at your local home center for pocket change.

The switch is the most likely culprit when your lamp won't light. Simply disassemble and disconnect the old socket and switch assembly and replace it as shown here. And if you wish, you can replace your old one-way switch with a three-way. If the cord is frayed, cracked, or broken, replace it at the same time.

Proper plug polarity is essential for a safely grounded lamp. Make sure the wire coming from the wide prong of the plug connects to the silver-colored screw of the socket/switch, the other wire to the brass-colored screw.

Replacing Plugs

Quick fixes for three plugs.

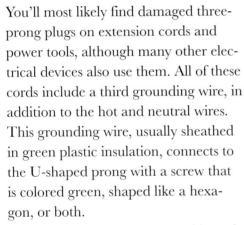

You'll most likely find damaged three-prong plugs on extension cords and power tools, although many other electrical devices also use them. All of these cords include a third grounding wire, in addition to the hot and neutral wires. This grounding wire, usually sheathed in green plastic insulation, connects to the U-shaped prong with a screw that is colored green, shaped like a hexagon, or both.

Round electrical cords, used in such appliances as vacuum cleaners and hand power tools, tend to get a lot of hard use. They're very flexible, but frequent plugging and unplugging can wear the cord badly where it joins the plug. When shopping for a new plug, buy one that you can grab easily so you won't be tempted to pull it out by jerking the cord.

THREE-PRONG PLUGS

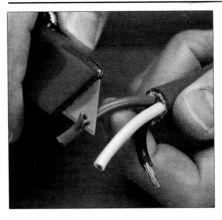

STEP 1 Whittle ⅝ inch of insulation off the wire ends using a utility knife. Avoid cutting the wire strands.

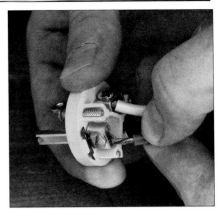

STEP 2 Connect the wires to the proper terminals: the black wire gets to the brass-colored terminal, the white goes to the silver, and the green goes to the green or hexagonal.

STEP 3 Align the wires properly and screw the parts of the two-piece plug back together.

STEP 4 Push the cord into the plug slightly and tighten the clamp to limit stress on the wires and screws.

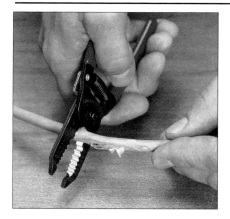

STEP 1   Clip off and discard any damaged cord. Strip 3 inches of outer insulation off the wires.

STEP 2   Insert the cord through the plug and tie an Underwriter's knot as shown. Pull the knot tight.

STEP 3   Trim the ends of the wires to about 1¼ inches and strip ⅝ inch of insulation off each with either wire strippers or a knife.

STEP 4   Twist the wire end and make a loop. Hook the loop around the screw and tighten to the clamp wire.

STEP 5   Draw the knot snugly into the plug. The cord should pull on the knot, not on the screw connections. Snap the plug together.

Electrical Safety

!   Protect pets who like to bite and chew lamp and appliance cords by covering the cord with clear plastic tubing. Pull about 3 feet of cord through it. You will probably have to remove the molded plug, run the cord through the tubing, and then replace the old plug with a new one. Or slit the tubing with a knife and press the cord through the cut.

Flat-cord Plugs

The plug shown below is one of several types designed for the thin, flat cord commonly used for floor and table lamps, lightweight extension cords, and other low-current devices. The plug's not polarized (the prongs are the same size), so it shouldn't be used to replace a polarized plug.

Simply cut the cord off squarely with wire cutters, slightly separate the wire ends, and push the wire firmly into its slot. Folding the lever down on top of the wires crimps them onto the metal posts and also locks the wire in place.

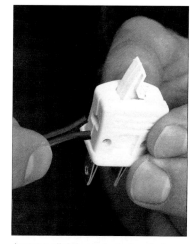

Insert a slightly separated end of a two-wire flat cord into the opening, then push the lever down to secure.

Work Better,
Work Safer

Electrical-box Nailer

To nail an electrical box to a stud when there's no room for you to swing a hammer, use a C-clamp. Just squeeze short nails through the holes in the sides of the box and into the stud by tightening the clamp.

Clamp and nail

No-cut Wire Stripper

Here's a way to remove the insulation from the end of wire without having to worry about cutting or nicking the wire. Heat the insulation with a match about where you want it to break away. You'll then be able to pull the softened plastic covering off with a pair of pliers.

Shed a Little Light

Create a mini trouble light from everyday components by plugging a small hooded incandescent night light into a household extension cord. This light takes the hassle out of using a cumbersome, heavy trouble light on small jobs in cramped spaces. When it's no longer needed, it can be disassembled and the components can be used elsewhere.

Handy Wire Fisher

When you have to fish a wire or cable inside a wall, an ordinary 25-foot metal tape measure will work well just about every time. It remains rigid for a long distance, and the hole in the end hook provides a convenient place to attach the wire. The tape measure also tells you at a glance exactly how far your wire reaches inside the wall.

Magnetic Attraction

When fishing electrical wire or cable where access is limited, try using two strong bar magnets instead of the usual wire and hook method. Tie one magnet to a string and drop it into the wall from the top. Tape the other magnet to the end of the wire which is inserted through the outlet opening. As soon as the magnets are reasonably close together, they will attract each other.

Extension Cord Repair

If you accidentally cut an extension cord in half, there is an alternative to splicing the cut ends together. Connect them to a double receptacle box instead. Now you have an extra outlet box as an additional power source rather than an extension cord with a makeshift joint in the middle.

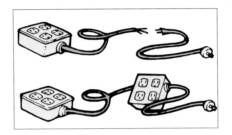

Handier than a splice

Glue Gun for Wiring

Low-voltage wiring such as telephone, thermostat, and door bell wire can be quickly and easily secured to walls and ceilings with a hot melt glue gun. Simply run a bead of glue about an inch long and $1/8$ to $3/16$ inch wide. Then, while the glue is still soft, press the wire into the bead and hold it in place for a few seconds until the glue sets up. Repeat this process every few feet. Using the hot melt glue gun eliminates the need for staples on wood surfaces and makes it easy to run wiring on concrete or masonry walls.

Circuit Marker

To ensure shutting off the right circuit when you need to do electrical work in your home, mark the number of the fuse or circuit breaker on the back side of each switch plate or outlet cover. If you need to work on an outlet, you must remove the outlet cover anyway, and the fuse/circuit breaker number is handy for quickly disconnecting power at the source.

Outlet Openings

Increase your accuracy and avoid measuring errors when installing drywall around electrical outlets. Instead of measuring, replace the top and bottom machine screws in the box with screws that have been sharpened on the ends pointed toward you. Align the drywall over the box and press it firmly against the screws. Use a spare electrical box placed over these holes and draw an outline of the shape for a perfect fit. Power to the outlet should be turned off at the main fuse or circuit box.

Bucket of Volts

Store electrical cords in a 5-gallon plastic bucket. Cut or drill a hole near the base large enough to pass the male end of the extension cord through to the outside. As you feed the remaining cord into the bucket, it will roll itself neatly into coils as it falls. Attach both ends of the cord together when not in use. When you're ready to use it, the cord comes out of the bucket as fast as you can pull it — tangle free!

Light Bulb Octopus

Every home has at least one light bulb that requires a ladder to change. Make a tool for changing bulbs in hard-to-reach locations by fastening a clip from a lampshade to a dowel of the right length (a 4-foot-long by 1-inch-diameter dowel will enable you to reach high bulbs in the garage or stairway). Wrap the bulb clip with electrical tape for a good grip on the bulb.

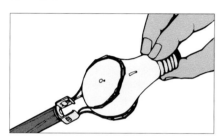

Bulb octopus

Tube It

Change a light bulb in a hard-to-reach location by cutting four slits in the end of a cardboard mailing tube. Slip a heavy rubber band over the end of the tube and gently push the bulb into it. You can use it to remove the old bulb and install the new.

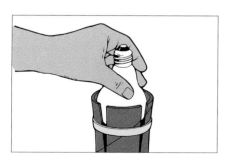

Tube changer

Light Bulb Handle

Removing a tight, burned-out light bulb from a recessed fixture can be next to impossible because there just isn't enough room for your fingers. Make a light bulb "handle" from a 15-inch strip of duct tape. Center the tape on the bulb; fold the two ends back to the middle, then fold each end over again on itself to form the handle.

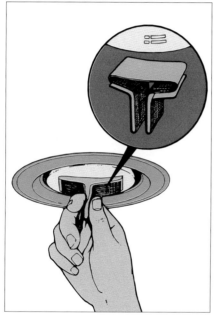

Bulb handle

Easy Light-bulb Removal

Outdoor light bulbs — and some indoors as well — always seem to be hard to remove. Make the job easier next time, and avoid the risk of breaking the bulb in your hand, by putting a light coating of petroleum jelly on the threads of the new bulb.

Organizer for Ugly Wires

All those wires hanging down behind your TV, VCR, or stereo can look like a jungle. Organize them into a neat, attractive cable with a coiled telephone cord. The cords are inexpensive and come in various lengths and a number of colors. Just clip the snap-in plugs off the ends and wrap the coils around the wires.

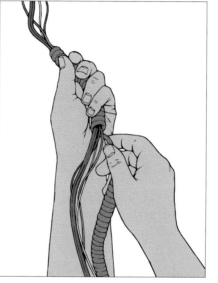

Coil organizer

Battery-charge Timer

Avoid overcharging your battery-operated tools: Plug the charger into an ordinary light timer that's set to shut off after the recharging time. Make sure the timer isn't set to turn back on.

Circuit Box Siren

To figure out which fuse or circuit breaker controls an electrical outlet, plug the vacuum cleaner into the outlet and turn it on. Even from the basement you'll be able to hear the silence when you switch off the right breaker or unscrew the right fuse.

Shock-proof Electrical Jobs

Place a heavy rubber insulating mat by your electric service entry panel and stand on the mat when checking fuses or circuit breakers. If your system uses fuses, keep a supply near the entry panel and be sure to keep a flashlight nearby for use if a light fuse blows by the panel.

White Hot Wire

A white wire is NOT, NOT, NOT always neutral! The box may be wired poorly, of course. But even in a properly wired box, white can be hot without any kind of black tape or other identification. The U.S. and Canadian electrical codes make an exception from the normal "black-hot, white-neutral" rule for wires in a "switching situation." This means that in a properly wired three-way switch, the white wire in the electrical box will be the hot wire. Even common single-pole switches can have a white wire that's hot.

This code exception has been in force for a long time and only requires that the wires be "manufactured" cable. This includes the nonmetallic sheathed cable you normally use for house wiring, the one that has the black, white, and ground wires together in a plastic cover. Professional electricians would not ordinarily mark a hot white wire with black tape, though there are many how-to stories for DIYers that say this is a must.

The moral of this story is simple: Shut off the circuit at the main panel and test all wires for voltage before you touch them. That $1 voltage tester belongs in your pocket whenever you work with wiring. Even a white wire can be hot.

White can be hot

Using Electrical Testers

Nothing strikes fear into the heart of the beginning do-it-yourselfer like electricity. With plumbing, the worst that can happen is you get soaked; with carpentry, you can cut yourself; and how badly can you damage yourself wallpapering? But when a beginner takes the cover plate off an outlet — it's a vision of the electric chair that comes to mind. Or at least it ought to. Electricity is dangerous, but with a couple of inex-

pensive testers, you can protect yourself and make electric wiring a safe and understandable project.

The Circuit Tester

This inexpensive tool should be in every DIYer's toolbox; it's unsafe to work around wiring without it. The circuit tester is just a neon bulb with two leads that's used to indicate the presence or absence of ordinary household voltage. Its most common use is to make sure the voltage is actually off at the switch, outlet, or light fixture you are working on, even if you've turned off what you thought was the right circuit breaker. A mislabeled breaker box, eccentric wiring techniques, or a faulty breaker all can mean that the wire you thought was safe to touch isn't. So test it first with your circuit tester.

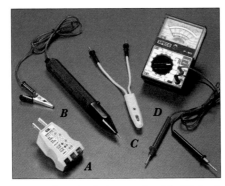

Four electrical testers: from left, (A) circuit analyzer, (B) continuity tester, (C) circuit tester, and (D) multimeter.

To use a circuit tester, hold the leads well back from their tips and make three tests: (1) connect the black

(hot) lead to ground (the metal box or bare ground wire); (2) connect the white (neutral) wire to ground; and (3) connect the black wire to the white wire. The light should not go on if you have turned off the power. If there is still power, the light will go on for one of the three tests. If you encounter the rare situation where you cannot find the white (neutral) wire, make a known ground by connecting a wire to a pipe or radiator, and check your black (hot) wire against that ground.

The circuit tester is a basic safety tool. Hold leads back from the ends and touch all combinations of wires to test for the presence of voltage.

Checking the ground connection is another good use for the circuit tester. The round hole of a three-pronged outlet must be properly grounded to get any safety benefit. Put one lead of the tester into the round hole and try the two other slots. A light from one of them means the outlet is grounded.

Similarly, if you plan to use an adapter between a three-prong plug

and a two-prong receptacle, the kind with a green ground wire that connects to the center screw on the outlet cover, first test that the screw is properly grounded.

The Circuit Analyzer

If you are adding a circuit to your home, or if you suspect there is something wrong with your wiring, the circuit analyzer can warn you of several potentially dangerous circuit problems. Just plug it in, and the pattern of lights will indicate any of these problems:

The circuit analyzer diagnoses faulty wiring, such as a disconnected ground wire or reversed hot and neutral wires.

- *Hot and neutral wires reversed.* This wiring problem may not affect lights and appliances, but it can give you a bad shock from an otherwise properly functioning device.
- *Shorted hot and disconnected ground,* or *reversed hot and ground.* Either of these two situations can give you a nasty shock from the junction box, switch, or light fixture.

■ *Open (not connected) ground.* This negates the safety benefits of grounded wiring and appliances.

If your circuit analyzer shows one of these situations, rewire the mistake, or if you have any doubts about where the problem lies, call an electrician.

The Continuity Tester

This tool is used to indicate whether a circuit is complete, that is, whether electricity can flow through it. If you plan on doing even a moderate amount of electrical work, get one.

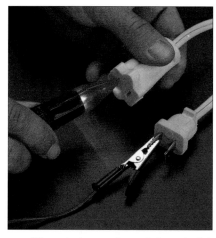

The continuity tester shows whether a circuit is broken or complete. Here it is used to see if an extension cord is faulty.

Caution: The power must be off when you use this tool. While the two previous tools were powered by the circuit they tested, the continuity tester has a battery and supplies its own power. When using this tester, if the light goes on, there is no break in the circuit.

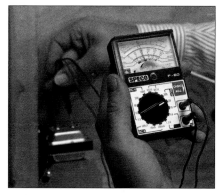

The multimeter measures resistance, current, and a large range of voltages, both AC (household) and DC (batteries).

Here are some practical uses of this tool for the DIYer:

■ *Testing a fuse or circuit breaker to see whether it is functioning.* This is useful for cartridge fuses, which show no external signs of having been blown.
■ *Testing a new circuit for shorts.* Let's say you have just added new circuits in your remodeled attic. Before you turn on the power, you should test all combinations of leads on the outlet or fixture farthest from the main panel. A complete circuit between black and ground, black and white, or white and ground indicates a short, which must be located and repaired. Be sure there are no tools, appliances, or light bulbs plugged into the new circuits, or you will get a false reading.
■ *Testing switches.* Check ordinary switches to help locate the problem in a defective circuit. Lamp switches are prone to breaking down and are easily checked.

For the Serious Do-It-Yourselfer: The Multimeter

The multimeter does everything the three basic testers do, plus a few more jobs. Instead of giving you a yes-no, on-off reading, it gives you a measurement of voltage, current, or resistance. Multimeters are available in a number of price ranges at hardware stores, home centers, and electronics stores.

The multimeter can measure voltage, both AC (the type in your house) and DC (the type in batteries); resistance (the ease with which current flows in a circuit); and the amount of current. To use the multimeter as a circuit tester, just set it to measure AC voltage. To use as a continuity tester, set it to measure resistance (an open circuit has plenty of resistance!). All multimeters come with users' manuals that tell exactly how to use a particular model. Here are some other household uses:

■ *Wiring for 240 volts.* If you are working with 240-volt circuits, as in a shop or electric appliance circuit, the multimeter can be used to distinguish 120-volt circuits from 240-volt circuits.
■ *Appliance and audio equipment repair.* The multimeter helps with general circuit troubleshooting.
■ *Working with low-voltage circuits.* Doorbells, security alarms, and thermostats all run on low voltage — too low for ordinary circuit testers. Is your doorbell sounding weak? Check the AC voltage; it should be within two volts of the voltage indicated on the transformer.

Electric Pail

You can take the 5-gallon bucket in "Bucket of Volts" on page 100 and jazz it up. After bolting the grounded outlet box to the outside of the pail, bolt a smaller pail inside the 5-gallon one. This makes a faster and neater job of winding 100 feet of cord flat against the inside wall of the larger pail, and also makes it easier to carry tools without interfering with the cord feed-out. Use large washers to bolt the pail and the electrical box to hold them securely.

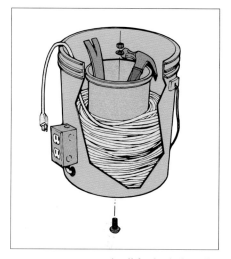

A pail for electrical supplies

Stuck Bulbs

To prevent a light bulb base from corroding and sticking in the socket, buy high-quality bulbs with brass bases instead of steel — brass will not corrode. To remove a stuck bulb, turn off power to the circuit, break the glass bulb, and remove the base with a pair of needle-nosed pliers.

Roof and Eaves

Patching a Roof Valley 106

Holes and open seams in valley flashing can allow water to seep into your attic. Both punctures and opened joints are easy to patch.

Fixing Leaky Gutters 108

A leaky gutter is more than a nuisance — it can lead to water damage in and around your house. Fix it before it gets worse.

Replacing Shingles   109

This repair isn't necessary very often, but when it is, save money by doing it yourself.

Replacing a Soffit   110

This is a major repair, but it requires more time than skill.

Replacing Vent Flashing   113

The seal between the roof's vent pipes and the shingles is just as important as the shingles themselves.

Work Better, Work Safer   114

Want to know how to straighten a gutter? Lift an asphalt shingle without breaking it? Or use an extension ladder safely? Just read these four pages for those tips, and more.

Patching a Roof Valley

First aid for holes and cracks.

WHAT YOU NEED

Wire brush

Gutter sealant

Putty knife

Paint thinner

Roofing cement

Winter ice and summer sun can do bad things to your roof valleys — the lines where two sections of roof meet. Worse, debris tends to gather in them, making the valley particularly vulnerable to wear and damage. A small leak in a valley may cause major water penetration, since the intersecting roofs concentrate the flow of water here.

Steps 1 – 3 show how to repair small punctures in aluminum or galvanized valley flashing — the kind of holes that often result from ice removal, a falling tree branch, hail, or other hard knocks.

While you're up there on the roof, seal the shingle joints along the flashing, as shown on the facing page. Roofers often neglect to seal this joint and, as the shingles age and begin to curl, they may pull away from the flashing and allow water to penetrate the roof.

REPAIRING A PUNCTURE

STEP 1   Clean the area around the puncture in the valley flashing with a wire brush to remove any loose dirt and debris.

STEP 2   Fill the hole and the surrounding area with gutter sealant, available in tube form at most home centers or a roofing supply outlet.

STEP 3   Spread the sealant with a small putty knife. Wet the knife blade with paint thinner to help you form a smooth finish on the sealant.

STEP 1 Seal shingles to the valley flashing by lifting the cut edge of each shingle and laying a bead of roofing cement on the valley flashing about ½ inch back from the edge. Keep the bead of cement a consistent width and thickness. Start from the bottom shingle and work toward the peak of the roof.

STEP 2 Drop the first shingle onto the cement, then lay another bead of cement along the bottom edge of that shingle. Continue this procedure up the valley to the peak.

STEP 3 After one side of the valley is completed, do the same on the opposite side. Press the shingles flat to make sure that they adhere to one another and to the flashing.

Sure and Safe Roofing: Working above the Ground

Here are some ideas that may make your roof repairs go easier and work better. They'll also keep you working safely.

■ Do your repairs on a warm day when shingles are soft and pliable. You'll be less likely to crack the shingles as you walk on them or fold them back, and roofing cement will adhere more readily. Always work with great caution on the roof. If the pitch is too steep for sure footing, construct a roof ladder that hooks in place over the roof peak or call a professional roofer to make the repair.

■ Don't ever touch the power lines that come to your home. They can be deadly.

■ On the roof you need to do a lot of nailing from a kneeling or squatting position, so try wearing your nail apron behind you. Just reach around when you need another handful of nails — you won't have to stand or straighten up each time. Also, the bag will hang open and won't dig into your thigh.

■ For both safety and comfort, it's important to set your ladder at the correct angle. To determine the proper angle, stand directly in front of the ladder and place your toes against its feet. Extend your arms straight out in front of you. If the rung nearest your hands falls around the middle of your fingers, the ladder is at the proper angle to ensure good balance and body mechanics, as well as maximum ladder strength.

■ There's a new product on the market that is another in a long line of no-mess caulks and sealants. It is a type of peel-and-stick roof and gutter caulk that eliminates smears of roof mastic on the roof shingles or gutters. It is guaranteed for 20 years when installed correctly. You can also use it to caulk around the roof vents of recreational vehicles. Check at your local home center in the caulk and adhesives aisle.

Fixing Leaky Gutters

Timely repairs can save you grief.

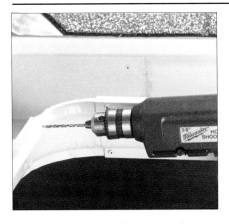

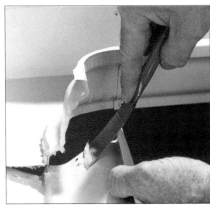

STEP 1   Open leaking seams in an aluminum gutter by drilling out the Pop rivets. Use a drill bit slightly larger than the hole in the center of the rivet.

STEP 2   Clean off the old sealant with a putty knife, or use coarse sandpaper if sealer is caked hard. Adjoining surfaces must be clean and smooth.

WHAT YOU NEED

Electric drill and bit

Putty knife

Coarse sandpaper

Gutter sealant

Pop rivets

Riveting tool

Leaky aluminum gutter seams have a disagreeable way of leaving dark water streaks on the outside of your house. Catch leaks before they make a mess by sealing up the offending seams.

Use one of the caulk sealants specifically intended for aluminum gutters. They're inexpensive, they adhere to metal, and they remain elastic even in extreme temperatures. They are available at all well-stocked home centers in white or a natural aluminum color.

Minor leaks can sometimes be cured without taking seams apart. Just force the gutter sealant into the joint from inside the gutter, using your finger. With larger leaks or where it's hard to get sealant all the way into the seams you have to take them apart. That way ordinary expansion and contraction won't quickly loosen them up again, and the water flow won't wash away the sealant.

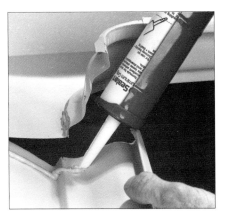

STEP 3   Apply a bead of gutter sealant about ³⁄₈ inch wide between adjoining surfaces. Work the sealant well back into the joint with the putty knife.

STEP 4   Install new Pop rivets with a riveting tool, using the old holes. Make sure the gutter surfaces match and the seam is tight.

Replacing Shingles

Keep your roof watertight.

WHAT YOU NEED

Pry bar

Hammer

Shingles

Galvanized roofing nails

Roofing adhesive

Replacing a few shingles that have missing or broken tabs (the visible flaps of the shingle) is quick and easy. Most roofing supply outlets or home centers will sell shingles in small quantities, or you can buy a full bundle. Take a piece of your broken shingle along to find a close color and size match. Shingles come in both metric and standard sizes, the metric being larger in both dimensions.

Each shingle usually has three tabs and is held in place with six roofing nails. These nails are accessible by lifting and folding back the two rows of shingle tabs above the damaged shingle.

Do your repairs on a warm day when the shingles are soft and pliable to avoid breaking or cracking the tabs. Always work with caution on the roof. If the pitch is too steep for sure footing, hire a professional roofing contractor.

REMOVE AND REPLACE

STEP 1 Gently pry up the two rows of shingle tabs immediately above the damaged shingle, loosening them from the thin self-sealing tar strip. Slide a pry bar along the full length of the tab before folding it back to expose the roofing nails.

STEP 2 Tap the pry bar under the nail heads and remove the nails without damaging the shingle below. Remove one nail from under each of the three tabs in the row just above the damaged shingle, and again in the row above that. Slide the damaged shingle out.

STEP 3 Insert the new shingle under the row of tabs above and renail with galvanized roofing nails the same size as those you removed and in approximately the same locations.

STEP 4 Spread a thin bead of roofing adhesive under the tabs of the new shingle and all those you folded back. Press the tabs flat and make sure they adhere to the adhesive.

Replacing a Rotted Soffit

Don't ignore this part of your house.

WHAT YOU NEED

Rolling scaffold

Pry bar

Hacksaw

Dust mask

Screwdriver

Hand saw

Galvanized wood screws

Plywood

Strip vent

Galvanized finishing nails

Exterior-grade paint

Paintbrush

Here's an ugly, awkward, dirty job, but if you do it right, you won't have to think about it again for a long, long time.

The soffit is the narrow band of ceiling that covers the bottom of the roof overhang. It shades the siding and protects it from bad weather, keeps rainwater away from the foundation, and provides ventilation that flushes excess moisture and heat away from the attic and roof.

When a soffit starts going bad, you usually get some clear signs. Watch for badly peeling paint or brown stains. Both signal water problems that are almost always caused by leaky roofs or gutters. In the north, ice dams are a major culprit. Once water seeps through worn shingles or under loose flashing, it'll run down rafters or roof boards and puddle on the top side of the soffit boards.

STEP 1 Pull the nails with a pry bar to release the gutter straps and lower the gutter. This job is easier if you have someone to help you.

STEP 2 Pry the fascia board off the rafter tails if it shows rot. You may have to cut through any badly rusted nails with a hacksaw.

STEP 3 Pry the soffit boards off the lookouts and remove the trim strip (sometimes called a "frieze board"). Remember to wear a dust mask, since this can be dirty work.

STEP 4 Probe the rotted areas with a screwdriver to find the extent of the damage. Let all the moist areas dry out before proceeding.

STEP 1   Screw a new section of rafter to the old one to reinforce the tail. Make the new section twice as long as the rafter tail.

STEP 2   Install new 2x4 lookouts to replace rotted ones or screw a new one to the old one if it's mostly sound. Install a new fascia board.

Parts of a Soffit

The *soffit* boards are nailed to lookouts that are fastened to the house and the ends, or *tails*, of the roof rafters. Whether the soffit is wood or metal, it should include sections of screening to admit air. The joint where the soffit meets the house is the *trim strip*. The *fascia* board encloses the soffit at the rafter ends.

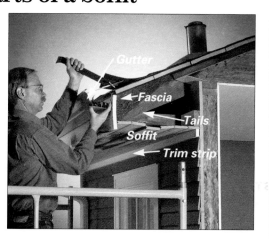

Rent a Scaffold for Above-ground Safety

Though you can work from ladders, there's a slick device that can make your soffit work a whole lot easier and safer — the rolling scaffold. One 6-foot-high section puts you up at a comfortable working height for most first-floor roofs, so you don't have to bend, stretch, and reach as you would from a ladder. The wheels allow you to push the scaffold back and forth along the house and soffit. Just make sure to shove two ¾-inch plywood pads at least 12 inches square under each of the four wheels and lock the wheels before climbing up.

Of course, working even a few feet off the ground can be dangerous. Make sure you follow all safety precautions, including fastening a railing on the outside of the scaffold. When you rent the scaffold, ask for full assembly and safety instructions. You shouldn't work any higher than the first story. Leave higher work for professionals.

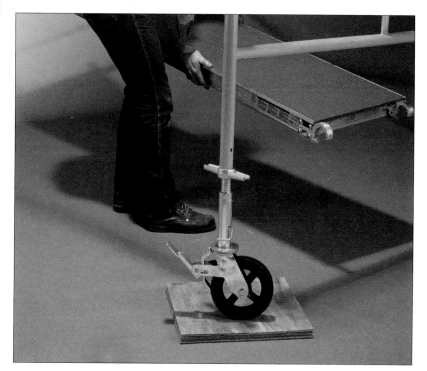

Rent a rolling scaffold for soffit repair work. The jacks adjust to the slope of your yard, and the plywood pads keep the wheels from sinking.

Watch Out for Bees!

Before you begin working on your soffits — or the overhang of any structure, for that matter — check for critters like bees and wasps, which often build their nests in these sheltered places.

Soffits, being well protected from bad weather, make a great home for these animals, as well as yellow jackets and hornets. Most of the creatures are worth having around — the bees pollinate flowers and wasps hunt down other insects — until you start hammering near their homes. You sure won't want them buzzing around your head when you're atop a ladder or scaffold.

If you're allergic to stings, take special care here. Check your soffits in advance for nests or signs of bee or wasp activity. You can simply knock smaller nests down with a pole but wait for nighttime when the insects are less active. For safety, work from the ground and use a flashlight or, even better, no light at all so they can't see you. A spray insecticide that's formulated for bees will work, too.

If you have the option of waiting, do your soffit work during cool weather, like the fall, when the insects become inactive or die. Keep in mind, too, that if the nest is softball size or larger, you're getting into a big colony and might want to contact a pest control service to remove it.

INSTALLING VENTS AND SOFFIT

STEP 1 Insert a strip vent (or other vents) in the new soffit to ventilate the attic and roof. Use galvanized finishing nails to fasten the soffit boards.

STEP 2 Cut the last soffit board to fit, then cover the sawn edge with the trim strip. Paint to finish up.

Replacing Vent Flashing

Add years to the life of your roof.

WHAT YOU NEED

Pry bar

Roofing cement

Caulking gun

Vent flashing base with telescoping sleeve

1-inch roofing nails

Utility knife

Are rain and melting snow bringing water into your home around the plumbing vent pipe? You could fix the problem with a minor touch-up of the lead caulking ring where the pipe and flashing neck join or with a few dabs of roofing cement in the leaking areas.

But if the vent flashing unit is beyond patching, replace it with an adjustable, frostproof unit. A telescoping sleeve adjusts up or down about 6 inches to accommodate almost any length of pipe protruding through the roof. The lead caulking ring lays on the vent pipe's lip and folds over the inner edge of the pipe to prevent leakage, even with expansion and contraction caused by freezing.

CAULK AND INSTALL

STEP 1 Carefully remove all the shingles that cover the old vent flashing (the shingles lap over only the top half of the flashing base). If you intend to reuse the shingles, make sure they are warm and pliable before you begin removing them.

STEP 2 Using a caulking gun, spread a bead of roofing cement evenly around the perimeter of the underside of the new vent flashing base.

STEP 3 Slide the flashing over the vent pipe. Adjust the sleeve to the length of the pipe. Drive 1-inch roofing nails around the flashing base. Bend the caulking ring over the top of the pipe.

STEP 4 Renail the shingles, trimming them to lay flat and overlap the top half of the flashing base. Apply roofing cement to the nail heads and shingle edges around the flashing base.

Work Better, Work Safer

Shingle-saving Roof Rake

An aluminum roof rake really cleans the snow off the roof, but it also scrapes off some of the shingle granules at the same time. To solve this problem, try attaching a vinyl door-bottom sweep to the rake. It still removes the snow, but it's much more gentle on the shingles.

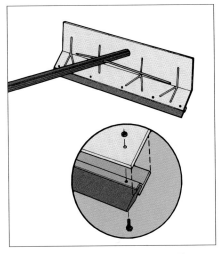

Raking snow

Reroofing Cleanup

As you tear off the old roofing, tear the pieces up and put them in 30-gallon plastic trash bags right on the roof. It's

a third as much work as throwing the pieces off onto the ground and then picking them up again. You also eliminate the danger of stepping on roofing nails, which always seem to land with the point up.

Buy the cheap bags that come in a roll and double bag them. Use masking tape to close the bag. Drop them off the roof gently; don't throw them down.

Level Scaffold

It is a good idea to rent a steel scaffold for those jobs around roofs, eaves, and gutters that require a safe work platform. But many home owners use odd scraps of wood to level the scaffold. For a dollar or two per day you can rent adjustable levelers that are not only easy to operate but also lock in place to guarantee safety aloft.

Need a New Roof?

If you buy an older house, the condition of the roof is a major issue. But no matter how it looks, as long as a roof doesn't leak, and if you can live with its looks, there's no reason to replace it. Check between the roof rafters for any

signs of leaking and make sure the roof decking is not wet or rotting under the shingles along the roof's bottom edges. Leaks don't start as gushers, all at once. They usually come gradually, allowing you enough time to replace the roof before major damage is done.

Shingle Raiser

Use a heavy mason's trowel to raise three-tab shingles to repair the roof or when replacing flashing. Starting at the edge of a sealer shingle, gently tap the edge of the trowel with the hammer to break the seal and lift the shingle.

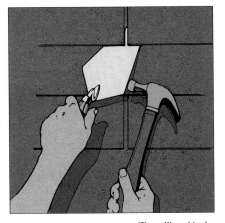

Trowelling shingles

Roof Tile Review

A tile roof is virtually maintenance-free. Made of clay or concrete, tiles need no patching, sealing, or recoating. Unlike other roofing materials, the only maintenance they may require is occasionally replacing broken tiles. Because tiles are fragile and tricky to handle, this should be done by a professional. The

fact is, a properly installed tile roof should last the life of your house.

You can get more information on tile roofs by writing: The National Tile Roofing Manufacturers Assoc., Inc., Dept. FH, 3127 Los Feliz Blvd., Los Angeles, CA 90039.

Snow-shoveling Sparrows

Does this problem sound familiar? Each winter the snow piles up on the roof and then slides off, taking your gutters with it. Try installing "snowbirds." For those unfamiliar with snowbirds, they're used to break up large sections of melting snow as it slides off a roof. This reduces the chance of a large chunk taking the gutter with it as it falls. They come in eagle, owl, or sometimes purely geometrical shapes. They are made of cast iron and are approximately 5 inches high. They attach to the roof about a foot above the bottom edge near the fascia or gutters. They should be placed every 2 feet on center to keep sliding snow chunks fairly small. They're used primarily on roofs with a steep pitch, because a steep pitch gives gravity an advantage, allowing large chunks to slide off easier. Snowbirds can be used on asphalt, metal, tile, or slate roofs.

Gutter Straightener

Ice coming off a roof can bend the spikes that secure your rain gutters to the soffit fascia. The spikes can seem impossible to straighten without removing both them and the gutters. But you can solve the problem using a 2-foot length of angle iron and a heavy metal chain link with the center section cut out of one side. Working from a ladder (be careful!), you'll find that the angle iron and chain link provide easy leverage to straighten out the spike and get the gutters back in alignment.

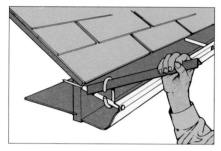

Spike bender

Care of Cedar Shakes

The best tip for prolonging the life of the roof is good housekeeping. Debris such as leaves, pine needles, or branches that accumulate on the roof surface contributes to the premature deterioration of cedar shake roofing. If allowed to remain on the roof, this debris will retain moisture and may result in the formation of moss and fungus. This debris can also impede the runoff of rainwater to a degree that could result in leaks in the roof.

Clean the roof using a stiff-bristled broom or brush or a high pressure washer (available at rental equipment stores). Be careful not to damage the shakes. And, use extreme caution if you stand on the roof — wet shakes are very slippery.

Most cedar shake roofs remain untreated after installation and on the whole, provide excellent service. Chemical treating (coating) of the roof is desirable if your local climate is hot and humid for much of the year, for roofs with low pitch or slope, or roofs beneath overhanging trees.

Copper Roof Blues

Okay, here's the situation: you have a copper roof over a bay window. It has turned dark brown and you can't get it clean. You've tried everything paint stripper, trisodium phosphate (TSP), ammonia, bleach, drain cleaner, and several polishes. Nothing seems to work. How can you restore the roof to its original luster?

Well, the bad news is, you can't. Copper goes through a natural weathering process, called oxidation, that is the very thing that makes copper roofs so appealing and maintenance-free. A roof that has gone from a shiny copper color to dull brown is far enough into the process that it would be impossible to restore its shine.

But there is good news: Your roof won't stay its current brown color forever. The brown stage is only the first of three. Next you'll see streaks of green begin to develop. Finally, the whole roof will turn a soft green.

If you're not willing to let Mother Nature take her slow course, you can artificially induce the final green stage with an acid-based solution. Because of the health hazards that acid poses, the

process is not for the do-it-yourselfer, but instead should be done by a roofer who specializes in metal roofs. Look in the yellow pages under "Roofing Contractors." The fact is, a copper roof in its natural state is a trouble-free, beautiful asset to any house.

Gutter Scoop

You can make a great gutter-cleaning scoop by cutting away the bottom portion of a rectangular motor oil container. It's just the right width to fit into the gutter, and the spout gives you a great hand grip.

Oil-jug scoop

Fungus and Asphalt Shingles

Fungal growth on roofs is typically found in hot, humid locales. While fungus does not shorten the life of asphalt shingles, fungus is unattractive because it discolors and darkens asphalt. You can temporarily lighten the shingles by cleaning them, but this won't stop the fungus altogether.

If you're planning to reroof in the near future, however, you can minimize future problems if you install shingles that are designed to inhibit fungus. Made by most major shingle manufacturers, they have a zinc granule that kills fungus. They cost about 10 to 15 percent more per square than standard three-tab shingles (one square equals 100 square feet).

In the meantime, if you want to temporarily lighten the shingles, use a clean garden spray pump to apply a solution of one part chlorine bleach and four parts water. (Don't scrub or you'll loosen and remove granules.)

Then gently rinse the solution off with your garden hose. Be sure to protect shrubs and plants with plastic coverings, and wet your siding down before you apply the solution. Then as you work, have a helper rinse off any solution that may drip onto the siding.

Caution: This solution will make the roof slippery. Don't attempt this if you have a steeply pitched roof. Use proper safety equipment and wear protective clothing: soft-soled shoes such as tennis shoes, and protective rubber gloves and goggles. Work cautiously. Be aware of and stay clear of power lines.

Using Extension Ladders

Every year 300 people are killed and 65,000 more hospitalized due to accidents involving extension ladders. For tools that can't be plugged in, with few moving parts, extension ladders are surprisingly dangerous.

Some Sensible Safety Rules

Ladders themselves rarely malfunction, but ladder users do. Emergency room doctors call this the "I'd rather spend three months in traction than three minutes setting this ladder up correctly" syndrome. Ladder safety is 50 percent common sense and 50 percent taking the time to do it right. Here's the common-sense advice, emblazoned on the side of every ladder sold today:

- Check overhead for electrical wires. Aluminum ladders are particularly hazardous, but dirty wood and fiberglass ladders can conduct electricity, too.
- Stabilize both the top and bottom of your ladder. If the bottom can't slide and the top can't tip, not much can happen in between.
- Lower your ladder and carry it parallel to the ground when moving it from one spot to the next.
- Face the ladder as you go up and down. Wear soft, rubber-soled shoes — leather soles can slip.
- Maintain three points of contact: Two feet and one hand or two hands and one foot should be on the ladder at all times.
- Avoid overreaching. Your belt buckle should remain between the ladder's two side rails at all times.
- Select a ladder that's the right height and sturdy enough for the job.

Raising Ladders the Right Way

Four hands are better than two when it comes to raising extension ladders, especially those over 28 feet long. Here's the best method:

1. Place the bottom of the ladder against the base of the house and raise it "flag at Iwo Jima style" by walking it hand over hand starting at the top of the ladder.

Walk ladder hand over hand.

2. When the ladder is vertical, pull the base out slightly from the house and extend the ladder to the desired height. Be sure the locks are fully engaged.

The safe angle is shown on the side of the ladder.

3. Move the base of the ladder away from the house and establish the correct angle of 75 degrees (above right). For each 4 feet of ladder used, the base should be 1 foot away from the house.

4. Secure the base. On grass or loose rock, use the ladder feet in the spike position . On hard, stable surfaces, use the feet in the flat-foot position. If possible, tie the base of the ladder back to the house with rope. If you're on a wooden deck, nail a cleat behind the ladder feet to keep it from sliding outward. When in doubt, have a helper hold the bottom.

Use the ladder feet in spike position for grass, landscaping rock or loose soil.

Safety Tips for Special Situations

When you're working on a roof, the side rails of your ladder should extend 3 feet above the roof edge so you have a good handhold as you climb on and off the ladder. Step onto the roof from the side, rather than over the top rung.

Use a ladder stabilizer bar to prevent damage to siding and gutters, to span window openings, and to provide better stability. All major ladder manufacturers offer these bars.

Never set a ladder on sawhorses or boxes to extend its reach.

Use a tool belt or your pockets to carry tools and supplies — not your hands. Better yet, use a bucket and rope to pull your tools up after you've climbed up.

Pulling Nails

It takes 65,000 nails to hold the shingles on your roof, secure the trim around each window, and keep the family portrait hanging safely in the hall. You tend to take these little guys for granted — until they have to come out.

Over the course of repairing or remodeling your home, unwanted nails, old and new alike, will inevitably rear their ugly little heads. But a dash of physics, coupled with the right tool used the right way, makes pulling nails safe, fast, and easy.

The Nail Puller's Toolbox

The flat bar is a must for any toolbox. If you add both a cat's paw and a crowbar to your arsenal, you'll be prepared for almost any nail-pulling encounter.

Grab, Hold, and Pull

Removing any nail involves two steps: grabbing, then pulling. Here's how to do it using your basic nail pullers, the flat bar and the cat's paw:

Position the claw ½ inch or so from the nail head at about a 30-degree angle to the wood. The deeper the nail, the farther back you must start or the steeper the angle should be.

Rap the tool's heel firmly with a hammer. Don't be shy — it's okay to dig up a little wood along with the nail head. Once the claw is snugged securely around the nail shank, pry it out. A well-defined "V" on the claw gives you the best grip with the least likelihood of slipping or stripping the nail head.

When you encounter a headless nail or a particularly stubborn one, use the "sidewinder" approach . A ripping claw hammer, with a nearly straight claw, works best for this. Beware of overstressing the handle, though, especially a wooden one.

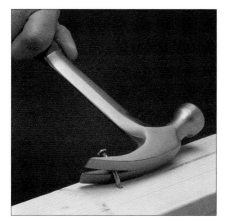
Sidewinding with a hammer

The common curved-claw hammer is best for straight-ahead nail pulling. Short, jerky pulls work best for stubborn nails.

Caution: Nails, wood, or even tools can give way suddenly. Wear safety glasses and make sure you're well braced, especially when working from a ladder or high up.

Cat's paw

Big Pull, Less Work

Despite their variety in shape and size, all pulling and prying tools are basically levers with a claw on one end and a fulcrum (the "prying-against point") close by. Keep in mind:

Nail puller

- The longer the shaft, the better the leverage; short-handled grabbers sometimes make poor pullers.
- A combined approach often works best — making the nail accessible with one tool, then switching and pulling with another.

When you feel yourself or your tools straining, it's time to switch to longer, more "influential" tools. The standard 3-foot crowbar will finish most jobs, although wrecking bars with shafts up to 6 feet long are available.

The specialized nail puller is indispensable for major salvage work or jobs like pulling nails out of an entire plywood subfloor.

Saving Face

All nail-pulling tools will cause some marring. But what if you want to reuse a hard-to-match piece of trim or save some perfectly good tongue-and-groove flooring or paneling?

One approach is to pry and remove the piece you want to save, finish nails and all, with a flat bar. Then with a carpenter's nipper or locking pliers, pull the head and shank out from the back side. Most of the time this prevents the splintering and paint tear-out that occur if you bang a nail back out through the face.

Another trick is to punch the nails all the way through the piece with a nail set before removing them. Either approach will result in an enlarged hole, but it will be well-defined and easily filled.

Here's a final tip that works particularly well on lap siding. Rather than digging at the nail head, just pry up the wood and then gently whack the board right next to the nail head. Often the head will pop up as the board goes down, and you can remove the nail without a blemish.

Gutter Shelving

Vinyl rain gutters make great storage shelves for long, thin items such as molding, light lumber, pipe and long tools. Lengths of gutter are inexpensive and will support a surprising amount of weight if you use the gutter's wrap-around support brackets. Just screw the brackets to the studs of your garage or basement and snap the gutters in place.

Gutter Bucket

Snip the wire handle of a 5-gallon bucket in half and bend the free ends into small hooks. Hang the bucket on the edge of your gutter, then slide it along and fill it as you work your way along the length of the gutter.

Gutter work made easier

Outdoor Fixes

If you include this job in your spring-cleaning to-do list, you may not have to repaint your house as often.

Replacing a broken deck board is a task that most home owners can accomplish easily. You need just standard tools, a little time, and not much money.

Fallen tree limbs and any number of other accidents can damage the wood lap siding of your house. But you can make a repair that looks as good as new.

You can remodel a house that is faced with stucco by installing new windows and doors or an addition. And here's how to patch the stucco after you're done.

A loose metal railing on steps or around a porch is unsightly and dangerous. Get rid of the wobbles in four easy steps.

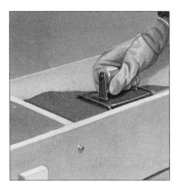

Power Washing Your House

Do it once a year, and your siding will look great.

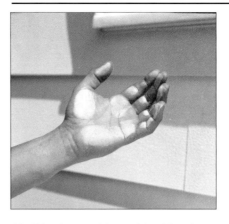

Chalking is a problem with white aluminum siding that's 15 to 20 years old. Power washing gets rid of the residue so that new paint will adhere.

Powerful and portable, power washing equipment is available at most rental equipment dealers. The telescoping wand makes it easy to reach the upper stories of the house.

WHAT YOU NEED

Power washing equipment

Garden hose

Duct tape

Plastic sheeting and drop cloth

Cleaning agent (optional)

The inside of your house, and your yard, usually get an annual or "spring" cleaning. But why stop there? A complete house cleaning should include power washing the exterior. After all, it's the first thing your guests see.

A thorough power washing will remove not only dirt, mildew, and moss, but also paint that is peeling, flaking, and chalking.

Power washing is a good way to prepare your house's surface for repainting, too. And once the siding is clean, you may just find out that you don't have to paint after all.

Handling the Equipment

You'll be working with a lot more water pressure than the average garden hose delivers. A power washer delivers about 1,200 to 2,500 pounds per square inch (psi), compared to 60 psi from a garden hose, making the washer wand a dangerous tool. But with a little practice you can control it.

A telescoping spray wand like the one shown (above right) can be a real handful, however, kicking back 3 to 4 feet when you pull the trigger.

Also, you'll get tired from fighting the pressure so when you begin to feel tired, take a break.

A power washer is not a toy and should not be operated by children. Never put your hands or fingers near the tip of the wand when it's operating, or aim the wand at a person or an animal. The water will penetrate the skin and cause severe injury.

When you're working near the main overhead electrical service line that runs into your house, be extremely careful. Accidental contact of the wires by the wand will kill you! Keep the wand at least 10 feet from the power line. If needed, clean the area around the line by hand, using a wood-handled scrub brush.

STEP 1 Wash from the bottom up to prevent the dirt and cleaning agent from running down onto the unwashed surface and streaking it.

STEP 2 Rinse from the top down to thoroughly wash away the cleaning agent and dirt and to avoid leaving streaks on the clean surface.

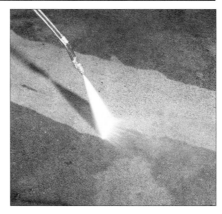

STEP 3 While you have the machine, clean other areas around the house, such as concrete patios, brick steps, decks, driveways, and trash cans.

Power Washing Do's and Don'ts

- Do keep the nozzle 10 to 12 inches from the surface, at about a 45-degree angle to the surface.

- Do make sure all windows are closed tightly.

- Do cover all outside light fixtures with plastic bags; secure the bags with duct tape.

- Do cover all electrical outlets on the exterior of the home with polyethylene film and duct tape.

- Do use extra caution on houses with aluminum or steel siding and fascia. A power washer can bend sections — even blow them right off the house.

- Place drop cloths over plants and shrubs. Move lawn furniture and other portable objects away from the house.

- Do watch the weather. If it's too windy, don't wash. There will be a lot of nuisance overspray, even if it's only water.

- Don't spray directly at windows. The water pressure can break them.

PSIs, Nozzles, and Soap

The recommended pressure rating, expressed in pounds per square inch (psi), of a washer intended for residential use is from 1,200 to 2,500 psi. Units rated less than 1,200 psi won't do the job as effectively; washers rated above 2,500 psi could cause damage if not handled properly.

The nozzle design and the width of the spray pattern are also important. The three recommended pattern sizes for power washing a house are 15, 25, and 40 degrees. You'll get better results with either a 15- or 25-degree nozzle, with the 15-degree nozzle probably working the best, giving you a thorough, yet controlled, cleaning.

Whether you need to use a cleaning agent depends on how dirty the house is. A power washing with clear water only usually does the trick.

However, if your siding is marred by chalking, oxidation, moss, or mildew, you'll probably need to use a general purpose cleaner, available by the gallon where you rent the power washing equipment.

Replacing Deck Boards

Rejuvenate your deck — and make it safer.

WHAT YOU NEED

Jigsaw

Pry bar

Treated 2x4 lumber

3-inch galvanized box nails

Hammer

Nail set

Belt sander

New deck board

Pity the poor deck board. It gets walked across, baked by the sun, rained on, even shoveled over — no other wood around our homes has to put up with that kind of abuse. No wonder deck boards often split, warp, and lose knots.

You can replace a short, damaged section of board without the expense and hassle of replacing the entire board. Begin by drawing lines to indicate the inside edges (not middles) of the two joists flanking the damaged area. Since you're cutting alongside, rather than directly over, the joists, you'll avoid cutting through old nails or into the tops of the joists. Make your cuts with a jigsaw rather than a circular saw so you don't slice into deck boards that run next to the damaged board.

CUT OUT BAD WOOD

STEP 1   Cut out the damaged section of deck board with a jigsaw. Saw along the edge (not down the middle) of the joist.

STEP 2   Pry out and remove the nails from the damaged section of board. Avoid prying against or damaging surrounding boards.

INSERT NAILER AND BOARD

STEP 1   Slip a nailer in place and secure it with 3-inch galvanized box nails. Do this on both joists. The nailer should be treated wood, long enough to fully support the end of the new board.

STEP 2   Nail the new deck board in place using galvanized nails. If the new board is thicker than the surrounding ones, sink the nails deeper and use a belt sander to even up the surface.

Replacing Wood Siding

Make your home look like new again.

WHAT YOU NEED

Nail set

Hammer

Pry bar

Mini hacksaw

Keyhole saw

Galvanized siding nails

Caulk

Exterior-grade primer

Exterior-grade paint

Paintbrush

Beveled lap siding, often known as "clapboard" siding, comes in many forms: It may be redwood, pine, or cedar in strips 3 to 12 inches wide, painted, stained, or left natural. But when it is time to replace damaged sections, the basic steps are the same.

The bottom edge of each clapboard is usually secured to the home's sheathing and underlying framework by nails every 16 inches. The top edge is pinched in place by the nails of the clapboard above.

You can find lap siding at most large home centers or lumberyards — though the older your home, the more difficult it may be to find an exact match.

STEP 1 Punch the nails through the damaged siding with a nail set. Also drive through the nails that hold the upper undamaged clapboard to release the bad piece below it.

STEP 2 You may have to pry the siding up and saw the nails off with a mini hacksaw if you can't locate the nails under multiple layers of paint.

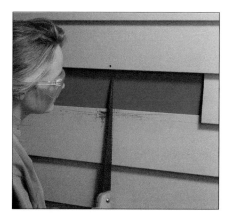

STEP 3 Stagger siding cuts, starting at the top and working down using a keyhole saw with blade reversed. Make straight cuts so the old and new clapboards meet clean and square.

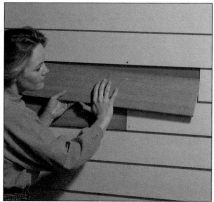

STEP 4 Install new clapboards, starting at the bottom and working up. Use galvanized siding nails. Apply caulk at windows, doors, and corner boards. Finish by priming and painting.

Repairing Stucco

Prepare and patch a broken exterior wall.

WHAT YOU NEED

Hammer

Safety goggles

Heavy-duty stapler

**15-pound asphalt-
impregnated felt**

**Preformed galvanized
drip cap**

Galvanized wire mesh

1¼-inch roofing nails

Metal-cutting shears

Steel trowel

Masking tape

Rake

Wooden straightedge

Sponge trowel

Stiff, long-bristled brush

Doing this repair yourself costs only about half as much as hiring a pro.

The job will require patience, because broken stucco admits water, which may damage underlying structures. Therefore, you first need to find and remove any rotting sheathing and nail on new boards to provide a solid base for the new stucco. If you're working around a window or door, set a copper or galvanized steel metal drip cap over the top casing. (Aluminum may corrode rapidly.)

You'll need metal-cutting shears to cut the galvanized mesh, and you need to be sure to buy self-furring mesh, which is dimpled to allow the first coat of stucco to get a solid grip on the wire.

Instructions for mixing the stucco are on the facing page.

PREPARING THE AREA

STEP 1 Break the stucco edge back to expose 2 inches of wire lath. Be sure to wear safety goggles.

STEP 2 Staple two thicknesses of 15-pound asphalt-impregnated felt over the exposed wood. Lap the edges about 2 inches.

STEP 3 Install a preformed galvanized drip cap over the top casing. Wire mesh will hold it in place.

STEP 4 Nail galvanized mesh over the felt with 1¼-inch roofing nails spaced every 6 inches. Overlap pieces of mesh 2 inches.

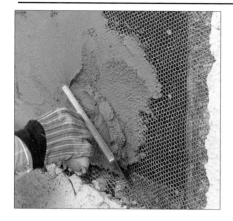

STEP 1 Follow the directions for mixing stucco at right. Press a ⅜-inch layer of stucco into the mesh with a steel trowel. Protect the finish trim with masking tape.

STEP 2 Score ⅛-inch grooves in the soft surface using a rake or the cut edge of a piece of mesh. Let it harden overnight.

STEP 3 Spread a second layer of stucco over the first with a steel trowel. Match the thickness of the old stucco.

STEP 4 Level the new stucco flush with the old with a board. Work the board upward in a sawing motion.

Mixing and Applying Stucco

The Scratch and Brown Coats

Use the first two coats — the so-called "scratch" and "brown" coats — to fill the patch to the level of the surrounding stucco. Prepare them by mixing one part Type M cement (a mixture of Portland and mason's cement) with three parts sand in a wheelbarrow. You can purchase these materials and special tools at a cement or masonry supply store.

Mix the dry materials with a hoe and slowly add water until the stucco becomes stiff but is still workable. It should press into the wire mesh and not crumble or fall out. Moisten the edges of the old stucco. Next, pick up a load of stucco on a steel trowel and push it through the mesh in an upward motion. Continue until the surface is covered with a ⅜-inch coat. This is the scratch coat. When the surface becomes stiff, score it with ⅛-inch horizontal grooves into which the second coat will bond. Let the scratch coat harden overnight. Try to avoid working in direct sunlight and very hot, dry conditions that would cause the stucco to dry out quickly. If you have to work under such conditions, moisten the stucco periodically by misting it lightly with water or cover it with plastic to slow its drying.

Mix the second (brown) coat to the same consistency as the first and fill the patch to the level of the old stucco. Use a sponge trowel to flatten ridges and roughen the surface to better hold the third, or dash, coat. Let the second coat harden overnight.

The Dash Coat

Mix two parts white Portland cement to three parts silica sand and powdered pigment for the dash coat. Add water until it reaches the consistency of a very thick soup. Then spread it about ⅛ inch thick with a large brush. Remix it frequently, since the sand tends to settle out.

It's tough to match the old and new stucco colors. Purchase pigments from your local masonry supplier and match the color of the old stucco when it's wet. The new and the old won't match initially, but as the patch cures over its first year, its color will change.

Making a Match

Matching the textures between the old and new stucco isn't always easy either. Here's where professional experience makes a difference. Before the dash coat hardens, apply the texture. The one shown here calls for flicking the same dash mixture from a special long-bristled brush.

It's not advisable to paint stucco unless absolutely necessary. Once the paint peels, it's very difficult to scrape the surface to adequately prepare for another coat. If you must paint, use porous paints such as latex and acrylics.

How to Repair Cracks

Cracks are usually the most common stucco damage you'll find on your home. It may be surprising that such hard material fractures, but temperature extremes alone will crack wide expanses.

But most cracks aren't really a problem. Even if a little water seeps through, the asphalt-impregnated felt underneath should block it. Here's a simple rule of thumb: if the crack doesn't cause any harm, leave it.

Cosmetic repairs to unsightly cracks are difficult. Whatever you use to fill the crack will usually be more unsightly than the crack itself. If you try anyway, use an acrylic caulk that closely matches the stucco color. Tint the caulk with latex paint if necessary.

If the crack is large, your wall probably has shifted, which indicates a foundation or other structural problem. You'll need to diagnose and solve this problem first, since any repaired crack will immediately open up when the house shifts again.

When repairing with new stucco, treat those large cracks like any other patch. Break back the edges and remove all cracked and loosened material. Unfortunately, you'll have the same problem matching colors.

STEP 5 Smooth the surface with a sponge trowel. Blend the edges, fill any holes, and flatten any ridges. Let the stucco harden overnight.

STEP 6 Follow the directions on the previous page to mix the soupy "dash" coat stucco. Apply the ⅛-inch dash coat with a large brush as if it were thick paint. Stir the mix often.

STEP 7 Texture the new patch by flicking stucco mix from a stiff, long-bristled brush. Practice on a scrap board first.

STEP 8 Draw a steel trowel lightly over the texture to flatten the peaks to match the old texture.

STEP 9 The new color of the finished repair won't exactly match the old, but the tint will change as the stucco cures.

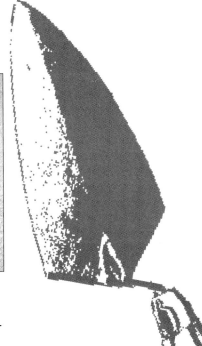

Anchoring a Railing

Tighten it back up for safety as well as looks.

WHAT YOU NEED

Wrench

Pry bar

Electric drill

Masonry bits

Galvanized bolts

Mounting flanges

Anchoring cement

Bonding agent

Waterproof cement sealer

Lock washers

Nuts

Paintbrush

If the thought of fixing a wobbly, old outside railing makes you as shaky as the railing itself, read on. Anchoring cement, bonding agent, and some upside-down bolts make this an easy repair. Before installing new bolts, use the old holes as guides and drill deeper and wider holes to accommodate your new fasteners. Use progressively larger masonry bits. Concrete bonding agent and anchoring cement can be found near each other at large home centers.

Mix the anchoring cement only when you're ready to use it. You'll have to work quickly because it begins to set in about 10 minutes. Don't touch the bolts after you've poured the anchoring cement; you might enlarge the holes and wind up with wobbly bolts again.

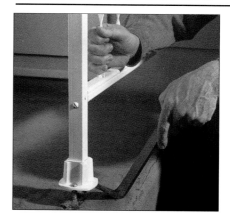

STEP 1 Remove the loose rail and the old fasteners. Detach the railing from the house, then use a pry bar to lift the railing and the old bolts. Enlarge the bolt holes.

STEP 2 Position galvanized bolts in the holes, head down. The bolts must be properly spaced and protrude far enough to accommodate the mounting flange, washer, and nuts.

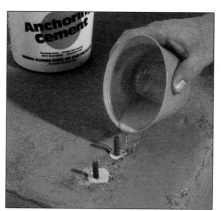

STEP 3 Pour anchoring cement after brushing the inside of the holes with bonding agent. The anchoring cement will usually set within an hour.

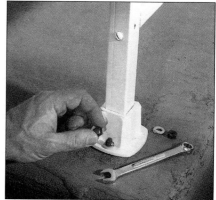

STEP 4 Apply a coat of waterproof cement sealer to the area and secure the railing back in place with lock washers and nuts.

Repairing Mortar

It's slow work, but it can prevent moisture from damaging your home.

STEP 1 Chisel out cracked or loose mortar to a depth of 1 inch or until you reach sound mortar. Chips will fly, so wear safety goggles.

STEP 2 Clean away all debris — use a stiff-bristled brush, blow it out with air, or flush it out with water from a garden hose.

WHAT YOU NEED

Small cold chisel

2-pound sledgehammer

Stiff brush

Trowel

Pointing tool

Jointing tool

Stiff-bristled scrub brush

Type N masonry cement

Masonry sand

Eye protection

Gloves

Brick houses are beautiful and long lasting. The rich color and deep texture of the brick exude strength. After all, even the big, bad wolf couldn't blow a brick house down.

It's estimated that a brick and mortar structure has a life expectancy of 50 to 75 years. And we all know of brick buildings still standing proudly after more than two centuries. Any weakness is not in the brick, but in the mortar that binds the building together. Age and the weather will take their toll over time.

Here is how to repair those joints (a process called "tuckpointing") so that your house not only looks better, but there will be less chance of moisture getting behind the bricks and causing structural damage.

STEP 3 Dry-mix three parts of masonry sand with one part of Type N masonry cement. Add enough water to make a stiff paste.

Is This the Project for You?

Consider the size of the area to be repaired. Most home owners can fill small cracks and a few missing mortar gaps. But if large areas need repair or if bricks are falling apart or missing, it's best to leave the job to a licensed masonry contractor.

Also, if you're afraid you'll ruin your house's brick, don't attempt to repoint your house yourself. Call a professional.

STEP 4 Push mortar from your trowel into a joint with the pointing tool.

STEP 5 Tool the mortar to match the existing joints. The mortar should be "thumb-print hard" before tooling.

STEP 6 Brush away any excess mortar from the brick surface after the mortar has stiffened.

Mortar Joints

These illustrations show the most commonly used mortar joints. One will probably match the joints used in your home. The joints are formed by using different shapes of brick jointing tools. These tools are available at most home centers and masonry supply stores.

V-JOINT
A brick jointer gives the concave "V" look.

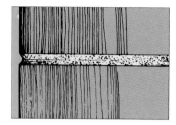

CONCAVE JOINT
Formed by the curved end of a brick jointer.

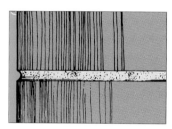

RAKED JOINT
Formed by removing mortar to a depth of ¼ inch with a wheel rake.

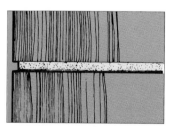

FLUSH JOINT
Formed by cutting off the mortar with the edge of a trowel.

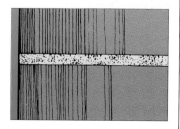

Fixing Concrete

Get rid of those broken eyesores.

WHAT YOU NEED

Chisel and maul

Pointing trowel

Edging tool

Wood float

Magnesium float

1x8-inch lumber

Heavy-duty work gloves

Safety goggles

Dust mask

Release agent

Liquid bonding agent

Sand mix

Paintbrush

Broom

Wire brush

Whether you're fixing a chipped step corner, a crack in the driveway, or a hole, the repair techniques are exactly the same. You need the same tools and materials — liquid bonding agent to help the new patch material stick to the old concrete, bags of dry premixed sand mix, and water.

The repairs shown here are fairly small, so you'll probably need only one or two 60-pound bags of sand mix. Sand mix leaves a smoother, easier-to-finish surface than concrete mix.

If the repair is really small, like filling a narrow ¼- to ½-inch-wide crack, a small 5- or 10-pound box of the pre-mixed material should be enough.

You probably own some, but not all, the tools you'll need. And since you probably won't be fixing concrete every year, it may be best to rent any special tools needed for your repairs.

STEP 1 Chip away any loose concrete using a 3-pound maul and brick chisel. You must get back to solid concrete so that the patch will hold. Blow away any loose concrete and dust. Wear goggles throughout the process.

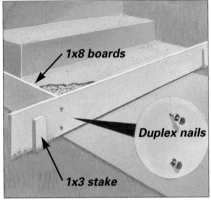

1x8 boards

Duplex nails

1x3 stake

STEP 2 Place forms (1x8 boards work well) around the broken corner and secure them with stakes. Coat the inside of the boards with a release agent such as motor oil to keep the patch from sticking.

STEP 3 Dampen the concrete, then apply a mixture of liquid bonding agent and fine, sifted sand mix. Cut the bristles of a paintbrush to half their length to work the mixture into the concrete.

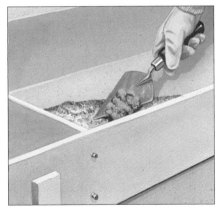

STEP 4 Fill the patch area a little less than half full using the pointing trowel. Pack the patch material down with a small board to remove all of the air bubbles and air pockets.

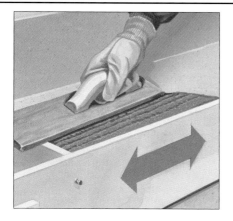

STEP 5 Fill the area to the top and level with a wood float. Tip the float on edge and move it back and forth over the patch to pack the material into the hole and level it.

STEP 6 Place the edging tool's curved edge between the patch and the form. Move the edger back and forth in short strokes to form the curved edge. Let the patch set for about 45 minutes.

STEP 7 Finish the top surface with a magnesium float when you can push your fingers into it and leave only light fingerprints. Broom-finish the patch to match the existing finish.

STEP 8 Remove the forms after 30 minutes. Use the edging tool to curve the corner's vertical edge. Keep the patch wet for about a week. The patch will cure fully in about a month.

Concrete Repair Primer

Begin by removing any loose concrete with the maul and chisel. To keep the form for a step corner in position, drive 1x3 stakes into the ground. If you're repairing an upper step corner, brace the forms against the step using 2x4s placed at about a 45-degree angle. Drive them from the ground so they slant up to the form.

To help the new patch bond to the old concrete, you need to apply a "scrub coat." This is a mixture of the liquid bonding agent and some pre-mixed sand mix sifted to a fine consistency. The mixture should look like the flour and water mixture you use to make gravy. Make sure that the scrub coat is still wet when you begin filling with the wet sand mix. If the scrub coat dries, the patch won't hold.

Before you mix the materials with water, empty the entire bag of dry sand mix into a large, flat container (a wheelbarrow is good) and stir it thoroughly with a garden hoe. Pour the material back into the bag and then scoop out only as much as you need.

Add water in small quantities; your goal is to mix in just enough water to form a workable material; when the moistened sand mix can be formed into a ball in your hand and doesn't crumble apart or have excess water drip from it, that's the right consistency. To get this, you may need to add more water or sand mix to the original batch.

Keep the patched area wet so it cures properly. This usually takes about a month. It is a must to soak the patch with a fine mist from a spray bottle or garden hose two to three times a day for the first two or three days. After that, moisten it at least twice a day for a week. Water evaporating too quickly from the concrete will weaken the patch, so cover the patched area with white plastic — a trash bag works well.

Route foot traffic around the patch for the first few days.

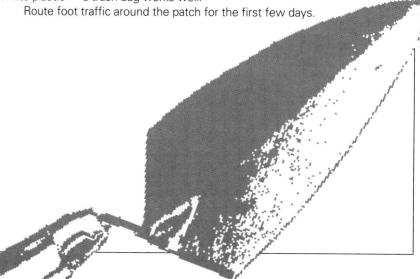

Safety Tip

! Both wet concrete and dry sand mix are caustic, so be sure to wear long pants, a long-sleeved shirt, heavy-duty work gloves, and safety goggles. Keep a dust mask handy, too, and wear it while you dry-mix the concrete. The premixed material is really dusty until you add the water.

There's no way to work concrete without being in close contact with it, and these precautions will let you work without worry.

Handy Hints

■ Unused motor oil makes a good release agent for small repairs.

■ If a hole is deep enough, drive a few masonry screws into the depression to give the patching material something more to grab on to.

STEP 1 Pound on the smooth concrete around the hole to see how much has been weakened and must be removed. Weak concrete will have a hollow sound when you pound on it. If you don't remove the weak concrete, the new patch won't last.

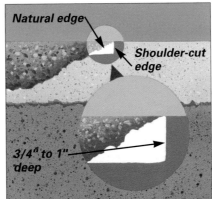

Natural edge · Shoulder-cut edge · 3/4" to 1" deep

STEP 2 Cut a ¾- to 1-inch deep square, or "shoulder," at the edge of the hole. If you attempt to fill the hole and leave the natural tapered edge, the thin edges of the patch will chip away from the old concrete.

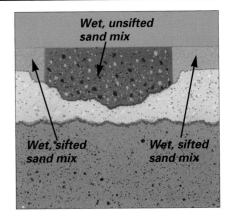

Wet, unsifted sand mix · Wet, sifted sand mix · Wet, sifted sand mix

STEP 3 Fill the hole with two different patch materials: a wet mixture of sifted sand for areas 1 inch deep or less, and a wet mixture of unsifted sand mix for deeper areas.

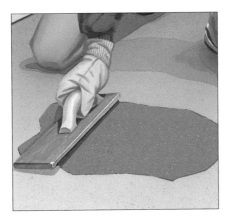

STEP 4 Pack and level off the patch using a wood float. Tip the float as shown as you move it back and forth.

STEP 5 Smooth the surface with a magnesium float. Broom-finish the patch so that it matches the surrounding surface.

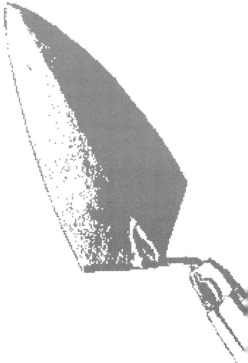

FIXING A CRACK

To repair a crack properly, you must widen it before you can start to fill it. Narrow cracks, ⅛ inch or less, can generally be filled with polyurethane caulk (sold by the tube at home centers and full-service hardware stores). Simply clean out the crack with a wire brush, apply the caulk, and smooth the top with a putty knife. This won't hide the crack, but will seal it.

For cracks that are wider than ⅛ inch, use a sand mix patch. Begin by making a "V" groove, enlarging the crack to about 1 inch deep and 2 to 3 inches wide with the maul and brick chisel.

Next, take a wire brush and scrape the area to remove any loose concrete. Rinse the area thoroughly to remove any loose stones. Now apply the scrub coat to the dampened crack in the concrete.

Because you're filling a shallow, narrow area, use sifted sand mix and water for your patch material. Fill the crack with the patch material and use a wood float or pointing trowel, whichever you're more comfortable using, to smooth the surface of the patch.

Wait about 45 minutes and then finish the surface with the magnesium float. Keep repaired cracks damp, too, just as you would corners and holes.

STEP 1   Enlarge all ⅛-inch or wider cracks to 1 inch deep by 2 to 3 inches wide using brick chisel and maul. Scrape out the loose concrete, dampen the area with water, and apply the scrub coat. Fill the crack with wet, sifted sand mix. Level off the excess, then finish with a magnesium float.

STEP 2   Sift the dry sand mix to remove larger aggregate, leaving a fine sand mix. The fine sand mix is used for filling cracks or other areas that are 1 inch deep or less. The sifter is constructed from 2x2s and metal window screen.

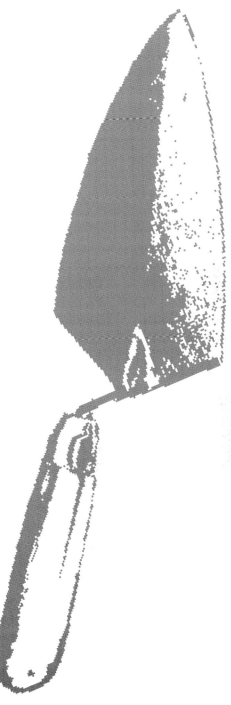

Pouring Concrete

For small jobs, be your own contractor.

WHAT YOU NEED

Wheelbarrow

Dry concrete mix

Hand float

Edging tool

Grooving tool

Finishing trowel

Push broom

Sledgehammer

Circular saw with masonry blade

Scrap 4x4 timber

Sand or gravel

Lumber for forms

1x3 stakes

Shovel and hoe

Motor oil

Broken, crumbling concrete is ugly and dangerous. If there's any around your home, no doubt you're tired of looking at it and picking chunks of it out of your lawn. And the mailman is tired of tripping over it. It's high time you repaired the mess. But, you say, you don't have the tools, know-how, or gumption to tackle such a big repair. Nonsense.

That little stretch of broken walkway is just the starter project you need to acquaint yourself with the tools, materials, and techniques involved in pouring a small concrete slab.

Walkways are most commonly damaged by creeping tree roots, frost heave, and impact. Small cracks can be filled and chipped corners can be patched, but when entire sections are buckled or severely cracked, replacement is the best solution. These 13 steps tell you everything you need to know.

STEP 1 Break up the damaged section of walkway. Use a sledgehammer, starting at an open side, then work carefully toward good sections. Wear eye protection because flying concrete chips can do real damage.

STEP 2 Cut and deepen the control joint to create a clean break between old and new concrete sections. Use a masonry blade in a circular saw. Wear a respirator for this job to keep harmful dust out of your lungs.

STEP 3 Remove loose dirt and roots, flatten the area, then compact it with the end of a 4x4. Fill low spots with sand or gravel.

Pro Tips for the Novice

Start small. A 3x6-foot section of walkway is manageable for a first-time DIYer.

Ideal weather conditions are 50 to 70 degrees, with no rain in sight. Hot, dry weather will speed the hardening of your concrete, so you'll have to work faster. Freezing conditions can ruin your project. Rain can spell real disaster. Keep a roll of thick polyethylene plastic on hand just in case.

STEP 4 Secure the forms in place with 1x3 stakes every 2 feet. Stakes shouldn't protrude above the forms. Mound dirt along the outer edge to stabilize the forms.

STEP 5 Brush motor oil onto the inside of the forms so they'll release from the concrete later on. Sweep the ends of the existing walkway sections so they are free of dust.

STEP 6 Mix the concrete in a wheelbarrow with a hoe or shovel. First dry-mix the ingredients, then add water. All ingredients should be thoroughly wet, but not soupy or runny.

STEP 7 Shovel in the concrete and level it with the top of the forms. Work the screed board in a side-to-side motion. Push the concrete into corners and edges.

Preparation: Steps to Success

The first step is to get rid of the old concrete. This is hard, heavy work and you'll want to move the stuff as few times as possible. Put broken pieces immediately into your wheelbarrow and wheel it directly to its final resting spot or trash bin.

Wearing safety goggles, long pants, a long-sleeved shirt, and work boots, break up the damaged sections with a sledgehammer. Start at an open edge and work inward. As you near the good sections of walkway, slow down. Older sidewalks are often cracked all the way through at the control joint (as they're supposed to be) and usually separate cleanly. But newer walkways may still be solid all the way through. Put a masonry blade in your circular saw and deepen the joint to at least 1½ inches in three or four successively deeper passes. Then carefully whack off the remaining concrete.

Clean out and flatten the area. If tree roots have broken your slab, you need to make a decision. You can chop off the offending root a foot or so past your walkway, then coat the ends with a root preservative (available at most large nurseries). However, if you chop through very large roots, those thicker than your arm, you can kill the tree. Oaks are especially vulnerable. Consult a tree expert before hacking away. If you love the tree and the root has to stay, your only option may be to reroute your walkway.

Smooth and level the soil. Tamp the area with the end of a 4x4. Fill low spots with sand. Sweep off the exposed ends of the good concrete sections.

Next, install the two straight 2x4 forms. The tops of the forms should be even with the existing walkway sections. Let the 2x4s extend past the good sections at least 6 inches. Install foot-long 1x3 stakes at the ends and every 2 feet in between. Secure the stakes to the forms with double-headed nails or drywall screws, making sure the tips don't extend inside the forms. Don't let the stakes protrude above the form or they'll be in the way when you level the concrete. Bank dirt up along the outside of the form for extra rigidity.

If the soil is extremely dry, dampen it lightly so it doesn't absorb water from the concrete you're about to pour.

Buying Concrete

One of the mysteries you'll need to unlock about concrete is how much you need for your project. Once you determine that, you can decide whether to hand-mix it from bags, order a truckload of ready-mixed concrete, or select an option somewhere in between.

Most concrete "flatwork" (basement floors, sidewalks, and driveways) is 3½ to 4 inches thick. Concrete is normally sold by the cubic foot or cubic yard. One cubic foot will create 3 square feet of concrete, 4 inches deep. One cubic yard will create 81 square feet of concrete, 4 inches deep.

■ Mixing by Hand

For an area smaller than 20 square feet, you can easily mix bags of concrete mix in a wheelbarrow, tray, or drum, then dump it in place. A 3x6-foot walkway repair (18 square feet) requires 6 cubic feet of concrete. This translates into a dozen 60-pound bags of concrete mix and about 40 minutes of total mixing time. Be sure to read the directions on the bag and make sure you're buying concrete mix — not other similar products.

When you get into projects in the 20- to 50-square-foot size, it makes sense to rent an electric or gas-powered drum mixer. These mix 2 to 5 cubic feet at a time and also provide a convenient way to dump it in place.

■ Haul It Yourself

Mixing concrete by hand on projects that exceed 50 square feet can be very time consuming; plus there's the danger that the earlier poured concrete will harden sooner than that poured later.

Many rental yards or ready-mix plants offer trailer loads of "haul-it-yourself" premixed concrete. The trailers can carry up to one yard of concrete. Of course the challenge is to get the 500-pound trailer and 3,500 pounds of concrete from the supplier to your house; a true challenge if you drive a small car and an impossibility unless you have a trailer hitch. There's also the danger that the mix will settle unevenly during transportation, creating a weaker mix. But for intermediate-size projects, where ordering a ready-mix truck is too expensive and mixing it by hand is out of the question, look into this option.

■ Ready-mix Truck Load

For anything over 100 square feet (and bear in mind, a project of this size is not recommended for a first-timer), order a ready-mix truck. The concrete is sold by the cubic yard (plus delivery charges if you order a partial load).

Ready mix is the only way to go for large projects, but you'll need to have plenty of help on hand, contend with heavy trucks, and be extremely confident and experienced in your concrete skills.

STEP 8 Even out the concrete surface with a hand float. The float smooths the surface and pushes rock and gravel farther down.

STEP 9 Round and compact the edges of the slab using an edging tool. Work in a series of short, jabbing motions and finish with a single pass.

STEP 10 Cut control joints, keeping them the same distance apart as those in the rest of the walkway. Lay a straight 2x4 across the forms as a guide for the grooving tool.

STEP 11 Smooth the surface with a flexible finishing trowel. Work in short arcs. A slurry of cement and water should rise to the surface and fill small gaps and grooves.

STEP 12 Drag a push broom across the surface of the concrete to create a slip-proof surface. The broom should not push liquid, but should just leave slight ridges.

STEP 13 Cover the area with plastic to allow the concrete to harden slowly. Keep it covered for three days, even if vehicles will be driving over it. Try to reduce use, however.

Concrete and Tools

B ecause this concrete repair job is a small project — 18 square feet — all you need is a wheelbarrow, some bags of dry concrete mix, and a few hand tools. Don't be confused when you go to buy concrete mix. Buy the type that has gravel and sand already mixed in it. Don't buy Portland cement, mason mix, or mason sand, because they don't have the necessary gravel and sand for your project. If in doubt, ask a salesperson.

Grooving tool

You'll need a float for leveling the concrete, an edging tool for rounding the edges, a grooving tool for cutting control joints, a finish trowel for smoothing the concrete, and a push broom. All of the special tools can be rented for about one quarter the cost of purchasing them.

That Final Finish

T he quality of a concrete finish is determined by how well it is worked after *screeding,* or leveling. Smooth the surface with a wood or magnesium float. Swing large arcs, holding the float at a very slight angle so the leading edge doesn't dig into the concrete. The float pushes the gravel below the surface and further levels small dips. Using a float also brings water and cement to the surface. Don't overwork the concrete, or you'll bring too much water and cement to the top, weakening the surface of the walkway. At this point, just smooth out ripples and ridges.

While the concrete is still pliable — usually within the first hour — edge the slab and cut control joints. Edging the slab, as the name implies, rounds and compacts the edges, making them less susceptible to chipping (and much friendlier to bare feet). Before edging, cut the concrete away from the form, about 1 inch deep, with a trowel. Push the edging tool in a series of short seesaw strokes. Once you've completed an edge, go back and take one long, continuous swipe to smooth it out.

Use the edging tool to round the new concrete where it meets the existing sections of walkway, too. You can lightly wet the tool to help it slide more easily. Cut control joints at the same spacing as the rest of the walkway, usually 3 feet. Use the screed board as a straightedge to guide the grooving tool. Again, work it in a series of short strokes; the gravel below the surface will want to block and misdirect the grooving tool, so be firm. Then go back over the cut with one long swipe.

Use the float to remove the marks made by the edging and grooving tools. You may have to use the edging, grooving, and float tools a couple of times to get the surface flat and the edges just right.

When all the surface water has disappeared and the concrete has set up hard enough so it's difficult to indent with your fingers, use a finish trowel held at a slight angle to further smooth the concrete. Work in a series of arcs. A thick "cream," or slurry, should rise to the surface to help fill small voids and grooves. Bear down hard. Go over the entire surface several times if the final surface is to be smooth. A single pass will suffice if you're adding a broom finish. If the concrete has become really hard, sprinkle a little water over the surface and work the trowel with both hands in a back-and-forth scrubbing motion.

Match the surface texture to the existing sidewalk. To give it a "broom finish" — one that's more slip-resistant — wait until the concrete has hardened sufficiently so a stiff-bristled push broom leaves crisp marks.

Wash your tools as soon as you're done with them; wet concrete slides off, but if it dries, you'll have to chip it away.

Asphalt Driveway

Quick steps for repair and maintenance.

WHAT YOU NEED

Push broom

Cold chisel

Trowel

Cold-mix asphalt patch

4x4 timber

Weed killer

Crack filler

Degreaser

Detergent

Driveway sealer

Sealing brush/squeegee

Roller

Home owners with asphalt driveways fall into one of two categories: Either they apply a sealer annually, or they never do a thing to maintain the surface.

Asphalt is formulated to withstand the elements, so why should you spend the time and money to seal your driveway? You shouldn't — unless you fill cracks and patch holes first. Regardless of your best efforts, asphalt will flex and crack. Left alone, cracks will become holes, and holes will turn into even larger and uglier voids. If you fix the damage, sealers help delay future problems.

Here are some easy steps you can take to fix the problems and then maintain the surface.

PATCHING A DRIVEWAY

STEP 1 Clean out all loose asphalt and gravel. Scrape around the edge of the hole until you have a solid edge. Fill the hole to within 1 inch of the top with asphalt patch mix.

STEP 2 Use a 4x4 timber to tamp the mixture into the hole. Make sure it's pressed firmly against the edges, as well as the bottom.

STEP 3 Add additional patch mix so the filled area is about ½ inch above the level of the driveway.

STEP 4 Tamp the area flush using the 4x4. If the hole is deep (3 inches or more), place a board over the patch and drive your car over it.

SEALING THE SURFACE

Before you apply the sealer, fill any cracks and sweep the driveway free of dirt and debris. Read the manufacturer's label for specific preparation steps.

The sealer can be applied with a sealing brush/squeegee, an old push broom, or a roller. If you don't plan to do the entire driveway at once, buy an additional applicator. The first one will dry and become too hard to use for a later application.

Before applying the sealer, mix it thoroughly. A 3-foot length of 1x2 or an old broom handle works nicely. To reduce the mixing time, usually 10 to 15 minutes, turn the buckets upside down the day before you plan to apply the sealer. Also, if you seal half of your driveway one day and plan to do the other half the next, mix the sealer again before applying it.

Don't pour out all of the sealer at once — it could begin to dry before you're able to spread. Seal about 100 square feet at a time. Once the entire driveway is sealed, block off the entrance and keep off the surface for the recommended drying time (usually 24 to 48 hours).

If your driveway has never been sealed, it may need two coats. The first coat usually needs to be completely dry before applying a second one. Follow the manufacturer's instructions.

STEP 1 Remove loose asphalt and kill all vegetation. Pour in crack filler until it is flush. Follow the manufacturer's instructions for drying time before applying a sealer.

STEP 2 Sweep away debris and remove oil and rust stains. Apply sealer, following the manufacturer's instructions. Block the entrance. Stay off of the asphalt for at least 24 hours.

Asphalt Know-how

What's Available

Asphalt driveway sealers usually come in 5-gallon containers that cover 200 to 300 square feet.

There are two types available: sealer or sealer/filler combination, which has tiny fibers that fill hairline cracks. Generally, you're better off using the sealer/filler, since most driveways have some cracks. Remember that a sealer is a preventive coating, not a repair.

Crack filler is available in caulk tubes and in one-gallon containers of pourable liquid. The caulk type is neater, but you'll use more tubes than liquid to fix a given crack, making caulk more expensive overall.

Asphalt patch is most often sold in bags weighing about 60 pounds. All of these products are available at home centers and hardware stores.

Cosmetic Improvements

Applying a cold sealer, the type sold at hardware stores and home centers, is 90 percent cosmetic, according to engineers at the Asphalt Institute. It will give a graying asphalt driveway a black, like-new appearance.

Most asphalt driveways are intended to last 15 to 20 years but begin to show signs of aging after just five to seven years. That's when you need to take steps to prevent further damage and possibly save the expense of replacing the driveway.

Watch the Weather

The conditions under which you apply these products is important. Check the weather report. If there's rain in the forecast within 24 hours, don't do anything or you'll be doing the job over, since the rain will wash the sealer away. Most manufacturers recommend that the temperature be at least 55 degrees; warmer and less humid conditions will speed the drying time.

Permanent Repairs

The way to achieve a permanent repair on an asphalt driveway is to use hot-mix patch, fillers, and sealers. The hot-mix materials and equipment, however, are not available to the do-it-yourselfer. For that reason, the repairs you make with cold patch may need to be done again in the future. If you choose to have hot-mix repairs done, contact an asphalt paving contractor.

Repairing Rotted Wood

Try this inexpensive alternative to replacement.

WHAT YOU NEED

Chisel

Electric drill with ³⁄₁₆ -inch bit

Liquid two-part consoli–dant

Two-part paste filler

Vinyl gloves

Putty knife

Fine sandpaper

Rags

Oil-based primer

Latex or oil-based paint

Paintbrush

What's the condition of your home's exterior wood? Are the window sills free of splits and cracks? Are the casing and sill joints still solid? Are the door thresholds sound and firm?

If you answered "no" to any of these questions, you probably have some rotted wood. If left untreated, it will lead to major, expensive repairs.

There are two ways to deal with rot. You can replace the wood; this eliminates the rot, but it is an expensive option. Or you can repair the rotted area; this saves you money, but if it is done incorrectly, it can actually promote further decay and damage.

These seven steps show you how to make the repairs using a two-part liquid-and-paste system that stops the rot and saves money, too.

STEP 1   Remove the loose, decayed wood. Some rotted wood can remain, since the liquid consolidant will impregnate and solidify the wood fibers.

STEP 2   Drill a honeycomb pattern of ³⁄₁₆-inch holes into the decayed wood. The holes will allow the consolidant to penetrate and bond well with the sound wood.

STEP 3   Pour the liquid two-part consolidant mixture into the decayed area. Make sure the wood is completely dry before applying the consolidant.

STEP 4   Apply the two-part paste filler. Wear close-fitting vinyl gloves that protect your hands but let you feel what you're doing.

STEP 5 Smooth the paste filler with a putty knife. Try to shape the area flush with the surrounding wood to reduce the amount of sanding needed.

STEP 6 Sand the repaired area with fine sandpaper to prep the paste filler for painting. Wipe off all dust and residue before applying the primer.

STEP 7 Apply an oil-based primer and two coats of latex or oil-based paint. Make sure the primer covers the joint between the repair and the wood.

Understanding Two-step Repair Systems

The first step of a two-part system uses a resin-and-hardener liquid consolidant, which impregnates and reinforces the wood fibers. The second step builds up and fills in the decayed area with another resin-and-hardener mixture. Once this mixture has dried, it can be cut, planed, or sanded to match the area surrounding the repair.

Cosmetic Repairs Only
The repairs illustrated on these pages are for appearance only — they are not structural. While there are epoxies formulated for making structural repairs, they are difficult to work with and beyond the ability of most home owners. Also, a structural problem often requires replacement rather than repair. Consult a professional, such as an architect or engineer, if a structural problem is suspected.

Safety Precautions
When working with chemicals as potent as these, certain safety measures should be taken. Use eye, skin, and respiratory protection, work in a well-ventilated area, and follow the manufacturer's directions.

What Will It Cost?
A two-step, two-part repair system will not come cheap. The amount you can expect to spend depends on the size of the repair. But if you weigh that cost against the price of buying and installing a new window — windows can cost several hundred dollars — the savings you can realize are substantial.

Detecting Wood Decay

Look for paint peeling down to bare wood. It may only be a paint application problem, but there's also a good chance that the peeling is due to underlying moisture, which eventually causes decay.

A wavy or rippled paint surface or a depression in the paint surface usually means there's decayed wood underneath.

Check window frame joints, especially at the sills. Look for tight, solid joints. Gaps and spaces, no matter how small, are the perfect areas for rot and decay to start and should be repaired before major damage can occur.

If you notice any of the above signs, probe the area with an ice pick or awl. Soft, mushy wood indicates decay. If the wood is solid, the ice pick should go in no farther than ¼ inch. Also, try to lift some splinters of wood with the pick. Long, thin, stringy splinters mean solid wood; short blocks or chunks of wood indicate decay.

As a final test, drill holes into a suspect area with a ⅜-inch twist drill bit. Solid wood will be light in color and dry; decayed or rotted wood will be dark and crumbly. Don't worry about drilling holes into good wood; the repair materials will fill the holes.

Work Better, Work Safer

Patio Paver Puller

After a winter of continual freezing and thawing, some individual bricks or pavers in your sand-based patio may have shifted and need releveling. To get the brick or paver out easily, make the pullers from two pieces of coat-hanger wire. Slip the wires down both sides of the offending paver, give them a quarter turn, and pull up the paver. For a large patio block, you'll need to make four pullers and get a second person to help you.

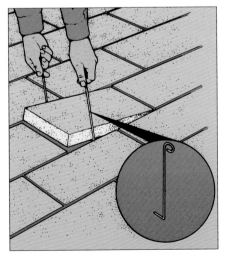

Paver puller

Removing Paint from Brick

There are two methods for removing paint drips from brick. One is cheap and guaranteed to be safe, while the other is probably much faster but requires experimentation.

The safe method is as follows. First, saturate the brick by spraying it with a hose. Then apply a solution of 2 pounds of trisodium phosphate in 1 gallon of water to the paint spots. (If TSP is not available in your area, use a nonphosphate cleaner.) After 5 to 10 minutes, scrub with a stiff nylon-bristled brush. Don't use a wire brush or other metal tool that might damage the brick and don't rinse the TSP down the drain — let it run into the soil. With older paint, several applications may be needed before the paint is completely gone. If some stubborn spots remain, try a commercial paint remover, experimenting first on a small spot in an out-of-the-way place.

The other, much faster method is to try one of the new water-based paint strippers, but since these are fairly new products, there aren't many guidelines for using them on brick. Experiment thoroughly in a hidden spot first. Be sure to follow the manufacturer's recommended safety precautions for any of these chemicals.

Driveway Cleaner

Clean the spots off your asphalt driveway: Thoroughly wet it down and sprinkle a nonpolluting powdered detergent over the surface. Brush it in with a stiff-bristled broom, then rinse.

Concrete Cleaner

Remove ground-in dirt and stains from concrete walks and driveways with household bleach. Pour the bleach over the stain, let it sit for 10 minutes, then rinse thoroughly.

Rusty Concrete

Rust stains on a concrete driveway — or any concrete surface — can be removed by mopping and scrubbing them with an acid/water mixture. Mop on a solution containing 1 pound of oxalic acid powder or thioglycolic acid per gallon of water.

Caution: Acid is extremely dangerous and toxic. Wear safety goggles, rubber gloves, and protective rubber clothing, such as rain gear. Avoid skin contact and inhalation of fumes.

Warning: Always add acid to water, never water to acid. Don't reuse the mop for any other projects.

After three hours, rinse with water, scrubbing at the same time with a stiff brush. Don't use a brush with metal bristles — it will leave small metal pieces or shavings that will also rust. Tough stains may require a second treatment.

Oxalic or thioglycolic acid can be purchased from commercial and scientific chemical suppliers (check the phone book under "Chemicals") or at some drugstores and hardware stores.

Easy Concrete Mixer

Here's a quick and easy way to mix concrete that uses a regular-sized plastic garbage can. Put in the concrete or concrete mix and the water, then tilt the garbage can about 45 degrees and twirl it as you would the steering wheel of a car. If you're using concrete and sand, dry-mix it before adding water. Don't use too much water to start but add water as necessary. And don't mix too much concrete at any one time or you'll have difficulty twirling it, rolling it on edge to where you need it, and pouring it accurately.

Garbage can concrete mixer

Safe Concrete Breakup

When breaking up or chipping away at concrete, keep the pieces from scattering all over, including into your face. Push the chisel through the center of a square of window screening, moving the chisel and screening along as you work. Wear safety goggles anyway, just in case.

Deck Board Spacer

It's easy to space deck boards evenly. Just insert ³⁄₈-inch wooden dowels that match the diameter of the spacing you desire into several pieces of scrap 2x4. Place the dowels between adjacent deck boards, fasten the boards in place, and remove the dowels.

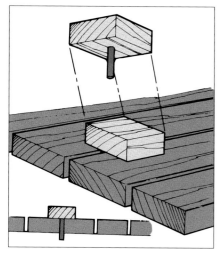

Dowel deck board spacer

Vinyl Siding Patch

You can patch a hole in your vinyl siding instead of replacing the whole piece of siding. Cut the patch from some left-over siding and mount it with ordinary PVC pipe cement (clean the area with PVC cleaner first). The patch will be secure and nearly invisible.

Mildew Ender

To get rid of mildew on outdoor wooden structures, try scrubbing the mildewed areas with straight vinegar rather than bleach, then finish the surface with two coats of wood sealer.

Siding Hold-up

When you install vinyl siding by yourself, use a piece of duct tape to hold one end of a strip of siding while you snap the other end in place. The tape works like another pair of hands.

Chalky Siding

Chalking is a natural characteristic of aluminum siding. The siding's finish is designed to gradually release its pigment — that's the chalking that you see. This action actually helps keep the siding clean by preventing dirt from sticking. The south side of a house usually chalks more because of greater exposure to the sun. Most chalking is simply washed away by rainstorms. If your house is surrounded by shrubs and trees, however, they could be preventing this from happening.

You can remove some of the chalking by washing the siding with a soft rag soaked in a solution of a nonabrasive, mild household detergent. Use ¹⁄₃ cup of detergent to 1 gallon of water and rinse well. A soft-bristled brush

used for cleaning cars also works. You can't expect to get rid of the chalking permanently, however.

Knotty Problem

Staining a pine deck can be difficult because the wood contains quite a few knots. Knots are extremely dense, so stains just don't penetrate them. If the knots occur in just a few boards, you might try replacing them with a higher-grade pine (the higher the grade, the fewer the knots). This would at least reduce the problem.

Restoring Color in Cedar

There are a number of products made to restore the color to a cedar deck. Once you've got the color back, though, the trick is keeping it. If your deck is fading very quickly, you may need to switch from a transparent sealer to a finish that contains pigment. A semitransparent stain that matches the red cedar color should last longer. Brush on (don't spray) the stain for best adhesion. Normally the stain will last two years or more.

Should You Seal Stucco?

During rainstorms stucco absorbs water like a sponge but it's nothing to worry about. The moisture it absorbs will just evaporate without damaging your house. Sealing the stucco would keep it from "breathing" and is likely to seal the moisture into the stucco. Sealing also makes it harder to renew the stucco finish. A stucco finish generally lasts

20 to 30 years, after which a thin dash coat of new stucco can be applied to renew it. But if you've put a sealer on, it'll have to be sandblasted off before the new dash coat can be applied.

The real problem for most people comes when moisture gets behind the stucco at small cracks, especially around windows and doors. This can lead to rotting wood. Seal up cracks in your stucco with a silicone caulk.

Fastening Wood to Concrete

During the past 15 years, the old chore of fastening wood to concrete has become much easier. Inventors have filled the marketplace with a vast array of fasteners designed to secure wood to concrete in almost any situation. The four most common types are nails, predrilled fasteners, expansion fasteners, and glue. Any one of them, or some combination, should be just the ticket to help you with your wood-to-concrete project.

If there's a secret to any of these methods, it's simply this: Use the right tool. When you're dealing with concrete and masonry, you're obviously dealing with extremely hard material. Woodworking hammers are too light and steel drill bits too soft. The concrete's brittle, too. Hard, sharp chips are likely to come flying out as you work on it, so always wear safety goggles to protect your eyes.

Nails. Nailing wood directly to concrete is probably the simplest, quickest, and cheapest method. Unfortunately, once driven, these nails may jar loose from a few hammer blows to the side of the board, so they are better for temporary fastening.

You'll usually find two types of special nails at the hardware store, cut nails and hardened concrete nails. It's difficult to predict which will work best for a particular project, so it can be well worth a small investment to buy both types in several lengths and use the ones that hold best.

Cut nail

Drive nails with a 2- to 4-pound hammer. Actually, it's very difficult to drive nails into cured (hardened) concrete, even with a 4-pound hammer. Nails work best in concrete that's cured for only a few days.

Nails can be quite effective in mortar joints, however. Mortar is softer than either the concrete block or brick, and it holds nails fairly well. For best results, drive them right along the joint edge. And here's a professional tip: For

improved holding power, run a bead of glue along the backside of your wood before nailing it up.

Predrilled Fasteners. This is a family of fasteners that can be driven into a predrilled hole. These not only fasten wood to concrete, but will fasten just about anything else to concrete as well.

They install easily — simply drill through the wood and into the concrete and then drive the fastener. Two types of fasteners are screws and *special nails*. Both types can be bought in packages that include the proper size carbide bit.

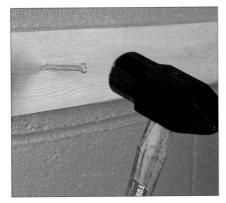

Special nail

Drilling the hole is the only difficult part. Use a carbide-tip bit. Because these holes are relatively small, your standard 1/4-inch or 3/8-inch power drill can do an adequate job, although each hole may take several minutes to bore.

A hammer drill, however, will drill your hole in a matter of seconds. A hammer drill is expensive to buy, but you can rent one by the day. If you have a lot of holes to drill, it'll save a lot

of time. Incidentally, be sure you buy or rent a carbide bit specifically designed for hammer drills.

It's a good idea to glue your wood to the concrete or masonry with this system as well, especially when using screws. Once screws are jarred loose, you may not be able to retighten them.

Expansion Fasteners. The illustration below shows how these excellent fasteners work. As the nut tightens, the cone-shaped shank forces the collar to expand and wedge tightly against the side of a predrilled hole. They're simple and effective and can carry a heavy load. In addition, they may be retightened without disturbing the job should they be accidentally jarred loose.

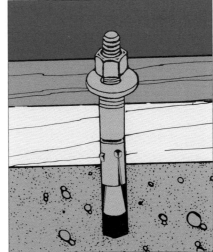

Expansion bolt

Because they require a larger hole, you really need a hammer drill as with predrilled fasteners to bore the concrete. If you don't have, or want to

rent, a hammer drill, you can use an ordinary drill. But follow these instructions: first bore a 1/8-inch hole with the carbide bit. Then use progressively larger carbide bits until your opening reaches the proper size.

Buy these fasteners long enough to wedge into the concrete as deeply as the wood is thick. Drill your hole an extra 1/4 inch deep, since the bolt draws back slightly when tightened.

Glue. Over the past 10 years, *construction adhesives* have improved and become more specialized. You can securely glue just about anything to a wall now. Since glued wood must be held tightly in place until the glue sets, it's handy to use an adhesive with another fastening system for mutual reinforcement; the glue damps the vibrations and jarring that may weaken the fasteners, and the fasteners hold the wood tightly until the glue sets.

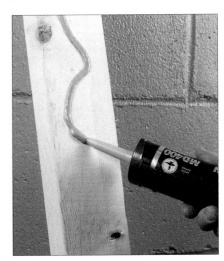

Construction adhesive

Proper preparation ensures a good glue bond. Be sure the wood and concrete surfaces are clean and dry. Loose paint, surface chalking, or moisture will cause the bond to release. When working with a very rough surface, apply a generous bead to bridge the wider gaps between the wood and concrete.

Using Caulks

If you're like most people, you'll leave a window wide open all winter long. It's not one in the basement or storage room or any of your ordinary windows — it's the 2-square-foot window you could make if you put together all the cracks and crevices that let air into your house. That's how leaky most houses tend to be.

Fortunately, there's a way to slam that window shut — by caulking. It's an inexpensive do-it-yourself job that will make your house warmer in the winter, cooler in the summer, and more resistant to moisture and insects all year round. Here are some tips on which caulks to use and how to apply them.

Tools of the Trade. You can buy a caulk gun very inexpensively. But if you plan to use your gun a lot, consider spending somewhat more for an open-sided, friction-drive gun. The friction-drive mechanism (as opposed to a ratchet design) is more durable and smoother, plus the thumb release button allows you to quickly back the plunger off to minimize caulk drooling. Open sides make the gun easier to clean if a tube splits open. Some guns

also have a handy spout cutter and rod to puncture and later seal the tip of the caulk tube.

Two Methods of Caulking. The goal of caulking is simple — fill a gap while leaving an attractive "bead," or line of caulk, along the surface.

Begin by cleaning the joint. Remove dried caulk with an old chisel or screwdriver (a heat gun may help). Remove loose paint and dirt with a wire brush. Wipe off oils with a rag soaked in mineral spirits.

There are two basic ways to caulk. Either of these methods will work well, as long as you force the caulk well into the crack. The *pull method* involves cutting the nozzle at 45 degrees, puncturing the inner seal of the caulk tube, then pulling the gun along at about a 60-degree angle to the surface. The tip should force caulk into the crack.

Pull method

The *push method* involves cutting a double angle on the nozzle. Then, with the tube at a 45-degree angle, force the caulk into the joint by pushing the tube.

Push method

Tips for Better Caulking

Whether you push or pull to caulk, remember:

Don't buy cheap caulk. You'll just be caulking again in a few years.

The angle at which you hold the caulking gun is important. Too low an angle produces a lumpy, irregular bead that just sits on the surface. Too steep means that the tip scrapes caulk out of the joint.

Bead width is controlled by how much you cut off the tapered spout of the caulk tube. Make this opening slightly smaller than your intended bead. For best results, both visually and functionally, it's best to keep the bead continuous, with a minimum width of $3/16$ inch and a maximum of $3/4$ inch.

Squeeze the handle steadily for an even flow. Applying a long bead of caulk takes several squeezes of the handle. Since each new squeeze disrupts the flow, try to release and resqueeze at a logical break — the start of the next clapboard or at the corners of doors and windows.

Carry a rag and frequently remove the excess caulk that tends to collect around the nozzle tip and mess up your bead. Try to lay down a good bead, then leave it alone. If you're a novice caulker, start in a seldom-seen part of your house, and by the time you get to the front, you'll be a pro.

Caulk will adhere best if it has three points of contact — two sides and a back. Push caulk into the crack thoroughly so it doesn't just float across the gap but grabs in back as well. If you encounter a very large crack, stuff a *cylindrical foam backer rod* into the space before caulking.

Foam backer rod

If you smooth your bead with a wet finger (as recommended by many brands), don't make the bead concave. Most types of caulk shrink about 25 percent and you need to leave a hefty enough bead so the caulk isn't pulled away as the underlying materials expand and contract.

Furniture

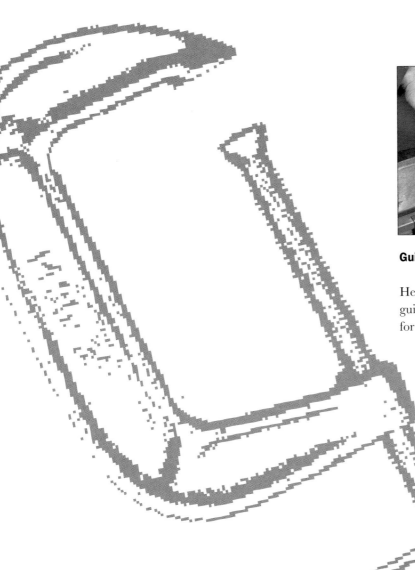

Guidelines   **148**

Here are some useful tips to guide all your repairs, whether for tables, chairs, or drawers.

Fixing Tables   **150**

A rickety table can be made sturdy and strong again, often quite easily.

Stabilizing a Bench   **152**

Have a bench that feels like it was a rocking chair in a former life? Here's how to make it rock solid again.

Reviving a Drawer   153

New life for drawers that are coming apart and drawers that won't slide right.

Repairing Chairs   154

Here's how to fix loose legs, repair broken rungs, glue split seats, recover, and recane.

Restoring a Finish   160

Simple fixes for your furniture's nicks and dents, scratches and spills, rings and dings.

Replacing Veneer   165

Repairing veneer is really no trickier than patching wallpaper. The results will make you proud.

Work Better, Work Safer   166

Here are some good ways to remove glue and put it on, tips on sanding without pain, and clamping techniques.

Guidelines for Repair

The simple keys to success.

WHAT YOU NEED

Chisel

Clamps and elastic tie-downs

Glue

Clean rags

Rubber mallet

Sandpaper

Screwdriver

Other items as needed

Other sections of this chapter will provide step-by-step directions for fixing tables, benches, drawers, and chairs, and refurbishing their finishes. Each type of repair usually requires its own tools (in addition to the generic repair list at left) and a few special techniques that you will find described in those sections.

But there are many tools and procedures common to all repairs — some guidelines, do's and don'ts apply no matter what it is you're fixing. They're good to know before you start any project and helpful to have handy as you progress. These two pages contain six tips to help you get started on the right track, so your repair efforts will let you restore favorite furniture to the place it deserves in your home.

BASIC FURNITURE REPAIR RULES

Rule 1   Don't use nails, screws, or metal mending plates or angle irons to put broken furniture back together. Glue is the proper material for joining furniture parts. Metal add-ons are just a temporary reprieve before the total failure of a joint. Although this sounds absolute, there are exceptions. Some furniture is designed to be held together by screws. And some glued furniture has screw joints, for example, where chair arms attach to the backrest. Drawers may also be held together with small nails.

Rule 2   Fix it before it breaks. Most breaks, unless from a serious accident or abuse, are caused by the pressures of ordinary use on loosened joints, and one loose joint leads to another. As you continue to use the piece, the rocking motion will wear, weaken, distort, or crack the wood, and what would have been a simple fix turns into a big one. So fix a joint as soon as it gets loose.

Rule 3 Remove all the old dried glue. Glue adheres by soaking in and attaching itself to wood fibers. It has almost no holding power on old glue. So take the joint apart and scrape off all the old glue with a sharp knife, chisel, file, or small paint scraper. Coarse sandpaper works only on glue that is fairly loose or flaky; it's pretty useless on glue that's hard and firm. Be careful not to remove wood. Otherwise, there will be gaps when you reglue.

Rule 4 Use the right glue. For most furniture, use ordinary white or yellow wood glue. The yellow variety gives a bit more strength and moisture resistance, but it begins to set in 8 to 10 minutes versus the 15-minute working time of white glue.

Hide glue, the traditional glue for furniture, is available in ready-mixed liquid form at some hardware stores and home centers or by mail order. Hide glue has great strength and doesn't begin setting up for nearly 30 minutes after application, so it's ideal for chairs, which take a long time to assemble and clamp.

Rule 5 Always hold a glued-together joint under pressure until the glue is dry. An unclamped joint is a lost cause. This doesn't mean you need a shop full of clamps. Clamps are fine if you have them, but they often won't work anyway because of the furniture's irregular shape. Instead, clamp glued-up parts using weights, such as books or tools; sticks or boards used as wedges; or elastic tie-downs. For smaller pieces use large rubber bands.

Rule 6 Clamping pressure must be sufficient to bring the two pieces of wood completely together and exactly aligned and matched the way they were originally. There should be no gaps, because the glue itself has almost no strength for bridging gaps.

Fixing Tables

Cracks, splinters, and splits can all be fixed.

WHAT YOU NEED

Electric drill

Circular saw

Screwdriver

Chisel

Wood glue

Shims

Small brush

Bar clamps

Hardwood

Vise

Wood filler

Toothpicks

Dowel

Straightedge

Elastic tie-downs

Pedestal tables are weak where the legs adjoin the center column; repair a break by refitting the dowels that hold the legs.

The legs of four-legged tables are attached to an apron with a leg-mount bolt through an angled leg support block. A loose leg can crack this block; you can prevent that by simply tightening the nuts on the leg-mount bolts.

Hinges on a drop-leaf table need to be kept tight to avoid damaging the table or the leaf. When replacing a hinge, use one that joins the table parts with the same spacing as the old hinge.

Simply gluing and clamping the halves of a cracked top rarely creates a permanent fix, but the repair shown on the opposite page will work for a top of any shape, as long as it can be unscrewed from its base.

STEP 1   Drill out the broken dowel after cutting it off flush. Use a bit $1/16$ inch smaller than the dowel; break out the rest of the dowel with a narrow screwdriver or chisel. Scrape off all the old glue.

STEP 2   Test fit the new dowel in the hole, then test fit the leg. If the fit is correct, glue the dowel in place. If not, redrill the dowel hole slightly larger and shim the dowel.

STEP 3   Apply a generous amount of glue to the dowels, the leg, and the center column base. Fit the pieces together snugly.

STEP 4   Exert pressure on all glued joints so that glue squeezes out uniformly. Scrape away excess glue after it solidifies, but before it hardens.

TABLE LEG SUPPORT BLOCK

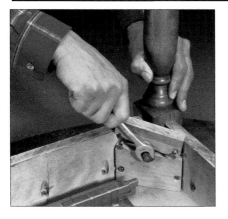

STEP 1 Replace a cracked table leg support block by removing the leg, then the block. Make a new block from hardwood, matching the size, shape, and holes exactly.

STEP 2 Screw the new leg support block to the table apron, using the old screw holes. If the leg-mount bolt hole doesn't line up, drill the hole larger.

HINGE SCREW TEAR-OUT

STEP 1 Remove bent or stripped-out screws from the drop-leaf hinge. If the hinge leaves are bent, remove the entire hinge and carefully straighten the leaves in a vise.

STEP 2 Pack the stripped-out holes with wood filler, adding a few toothpick tips in each hole for added bite. Drill pilot holes for the screws.

REPAIR A CRACKED TABLE TOP

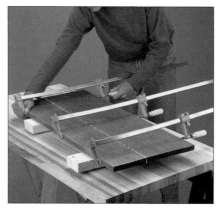

STEP 1 Remove the screws that secure the table top to the legs. (Tops that are glued or nailed in place cannot be easily fixed by this method.)

STEP 2 Saw the top in two, using a straightedge as a guide for cutting down the center of the crack. Two or three saw passes may be required.

STEP 3 Glue the two sections of the top together again. Drill new mounting holes and secure the top to the legs.

TABLE TOP TIPS

For wide or uneven cracks, move the straightedge several times and make repeated passes with the saw.

When you reattach the top to the base, use new holes drilled at least $1/2$ inch away from the old ones. If you use existing holes, the screws could meander over to their old positions and wedge the top apart.

Stabilizing a Bench

A little glue is all it takes.

STEP 1   Pull the joint apart and drill two or three ⅛-inch holes at an angle into the joint in an inconspicuous spot.

STEP 2   Inject glue into the joint. Force in glue until it oozes from the joint. Wipe off excess immediately.

WHAT YOU NEED

Electric drill with a ⅛- inch twist bit

Glue injector

Epoxy glue

Bar clamps

Pads

Some wobbly pieces of furniture are best fixed without taking the whole piece apart — especially if it's an upholstered piece such as the padded bench shown in these steps.

Pull the joint apart, then use a glue syringe to inject glue into the joint. If you can't force glue into the joint, drill a hole in an inconspicuous spot and complete the repair as shown.

Using a slow-setting epoxy glue gives you about 30 minutes to inject the glue and apply the clamps. Glue and syringes, often sold as kits, are available through well-stocked hardware and specialty woodworking stores. Don't use carpenter's glue; it sticks poorly to existing glue in the joint.

STEP 3   Press the joint together with bar clamps. Use pads to protect the furniture from the clamps.

Reviving a Drawer

Make all drawers work smoothly.

WHAT YOU NEED

Plastic- or metal-headed tacks

Hammer

Sandpaper

Bar soap or candle wax

Mallet

Coarse file or utility knife

Wood glue

Elastic tie-downs

Wood blocks

4d brads

Carpenter's square

A drawer that is coming apart simply needs to be disassembled and reglued.

However, drawers that don't slide easily need a different cure. They got that way because of wear. Usually, the bottom edges of the drawer sides wear down, causing the front to scrape.

The solution: Sand down parts that are getting too tight and rub a bar of soap or a candle on sliding surfaces.

If the wear is more significant, tap tacks with large plastic or metal heads into the fronts of each drawer runner and into the rear bottom edge of each drawer side to provide a new sliding surface that also brings the drawer up to the proper height.

On drawers with a centrally mounted wooden slide under the drawer bottom, the slide must align with its guide. If it does not, reposition the guide.

REBUILDING A DRAWER

STEP 1   Tap the drawer apart with a mallet. If the maker used dovetail joints, knock the sides away from the front and back.

STEP 2   Clean old glue off the dovetails with a coarse file, sandpaper, or a utility knife. Take care not to split or remove wood from the dovetails.

STEP 3   Glue and reassemble the drawer with elastic tie-downs and wood blocks. Use 4d brads on drawers without dovetails. Check for squareness.

STEP 4   The worn sides of drawers can be made to slide much more easily by installing tacks to minimize friction on vulnerable spots.

Repairing Chairs

*Chairs suffer a lot of abuse,
but they can be healed.*

WHAT YOU NEED

Masking tape

Rubber mallet

Hammer and screwdriver

Utility knife and chisel

Sandpaper

Cotton thread

Wood glue

Small, stiff brush

Cotton swabs

Bar clamps

Clean rags

Electric drill

C-clamp

¼-inch reinforcing dowels

Furniture touch-up stick

Elastic tie-downs

Chairs suffer more stress and strain than any other type of furniture. In time, the glue dries out and joints come loose. You can repair a few loose joints, but eventually you'll have to take the chair apart and glue it back together.

The sooner loose joints are repaired, the more likely it is that you will avoid broken parts.

In the following pages, you'll find step-by-step directions for regluing both stick and frame chairs, repairing broken parts, recovering upholstered pieces, and even recaning a chair seat.

Before you start any of these projects, it's a good idea to review the repair guidelines on pages 148 and 149 for some helpful tips common to all furniture repairs.

STEP 1   Mark joints to be taken apart so you'll know how to reassemble the chair. Use masking tape tabs coded with letters or numbers and lines to indicate alignment of the pieces.

STEP 2   Remove parts that are not securely glued by gently rocking, twisting, or tapping them with a rubber mallet or with a hammer and padded block of wood.

STEP 3   Remove all old glue from the dowels by scraping them with a utility knife or a chisel, then sanding lightly. Take care not to misshape the wood.

STEP 4   Sand the socket sides using sandpaper wrapped around a wood dowel. Remove built-up glue from socket bottoms with a narrow chisel.

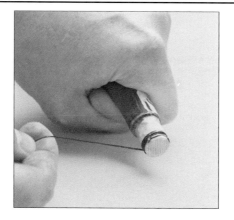

STEP 5 Assemble the chair without glue to test fit the cleaned joints. Tighten any loose joints by wrapping cotton thread around the dowel ends and coating it with glue.

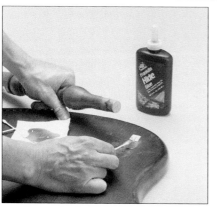

STEP 6 Apply a thin coat of liquid hide glue evenly to both the dowel ends and the sockets. Use a small, stiff brush or cotton swabs.

STEP 7 Fit glued parts together, beginning with the legs, then the rungs, and finally the stretchers. Be sure the alignment marks match up.

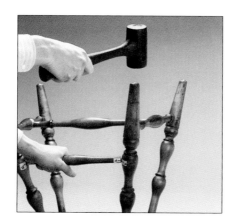

STEP 8 Tap all dowels firmly into the sockets with a rubber mallet or a hammer and padded block. Then turn the chair over onto a flat, level surface.

STEP 9 Draw joints tight with bar clamps, elastic tie-downs, or a combination of these. Make sure all joints are snug and that all legs touch the floor.

STEP 10 Glue and join disassembled backrest parts after the base section has dried; draw joints snug with tie-downs and wipe away excess glue.

Chair Tips

■ Dismantle as much of the chair as possible, gently working the pieces loose by hand, or use a rubber mallet or a hammer and a padded wooden block. Place chairs in a warm, dry room for a few days before disassembly.

■ Leave tight joints undisturbed.

■ If dowels or tenons fit loosely, build them up by gluing on string or wood shavings, then trim to fit.

■ After the old glue is removed, test fit the chair without glue to be sure all the joints fit properly.

■ Align the chair before the glue sets. Place it on a flat, level surface and make sure all the legs touch.

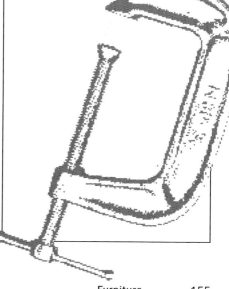

Frame Chairs

- A frame chair has a rectangular box frame secured to a leg at each corner by means of mortise and tenon joints. The back legs and outside backrest supports are all of one piece. The removable seat, usually covered with cloth, is attached with screws through the angled corner blocks.

- The most common breakdown in this kind of chair is the joint where the side seat rails join the back leg/backrest support. This joint is usually secured with dowels and is repaired much the same way as the doweled joint of the pedestal table leg, shown on page 150.

- If the seat of a frame chair splits, it's usually best to replace it rather than reglue it. Most other frame chair repairs are similar to the general chair repairs shown in these steps. The main difference is that the entire chair must be glued up in a single operation, since the back legs and the backrest are one piece.

- A broken back leg is a common affliction of frame chairs. However, if the break is along the grain and presents a sizable gluing surface, it can easily be repaired.

REFASTENING FRAME CHAIRS

STEP 1   Glue both surfaces of a broken leg and fit them together exactly. Make sure that any rungs intersecting the break are fully inserted.

STEP 2   Clamp the break with a C-clamp. Use wood strips to distribute the pressure and prevent damage. Glue should squeeze out on all sides.

STEP 3   Drill holes for ¼-inch-diameter reinforcing dowels after the glued joint has dried thoroughly. Use two dowels in each side of the leg.

STEP 4   Glue dowels in place so the dowel ends come to rest just below the surface. Fill the holes with a color-matched putty stick.

STEP 5   Remove loose corner blocks, then scrape or sand off all traces of old glue. Apply a generous coat of yellow wood glue to the blocks and the chair frame.

STEP 6   Remount corner blocks using the original screw holes in the frame. Tighten the screws thoroughly so glue squeezes out all around.

STEP 1 A broken rung end will quickly result in several additional broken rungs. The end shown above is probably impossible to remove intact.

STEP 2 Apply glue to both of the broken segments and rejoin them exactly as they came apart. Clamp the assembly tightly.

STEP 3 Drill a hole for a ¼-inch-diameter by 2-inch-long wood dowel. Drill at least 1 inch into the rung body. Keep the hole centered and straight.

STEP 4 Tap a dowel, liberally glued, into the hole; countersink just below the surface. When dry, fill the hole with a color-matched putty stick.

MAKING SPLIT PARTS WHOLE

Split Seat Repair a split seat by applying glue to both split edges, then clamping securely. Make sure the two surfaces and edges are exactly aligned.

Split Rung Glue a split rung with a small C-clamp. Use pieces of scrap wood to equalize the clamp's pressure over the split and to protect the rung.

Easy Does It

Most of these repairs require gluing and clamping; bear in mind, though, you can overdo both. Use too much glue and you'll not only create a mess, but weaken the joint or connection by creating a thick, easy to break glue line. Aim for a thin, even glue line.

Likewise, don't overtighten your clamps. You can drive too much glue out, creating a starved joint. Or you can compress the wood so much that when the clamps are removed and the fibers spring back to shape, they weaken the repair.

Worn or dated chairs with removable wrap-around seats can usually be reupholstered without having to remove the old fabric. Select a cotton or synthetic fabric that has the color or pattern woven into it. Polished cotton with the pattern printed on the surface is less durable.

Protect the new upholstery fabric from future spills and stains by spraying it with one of the many fabric protectants available.

STEP 1 Remove the chair bottom by taking out the four screws that secure it to the frame. Save the screws for reassembly later.

STEP 2 Cut the new batting 2 inches oversized on all sides, using the seat bottom as a pattern. Most large fabric stores carry batting.

STEP 3 Secure the batting by pulling it tight around the chair bottom and fastening it with ¼-inch staples. Trim any excess.

STEP 4 Mark center lines on the chair bottom and the fabric, then match them so that the fabric pattern runs straight from front to back.

STEP 5 Staple the fabric in place, first completing the front and back edges, then the two sides. Staple from the center toward the corners.

STEP 6 Fold the fabric at the corners, then secure it with staples. Trim excess fabric with sharp scissors after all corners are complete.

Caned chair seats may be constructed two different ways. Hand-woven cane is threaded, strand by strand, through individual holes in the chair's frame. It's a time consuming process we're not covering here. Other chairs, especially those less than 60 years old, were most often covered with machine-woven sheet cane which we do show how to repair. Regardless of the chair's original cane construction, sheet cane can be used to repair any piece of furniture that has a groove in which to secure a spline.

You can buy sheet cane by the running inch or foot in widths from 12 to 24 inches. Spline is sold by the running foot and is available in different widths.

Give your supplier the exact width of the groove in the chair so you get the right size spline. You'll also need one or more packs of caning wedges.

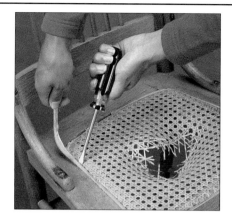

STEP 1 Remove the old spline by prying with a screwdriver. Cut along both edges with a utility knife beforehand to break loose the old glue. Remove the broken cane.

STEP 2 Soak the new cane in warm water for an hour. Precut the cane large enough so it will extend 1 inch past the chair groove on all sides.

STEP 3 Drive in the caning wedges around the seat, making certain the cane is lightly stretched and the pattern is running straight and square across the seat. Press the cane into the groove around the whole seat.

STEP 4 Remove the wedges, soak the spline in water for 15 minutes and run carpenter's glue in the groove. Press the new spline in place.

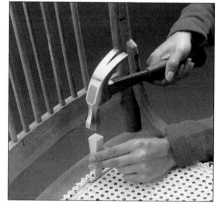

STEP 5 Tap the spline into the groove using a wedge. Trim the cane with a utility knife. Lightly sand with fine sandpaper, spray with lacquer, and set the chair aside for two days.

Restoring a Finish

Time-consuming stripping and staining are not always necessary.

WHAT YOU NEED

Mineral spirits

Cotton swabs

Clean rags

Rubbing compound

Extra-fine steel wool

Aerosol lacquer

Furniture wax

Alcohol

Rottenstone

Fine-grit sandpaper

Mineral oil

Danish oil

Furniture touch-up sticks

Oil soap

Plastic credit card

Many pro furniture refinishers will tell you that more good furniture is ruined by stripping and refinishing than is saved by it. Stripping with chemicals can loosen glue joints and veneers, and sanding and scraping remove the glow that gives old furniture its character. These drastic steps should be reserved for pieces that are hopelessly scratched, painted over, or worn through.

On the other hand, cleaning, touching up, and reviving a finish can bring a shabby-looking piece to a point where you'll be proud to restore it to its place of honor. Better yet, you won't spend a lot of time or money.

On this page you'll find some simple fixes for your furniture's daily dings and dents. Renovating more extensive damage is described on pages 162 and 163, and the steps to a thorough renewal are on page 164.

DINGS, DENTS, AND RINGS

Dings and scratches and other signs of daily use that really aren't all that bad, but still, they bug you. Most of these problems can be touched up very easily and quickly. All it takes is about 10 minutes and the right tools and techniques, shown on these pages.

There are only a few special supplies needed for basic touch-up. Alcohol, 0000 steel wool, and wet-or-dry sandpaper are standard hardware store items. Mineral oil (or baby oil) will be at your drugstore. Dark paste wax may be a little harder to find, but you can order it through the mail.

Furniture touch-up pens and sticks are available from larger hardware stores, large furniture dealers, or by mail. Although the touch-up pens look like ordinary markers, don't try to substitute — a garden-variety marker won't work.

WHITE RINGS Remove wax with mineral spirits and a soft cloth, then wipe with rubbing alcohol and a new cloth. If the ring remains, sand lightly with 600-grit wet-or-dry sandpaper and mineral oil. Wax to restore the shine.

WORN-THROUGH EDGES Clean the worn area with mineral spirits and a cloth, and scuff the edge with 400-grit sandpaper. Draw along the edge with a special touch-up pen of the appropriate color. Blend the repair by rubbing gently with your finger.

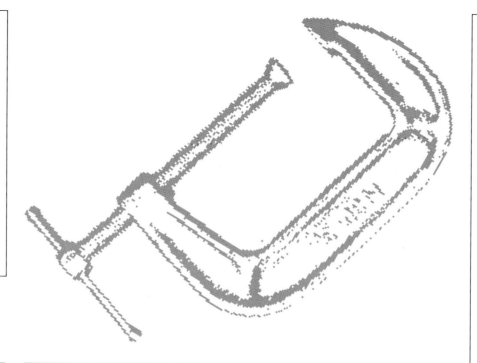

Careful

- **Fingernail polish**
  Whatever you do, don't try to wipe it up! The solvents in fingernail polish soften most furniture finishes, so if you wipe, you'll take off the finish.

- **Nicks and gouges**
  Don't try the fix on this page on table tops. Deep scratches on table tops require melted-in shellac and are best left to a professional.

Safe and Simple

No matter how many steps are involved, furniture finishing is a simple process. Keep it safe and simple by following these steps when you work:

- Thoroughly clean your piece with mineral spirits. Otherwise, silicone from old polishes will create unsightly "fish eyes" in the newly applied finish.

- When in doubt, check out the product or process on an inconspicuous area before risking the whole piece.

- Work outdoors or in a garage, basement, or other space that can accommodate a small mess. Be sure to provide adequate ventilation while you work.

- Set rags outdoors to allow mineral spirits and other products to evaporate, then dispose of them properly.

SMALL SCRATCHES Sand with the grain, using 600-grit wet-or-dry sandpaper lubricated with mineral oil. For a satin finish, rub with 0000 steel wool lubricated with oil soap. If there is streaking, add a little pumice. For a higher shine, use wax, then buff.

SPILLED NAIL POLISH Let the polish dry completely, then gently scrape it right off with a plastic credit card or similar tool. If the finish underneath has dulled, use paste wax and 0000 steel wool to bring back the shine.

NICKS AND GOUGES Clean the area with mineral spirits. Fill the larger gouges with a soft filler stick. Smooth with a small piece of wood and buff lightly with 0000 steel wool. Fill scratches with dark furniture wax.

Marred surfaces, nicks, scrapes, and scratches need not doom furniture to a major refinishing. A close look at the scarred finish of the table in step 1 (right) shows the problem: small cracks and scrapes in the top layer of the finish that do not penetrate through to the stain or wood. This is the most common flaw in a finish, and it can be repaired almost flawlessly by an amateur who uses patience and the right materials and techniques.

Rub the entire surface with very fine 0000 steel wool, lubricated with Danish oil, to remove the top layer of finish. Stop rubbing when the scars are gone. Don't use a rigid sanding block, which tends to cut the highest points of finish first removing stain in those areas before removing surface marks in the low areas. Above all, don't hurry the process of rubbing out the flaws. Finish off this stage by rubbing the surface with rottenstone.

Rottenstone, a fine abrasive, cuts better when lubricated with water; however, use oil when fine cracks in the finish could permit the water to penetrate to the wood. A final coat of lacquer or polyurethane gives a hard, moisture-resistant finish.

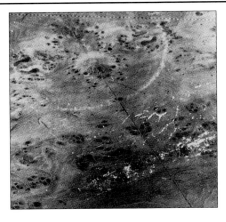

STEP 1 Examine the surface. As bad as they look, these abrasions do not penetrate completely through the varnish to the wood.

STEP 2 Rub out the marks with very fine 0000 steel wool, moving with the grain. Use Danish oil as a lubricant.

STEP 3 Rub rottenstone and Danish oil across the surface with a soft cloth for slower and finer cutting.

STEP 4 Wipe the surface with lacquer thinner to remove the oil. For a water-resistant surface, spray on several coats of lacquer or polyurethane.

Use Rejuvenators with Care

The "refinishers," "rejuvenators," and "restorers in a can," which revive finishes without stripping or touching up, work by dissolving a thin layer of the original finish, combining it with tung oil or other finish, then recoating the entire piece with this new, light film. This process disguises blemishes and enlivens some finishes, but it can ruin others if it dissolves too much of the finish or affects the stain. Always test these products in an inconspicuous area of the piece first, wear gloves, and work in a well-ventilated area.

Careless placement of wet glasses, bottles, or vases can create what appears to be severe damage. A closer look, however, shows that the wood and the stain are intact; only the hard, clear surface finish has been destroyed.

Use a refinisher to dissolve the old varnish, lacquer, or shellac and rub out the marks.

For a more durable finish, smooth the refinished surface with fine steel wool and Danish oil, clean with thinner and, when dry, coat with a water-resistant finish such as lacquer or polyurethane. See the box on the previous page for some cautions regarding refinishers.

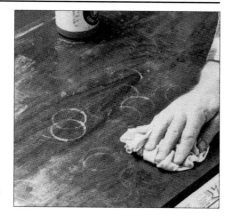

STEP 1 On this piece, the stain beneath the varnish is intact. Clean the damaged surface with an oil soap. Allow it to dry thoroughly.

STEP 2 Pour a small quantity of refinisher into a pan. Rub the entire surface with fine steel wool dipped in refinisher. Follow product directions.

STEP 3 Clean off the resulting gunk with fresh steel wool dipped in refinisher. Allow the remaining finish to harden again.

Deep Scratches and Gouges

For scratches that are narrow, yet cut all the way through the finish and stain, you need to recolor the light streak with matching stain, ink, iodine, or commercially available touch-up markers. A good coat of furniture polish will complete the job.

When you use a colored putty or wax touch-up stick or marker, be sure to confine the stain from the stick or marker to the scratch only. Start with a light shade, darkening the repair gradually until it matches.

A scratch into the wood itself requires filling in addition to coloring. (For scratches in very fine pieces of furniture, you may wish to consult a professional.) For shallow scratches, color and brush several coats of the appropriate finish into the scratch to build it back up to the surface level. Then renew the surface smoothness with a clear lacquer or polyurethane spray as shown on page 162. For deeper scratches, use shellac sticks, available through most woodworking stores.

STEP 1 Examine the piece carefully to determine what the problem is: cracked or alligatored finishes can't be revived. White water rings, black water rings, light finish scratches, or deep scratches can be touched up.

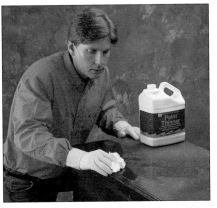

STEP 2 Clean all surfaces with mineral spirits and a soft rag. Do this two or three times to make sure all silicone polishes are removed. Use cotton swabs to clean small recesses or carvings.

STEP 3 Fill gouges and deep scratches with wax sticks. Blend different colors for a close match. Reshape the edges and smooth flat surfaces with the back of a piece of fine sandpaper.

STEP 4 Recoat the surface with aerosol lacquer. Spray with the grain of the wood. Wait 15 minutes, then spray again. Three to five coats (sometimes more) may be necessary.

STEP 5 Rub out the surface with car paint rubbing compound and extra-fine 0000 steel wool once the lacquer is dry. Rub with the grain. Wipe with a damp rag. Repeat if necessary.

STEP 6 Protect the piece with furniture wax. In the future, dust with a light spray polish and soft cloth. Avoid heavy-bodied oils, which give a temporary high-gloss shine but attract dust.

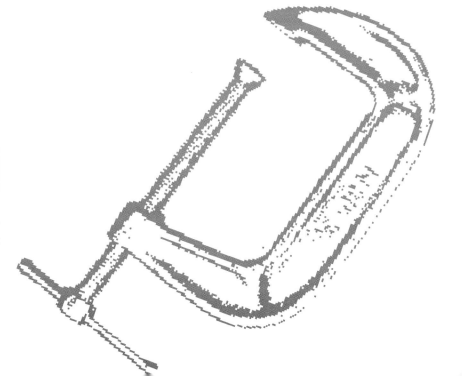

Replacing Veneer

This takes a little patience, but it's worth it.

WHAT YOU NEED

Veneer

Contact cement

Utility knife

Stain

Sandpaper

Paper

Pencil

Paintbrushes

Touch-up putty stick

Varnish

Replacing small sections of chipped-out or damaged veneer is easy to do, but it takes a bit of time and careful fitting. Pieces of veneer are sold by the square foot. They are readily available in oak, mahogany, or walnut.

You can use the thick contact cement sold in small bottles at most hardware stores. Be careful, though, because it is toxic and flammable.

Coat both surfaces being joined, and follow directions for drying time before sticking it down.

The best part is that if you don't like the look of the repair before you finally glue it, you can take it apart and try again. Once you're pleased with the result — and only then — apply glue.

REPLACING SMALL PIECES

STEP 1 Remove a piece of veneer surrounding the damage. Cut straight edges as near to parallel to the wood grain as you can to hide the seam.

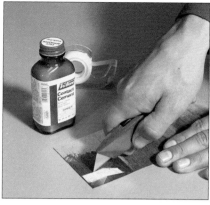

STEP 2 Cut an exact replica of the cut-out from a template. Make the template from a paper rubbing of the cut-out using the side of a pencil point.

STEP 3 Test fit the veneer patch and trim it if necessary. Glue it down with contact cement. Apply glue to both surfaces; allow it to dry before joining the surfaces.

STEP 4 Hide the seam with a furniture touch-up putty stick in a matching color. Varnish or oil the patch before using the putty stick; the finish won't adhere to the stick's wax.

Work Better, Work Safer

Spindle Painter

A neat, fast way to paint stair spindles or other hard-to-brush objects is to take a plastic food-storage bag and an old white sock, slip the bag over your hand, and then put the sock over the bag. Now dip the hand covered by the bag and sock into the paint and apply it. You'll cover all those areas that are difficult to reach including the nooks and crannies. It's as easy as that.

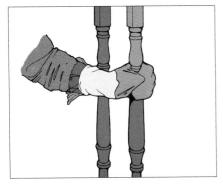

Spindle sock

Loosen Old Glue

After taking apart a chair or any piece of furniture for regluing, use this old cabinetmaker's trick to loosen and remove the old glue in the joints. Spray,

dab, or brush vinegar into the joint. It usually works in minutes, but a thick glue buildup could take up to an hour to loosen. It won't harm any finish and it leaves a white film that simply wipes off after it dries.

Sponge Painter

Cut a piece of flat, smooth sponge to cover a square area with paint or varnish. The paint goes on smoothly with no brush marks, and you can get into tight areas and around spindles easily. After you finish the paint or varnish job, just throw the sponge away. There's no cleanup.

Neat Stain Applicator

Here's a neat, efficient way to finish a furniture project by applying furniture stain: Use a hacksaw to cut a thick-nap, 9-inch paint roller into three equal sections. Hold the roller piece in your hand to wipe on the stain. The roller absorbs more stain than a brush and applies it more evenly than a rag. Wear a rubber glove and when you're finished, peel the glove off while holding the roller and discard the whole mess.

Joint Injection

Inject glue into thin cracks and joints in wood by flattening one end of an ordinary plastic drinking straw about 1 inch. Carefully draw up the glue by suction, wipe off the end of the straw, reflatten it, and gently blow the glue into the joint.

Wood Filler

Many types of wood filler tend to set up while you are mixing the filler with pigment to match the workpiece. To avoid this, try kneading them together in a small plastic bag — an ordinary kitchen bag will do. Punch a small hole in the plastic bag and squeeze small amounts of the filler out through the hole. This will reduce both mixing time and waste.

Furniture Joint Filler

If you're regluing furniture and have joints that are too worn or loose for the glue to properly join the pieces, thoroughly soak cotton balls in glue and use them as gap fillers.

Fine Furniture Finish

One recipe for a fine finish is to rub the piece with multiple coats of a mixture of boiled linseed oil and turpentine. There are times, however, when you might want a harder finish — one with varnish in it — but one that you can still rub on instead of brush.

To get this, simply add alkyd varnish to the mixture. Start with equal portions of each, then experiment with the proportions to get the best results.

Picture-perfect Pads

Make no-mar spacers for your metal C-clamps. Glue caps from plastic 35mm film containers to the swivel ends of your clamps with hot-melt glue. The caps will protect the surface of your projects, and you can pop them off when you don't need them.

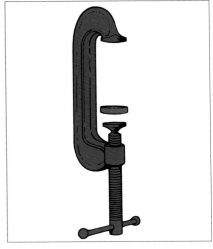

Padded C-clamp

Easiest Furniture Finish

There isn't any way to eliminate sanding when finishing furniture. Sanding between coats of varnish or oil not only provides the smoothest finish, but with varnish it also helps each subsequent coat adhere to the previous coat.

You can make the finishing job easier, however, by using Danish oil. With an oil finish you don't have to be picky about brushing, and it's much easier to sand smooth.

Here's how to use oil: Sand the wood quite smooth (220-grit sandpaper works well), remove all dust with a tack cloth, then apply the oil and give it time to soak in (according to manufacturer's recommendations). Thoroughly wipe off any oil that remains (be fanatical about this), and lightly sand the piece with 600-grit wet-or-dry paper, either used dry or lubricated with a little Danish oil. Repeat this procedure, applying several coats of oil. Then follow with a furniture wax.

Don't Break a Leg

To prevent wooden chair legs from breaking when you're taking apart a chair for regluing, remove the rungs or spreaders by supporting the chair so the leg rests lightly on a carpeted surface, as shown below. Then tap on the leg with a rubber mallet. The bond will loosen and allow you to pull the spreader out without damaging it or the leg.

Save a leg

Breaking Wood Glue Joints

Muscles alone probably won't break a glued joint. Carpenter's wood glue is tough stuff and is formulated so it won't come apart. But you might try the shock and steam method. Here's how to do it: To shock the joint, use a soft-faced mallet or a hammer and a block of wood, and give the glued joint a good rap.

To steam the joint, use a wet rag and a hot clothes iron. Place the wet rag over the "shocked" joint. Rub the hot iron over the rag as if you were ironing clothes. You may have to repeat these steps a few times, but this should soften and break the joint.

Nontoxic Clear Finishes

Any clear finish such as lacquer or polyurethane is nontoxic once it has cured, or dried. While a clear finish may contain solvents when the finish is in a liquid state, these solvents evaporate during the curing process.

When choosing a finish, consider both durability and repairability. For example, polyurethane gives a very hard, long-lasting surface, but should the finish get damaged, it cannot be repaired. Lacquer, on the other hand, is not as durable a finish as polyurethane but it can be repaired. Oil finishes are easy to apply but don't wear well.

Whichever finish you decide to use, ensure proper curing by applying the finish in light, thin coats. Then don't use the piece until the finish has cured (in most cases, a month should be

ample time). If you have doubts about curing time, check with the finish manufacturer (look for an address or phone number on the container).

For more information on nontoxic finishes, including paint, write to: Freedom of Information Division, Dept. TFH, Consumer Product Safety Commission, Washington, DC 20207.

When Strippers Won't Work

Ever try to refinish an old painted piece but find that the paint seems to resist every kind of stripper?

Don't despair! There's an almost magical solution: ordinary household ammonia. It should take that old paint right off. If strippers won't touch it, the paint is almost certainly an old-fashioned milk paint. Rural folks, especially in the Northeast, made this using milk, linseed oil, and a natural pigment like lime or rust-colored soil. You can find it on furniture and house trim dating from the 1700s to mid-1800s. While crude, milk paint is actually quite durable, though it could produce only soft colors (because of the milky base) and didn't have any gloss. And it's also impervious to normal paint strippers.

(Note: If the original milk paint is in good condition, a piece of furniture is probably worth quite a bit more with the paint on than it would be stripped.)

DIY Fluted Dowels

Whenever you need a fluted dowel for gluing and joining wood, crimp a plain dowel rod with the serrated jaws of

your pliers. Cut it to length and presto, you have a fluted dowel the exact size and length you need.

Basic Hand Sanding

Sanding will make or break the appearance of anything you build from wood. You just can't be too thorough or too fussy about sanding properly.

Use the Right Sandpaper. Sandpaper is made in a bewildering number of types. Here are the main choices and what they're good for.

Flint paper is the cheapest and shortest lived and it's usually not worth the money — don't bother with it.

Aluminum oxide is the familiar light-brown sandpaper. It has hard, uniform, and long-lasting grains. This is the best general-purpose sandpaper for the money and is especially good for power sanding.

Garnet paper is reddish in color and is also a good all-purpose abrasive. Garnet grains fracture as they are used, continually exposing fresh, sharp cutting edges. Garnet paper cuts easily but wears quickly and is particularly good for hand sanding.

Silicon carbide is the hardest grit—hard enough to sand metal—so it removes material very quickly. It's commonly found as black wet-or-dry paper. Wet-or-dry carbide paper is ideal for very fine sanding between coats of varnish and other finishes. The paper is waterproof so you can lubricate it with water or oil while you sand to keep the sandpaper from gumming up. As the name implies, you can also use this sandpaper dry. It's available only in fine grits.

Wet-or-dry sandpaper

Stearated paper is either a carbide or an aluminum oxide paper that has been coated with a light gray or white compound, called zinc stearate, which keeps the paper from getting clogged with dust. You will see this type of paper described as "no-fill." Stearated paper is extremely good for woodworking; it is fast cutting and long lasting, especially for softwoods, which can gum up ordinary papers. Unfortunately, it's also more expensive.

As a general rule, use aluminum oxide paper unless you are wet-sanding a finish (use wet-or-dry carbide) or you're willing to spend the extra money for stearated paper.

Use the Right Grit Size. Sandpaper is classified by grit size (80, 120, 150, 180, etc.), with higher numbers indicating smaller grains for finer sanding.

Start sanding with 100- or 120-grit paper, depending on how smooth the

surface already is. Hardwood plywood, for instance, is usually smooth enough to start at 120 grit. Use 60 or 80 grit only for coarse removal of material — not for smoothing.

After the initial sanding, progress through finer grits as necessary without skipping any grit steps. Your first, coarsest sanding should flatten the high spots. All subsequent sanding just replaces the large scratches with progressively smaller ones — until finally they're too small to notice. Where to stop depends on your project; if it's pine, for example, you could stop at 120. If it's oiled maple, you might go through 120, 150, 180, and 220, then polish the wood, while oiling uses 400-grit wet-or-dry paper.

In general, surfaces to be painted need sanding to 150 grit; those to be stained and varnished need to be sanded to about 220. However, the coarser the grain (oak, for example), the coarser the grit that can be used.

Sanding the Right Way. Here are the right techniques for sanding wood — the ones a lot of people end up learning the hard way:

Do final sanding by hand. Oscillating power sanders are great but they leave swirl marks that look bad when the wood is finished. Sand even the perfect-looking surfaces on factory-planed or -sanded wood to open the grain, give the wood a uniform appearance, and promote even staining.

Don't sand out large gouges and dents — you'll just get a wide, shallow

crater that will be very noticeable. Dents can often be eliminated by raising the crushed fibers with steam (put a damp rag on the dent and touch with a hot iron). Use wood putty to fill deep dents and scratches rather than trying to sand them out.

Sand with the grain. Sanding at an angle to the grain can leave scratches that are difficult to remove. Overlap sanding strokes and apply equal pressure on both your forward and your backward strokes so wood fibers are cut rather than combed down. The only exception to this rule is when you want to remove a large amount of wood. In that case, sand across the grain, then follow up by thoroughly sanding with the grain.

Sand with the grain

Use a block behind your sandpaper to knock down the ridges and span the low spots. A half sheet of paper will fit around a ¾ inch x 4½ inch softwood

block nicely. There are also numerous commercial sanding blocks available. Don't use your fingertips — the paper will follow surface and grain irregularities, leaving a wavy surface.

Use a sanding block

Don't skip grits. Sanding can be tedious, so it's tempting to jump from, say, 100 grit to 180. Don't. It'll be so hard to remove the 100-grit scratches with the fine paper that you'll end up losing, not saving, time.

Putting Everything Together

If a colonial carpenter were to open your toolbox, the tools he'd probably be most impressed with would be your C-clamps. In his day, clamps were expensive handmade tools, but today's clamps are so cheap, powerful, and versatile that no home owner should be without an assortment. Here are some tips for using them.

When you tighten a clamp, the pressure is exerted in a cone-shaped area in front of the clamp heads. The farther the glue line is from the clamp heads, the more widely the pressure is distributed. Using a caul (which is just a piece of scrap wood that you place between the work and the clamp) helps this pressure distribution, so you won't need as many clamps.

How tightly should you clamp? That's a good question, but there's no single answer. Sometimes you need only gentle pressure, as when clamping a doweled joint, gluing a sliver back into place, or gluing edging onto plywood. Other times you can hardly get enough pressure, as when edge-gluing boards that must hold weight or when face-gluing where the surface area of the glue joint is very large. One thing is certain: clamping pressure must be evenly distributed.

Another general rule to keep in mind: Even hardwoods will dent under the pressure of clamps, so have pads handy to protect your work. Keep a coffee can full of masonite pads right with your clamps.

There are many, many kinds of clamps, some very specialized and exotic looking. Most home owners need to use only a few.

C-clamps are versatile, basic, and inexpensive. Everyone should have a few in the workshop. They are slow to adjust, but they come in a great variety of sizes. The large ones are extremely powerful.

C-clamp

Lightweight *bar clamps* adjust very quickly, are only slightly more expensive than C-clamps, and come in much longer sizes. The long ones are especially useful for holding pieces in place before nailing or for screwing them together, as shown in the photo below.

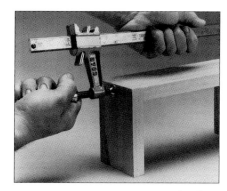
Bar clamp

Pipe clamps are best for edge gluing boards and assembling cabinets. You can make them any size you want. Heavy-duty bar clamps are available that work the same way as pipe clamps, but they are considerably more expensive. When you use pipe clamps, be sure the screw of the clamp lines up

with the center of the board's edge; thin boards will need to be held up with blocks. Alternating clamps on the top and the bottom keeps the boards from bowing. If you are clamping a thin edging to a board, use a wide caul between the edging and the clamps to distribute the pressure.

Pipe clamps

Spring clamps are great general-purpose helpers. They range in size from minuscule to monstrous and are surprisingly powerful.

Spring clamps

Hand screws seem ungainly to use at first, but they are amazingly versatile. Since they have wooden jaws, you

don't need pads (which have an annoying habit of falling off in the middle of a complicated glue-up). The jaws adjust so you can clamp surfaces that are not parallel, as well as those that are not in a line. Adjusting the hand screws is easy once you get the knack of spinning them. Hold a clamp handle in each hand and move the handles as if they were being used to pedal a bicycle.

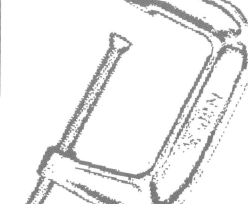
Hand screw

There are many more exotic clamps available, but with the five clamps described here, and a little ingenuity, you can clamp just about anything you'd ever want to.

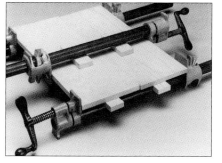

Home Safety

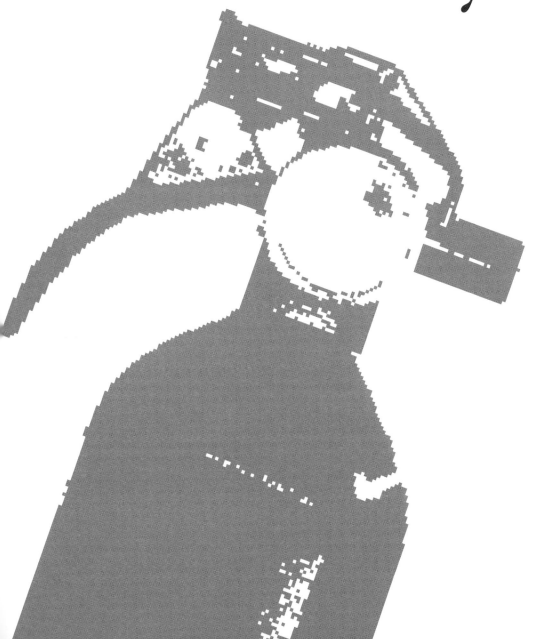

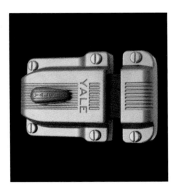

Home Security   172

If you don't have basic, common-sense, inexpensive burglary protection on and in your house, you are posting an invitation to burglars on the front door.

Garage Door Safety   175

Automatic garage door openers are seen in almost every house that has a garage. But these devices can be deadly unless you take some simple precautions.

Fire Safety 176

A fire is perhaps the home owner's greatest fear. Here's how you can keep it from happening — and how to protect yourself and your family if a fire should break out.

Carbon Monoxide 178

Half of all fatal poisonings in North America are caused by carbon monoxide, a colorless, odorless gas that can emanate from your furnace or fireplace.

Work Better, Work Safer 180

Here's how to save small fingers and your own eyes, plus a pro's look at lung protection.

Home Security

Protect your home from intruders.

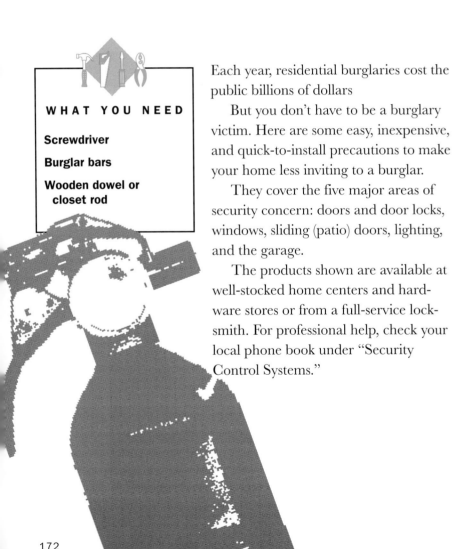

Each year, residential burglaries cost the public billions of dollars

But you don't have to be a burglary victim. Here are some easy, inexpensive, and quick-to-install precautions to make your home less inviting to a burglar.

They cover the five major areas of security concern: doors and door locks, windows, sliding (patio) doors, lighting, and the garage.

The products shown are available at well-stocked home centers and hardware stores or from a full-service locksmith. For professional help, check your local phone book under "Security Control Systems."

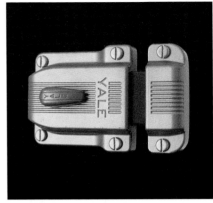

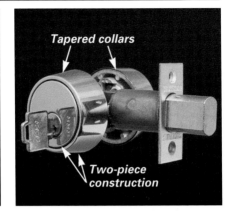

DEADBOLT   A deadbolt is the first item police and security experts recommend. The surface-mounted style (above) is the easiest to install and provides the best protection, according to recent consumer lab tests.

CYLINDER DEADBOLT   This is the most commonly used type. When properly installed, it provides good resistance to forced entry. Look for solid metal, tapered collars, and two-piece construction.

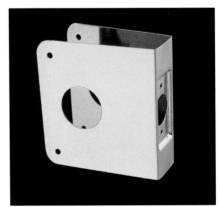

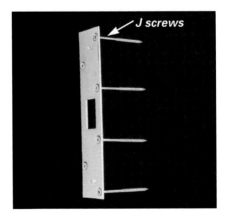

WRAP-AROUND KNOB REIN-FORCER   This device reduces the chance of having the knob area of the door kicked in during a forced entry. It is also available for a deadbolt.

REINFORCED STRIKE PLATE This plate prevents someone from tearing away the wooden door jamb. The screws must be long enough to penetrate into the house framework.

PEEP HOLES

A door, especially a side or back door, is most often the first place a burglar will try to enter. That's because a door offers a large opening that makes it easy to remove the items the burglar has stolen. It is also usually the quickest point of entry.

Installing a deadbolt is the No. 1 antiburglary recommendation from police and security experts. Cylinder deadbolts are available in two forms: the single-cylinder lock with a thumb turn on the inside and a key lock outside, and the double-cylinder lock, which requires a key for both the inside and the outside.

An additional security item for beefing up your entry doors is an inexpensive "peephole" or door viewer. This device lets you see who's outside without having to open the door. Door viewers can be installed in most wood or steel entry doors. All you need to do is drill a hole and pop in the viewer.

WINDOWS

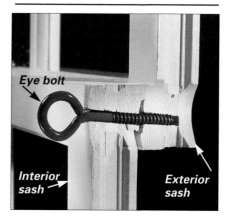

PINNING THE SASH This is an economical, effective way to prevent opening a double-hung window from the outside. Drill a hole slightly larger than the pin diameter into both sashes where they overlap, but don't penetrate the exterior sash.

BURGLAR BARS These bars keep intruders out, even if the glass has been broken. They are secured inside the window to the framing in the wall and swing open for emergencies.

Second Choice Entry

After a door, a window is the second choice for entry by a burglar, although many burglars begin there if they find an unlocked window. If a window is secured, the burglar probably won't try breaking the glass to release the lock. Shattering glass is noisy, and noise attracts unwanted attention.

Window style can be a natural deterrent to entry. A casement window (or "crank-out" window) is extremely difficult to open from the outside. However, a double-hung window is fairly easy even if the sash lock is engaged. Shown at left are the best ways to secure a double-hung window — sash pins and steel burglar bars.

In the case of the pins, you don't have to worry that they are visible, either. Remember, burglars don't like making noise, so it's unlikely they would break the glass to remove the pin.

Burglars are also in a hurry. Anything you can do to slow down a break-in artist will increase the likelihood that you'll be left alone.

CLOSET ROD Cut a wooden rod to fit and place it on the door track between the operating door panel and the opposite jamb. This is an effective and inexpensive way to secure the door. A rod costs just pennies per foot.

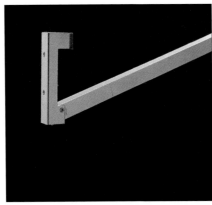

CHARLIE BAR This device prevents the door from being forced open. It attaches to the door frame and has a locking catch fastened to the operating door panel. The bar can be swung out of the way to allow normal door use.

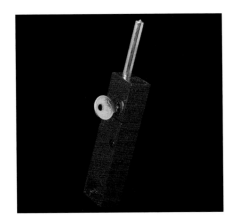

PATIO DOOR LOCKS Those with keys provide protection as long as the lock does more than just hold the two door panels together. You should buy a lock that has a bolt that slides into the door frame.

Secure Thoughts

■ **Sliding Doors**
A sliding patio door is an easy mark for a burglar. Most of these doors have flimsy latches. While many products on the market claim they'll keep intruders out, those shown at left have proven to be effective.

■ **Lighting**
A well-illuminated exterior is one of the most effective ways to deter a potential intruder. Ideally, all points of entry (doors and windows) should be illuminated. Remember, too, to use these lights every night, not just when you're away. To give the interior of your home a lived-in look even when you're not home, use plug-in timers to turn lights on and off.

■ **Garages**
Everyone keeps valuable items in the garage — the most obvious is the car. But tools, lawn mowers, garden tractors, motorcycles, and bicycles are also enticements for a burglar. You can do three things to make your garage more secure.

An automatic door opener is the best way to make sure the overhead garage door will remain closed since you need the transmitter to activate the opener when you're outside. Remember to check the opener's operation and safety reverse mechanism regularly and see the door safety tips on the facing page.

Paint or cover the window glass of an overhead or side service door so burglars can't see what they're missing.

A long-shackled padlock through the door track, just above one of the door rollers, prevents entry via the overhead door when you're gone for an extended length of time.

■ **Neighborhood Watch Programs**
A neighborhood watch program can be summed up as "neighbors watching out for each other." This program serves as a warning to burglars that the residents are concerned about crime and will call the police when any suspicious activity is observed. A neighborhood watch program also gives residents a better awareness of crime, reminding them to remove and reduce opportunities for criminals to act.
Neighborhood watch programs have directly contributed to the decline in burglaries where there was no watch program before. And even if you live in a low-crime area, you can establish a program in your neighborhood to ensure that it will remain safe.

Garage Door Safety

Don't let convenience lead to tragedy.

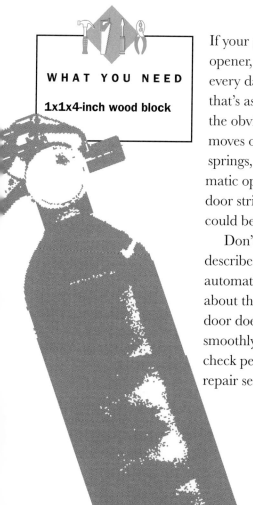

If your garage door has an automatic opener, you probably zip in and out every day without a worry or care. And that's as it should be. But don't overlook the obvious: A 300- to 400-pound door moves over your head on wheels, springs, and a metal track. If your automatic opener fails to reverse when the door strikes a person or a pet, the result could be tragic.

Don't be misled — the safety test described here will only tell you if the automatic safety reverse is working, not about the door's overall health. If your door doesn't seem to be operating smoothly, you should have a complete check performed by a professional repair service.

Safety Guides to Follow

Test Your Opener Today

■ Get a 1-inch thick piece of wood — two scraps of ½-inch thick plywood will work fine; just make sure it's a true 1-inch thick. Place the piece of wood on the garage floor under the door and activate the opener.

■ When the door hits the piece of wood it should reverse and reopen within 2 seconds. If the door does not reverse, disconnect the opener immediately and operate the door manually until the opener is repaired or replaced. Check your owner's manual or call a professional repair service listed under "Garage Doors and Openers" in the yellow pages.

■ Safety experts recommend that you conduct a test at least monthly of the door's automatic reverse mechanism.

Additional Safeguards

■ Buy only a UL-listed opener equipped with an automatic safety reverse mechanism.

■ Keep the remote control device in your glove compartment.

■ Locate wall-mounted controls high up, out of the reach of children.

■ Teach older children how to safely operate the garage door.

■ Never allow young children to operate or play with door controls.

■ To operate the door manually, use the emergency release handle.

■ An electric eye that detects motion, required in some states, can be used with some openers. You can have it installed or install it yourself for about half the cost.

Fire Safety

Learn how to avoid and escape disaster.

WHAT YOU NEED

Smoke detector

Batteries

Screwdriver

Floor plan

According to the National Fire Protection Association's most current figures, nearly 5,000 people die in home fires in North America each year. And, unfortunately, these deaths occur in the places most people feel safest — their homes.

Take the information here and go through your house from top to bottom looking for fire hazards.

Also, consider the worst case: If the unthinkable were to happen, how would you get out of your burning house? If you don't know, the seconds you spend deciding could be the difference between life and death. You need to have an escape plan and then teach the plan to everyone in the family. And finally, practice your plan.

REDUCING FIRE HAZARDS

◼ Careless Smoking

Smokers should use extreme caution when smoking and use large, heavy ashtrays to extinguish smoking materials. And never smoke in bed!

◼ Faulty Heating Equipment

Have your furnace cleaned and inspected by a professional once a year, before the heating season begins. Also, check around the furnace and water heater for any combustible materials.

Turn off portable space heaters before leaving the room or going to bed. Keep all heating appliances at least 3 feet from furniture, walls, or anything that can burn. Never add fuel to a space heater if it's hot or if the area is unventilated.

◼ Electrical Dangers

Never overload an electrical outlet or circuit. If you find overloaded circuits, it's probably time to upgrade the system. Contact a licensed electrician for advice.

Check all plugs and cords. Replace frayed or cracked cords.

Never run cords across traffic areas or underneath rugs, or pin them to the wall with furniture.

◼ Blocked Exits

Make sure exits are clear and doors and windows open easily.

◼ Matches and Lighters

Keep them out of children's reach. Teach children to bring any matches, lighters, or other strange items they find to an adult.

◼ Kitchens and Cooking

Wear short or close-fitting sleeves. Keep all pot and pan handles turned in. Don't leave cooking food unattended. Don't let spilled food or grease build up.

Smother the flames of a grease fire by sliding a lid over the fire, then turn off the burner. Never pour water on a grease fire! If you doubt your ability to extinguish the fire, get out and call your fire emergency telephone number.

◼ Flammable Liquids

Store all combustible liquids in labeled and approved metal containers away from heat or flame.

Never store gasoline in your home. Keep only enough on hand to power your lawn mower or similar equipment for a few hours.

◼ Additional Precautions

When you purchase an appliance, look for testing laboratory labels (such as Underwriter's Laboratory, or UL; in Canada, Canadian Standards Association, or CSA) on the appliance *and* its cord.

Your Escape Plan

■ Plan

Draw a floor plan of your home. Show landmarks outside the house such as trees, shrubs, the driveway, or a street lamp.

Locate a primary and secondary exit from each room — especially bedrooms. Most house fires occur while the family is asleep. Primary exit: the door. Secondary exit: usually a window. Make sure windows and window screens operate easily.

Mark on your map a designated meeting place outside the house. Make sure everyone knows where this is so all can be accounted for.

See that each exit works. Can all of the exits be used by everyone? Assign an older child to assist a younger sibling who can't handle even one of the exits.

Designate someone to call the fire department, usually from a neighbor's house.

Consult your local fire department about your escape plan.

■ Instruct

Review the escape plan and exits with everyone, especially young children.

Teach children that they can't hide from fire. They must escape from it and go to the designated meeting place.

Stay out of the house once you're out — never return for any reason, no matter how urgent.

■ Practice

Hold an unannounced, surprise fire drill every six months. Vary the location of the "fire."

Drill alternative escape routes. Pretend at various times that a fire is blocking the main route.

Escape quickly but don't make a race out of it. Learning what to do and how to do it is more important than speed.

Coach or assist children during the first or second drill. The goal must be for them to learn to get out on their own.

Change your escape plan as children grow.

What to Do If There's a Fire

■ Stay calm.
Panic can spell disaster in an emergency.

■ Alert everyone.
Make sure everyone knows that there's a fire.

■ Escape.
Get out of the house, now. Don't get dressed or gather valuables.

■ Feel a door before opening it.
If the door's hot, or there's smoke coming in underneath, don't open it! Use the secondary escape route.

■ Smother burning clothing.
Stop, drop, and roll. Cover your face with your hands. Never run; running fans the fire.

■ Meet.
Go to the designated meeting spot. Count heads to see that everyone's accounted for. Don't go back into the house!

■ Call.
If there's a fire alarm box nearby, use it. Or, go to a neighbor's house to call the fire department. Don't attempt to use your phone; it's too dangerous.

Smoke Detectors

One smoke detector is not enough. There should be at least one on every level of your house and one outside each sleeping area.

Install the detectors on the ceiling near the center of the room at the top of a stairway or on the highest point of a sloped ceiling. If you mount one on a wall, make sure it's 4 to 12 inches below the ceiling and never in a corner, or what's considered "dead air" space.

Test the detectors weekly and be sure to replace the batteries at least annually. Follow the manufacturer's instructions for recommended maintenance.

Never disconnect a smoke detector. If nuisance alarms, such as from cooking, are a problem, consider relocating the detector.

Carbon Monoxide

Keep this silent killer out of your house.

Carbon monoxide (chemical symbol CO) is a by-product of incomplete combustion. Sources of this gas include automobile exhaust fumes, furnaces, natural gas stoves and water heaters, fireplaces, charcoal grills, and lawn mowers. There are also unexpected sources such as the vapors of some solvents like paint strippers.

We also tend to make the situation worse in pursuit of energy efficiency. Some houses are simply too airtight for safety. Besides that, as thermostats have been turned down, a variety of room heaters have taken their place, or a fireplace or wood stove installed. In addition, if you build an enclosure around the furnace or water heater when you remodel the basement you have to provide for adequate fresh air flow or else you may create a perfect opportunity for carbon monoxide to build up.

Can Your House Breathe?

Houses need to breathe because fresh air is necessary for the furnace, water heater, and stove. If there isn't enough fresh air available inside the house, it will be pulled into the house down the furnace or fireplace chimney. This is called "backdrafting." Backdrafting reverses the chimney's normal siphoning effect, so the carbon monoxide produced by the furnace and water heater stays inside the house instead of going out the chimney.

To determine whether your house is receiving enough fresh air, conduct this test:

1. Close all doors, windows, and fireplace dampers.

2. Turn on all exhaust fans, such as those in the kitchen, bathrooms, attic, and your clothes dryer.

3. Turn on all vented gas appliances, such as the furnace, water heater, and clothes dryer.

4. Wait about 10 minutes for drafts to stabilize.

5. Hold a lighted wooden match below the furnace draft hood air intake (typically on one side of the furnace or an open section of ductwork near the furnace).

6. If the smoke is pulled up toward the draft hood (below left), there is sufficient fresh air.

7. If the match flame goes out (below right), backdrafting exists. Immediately call your local utility for assistance.

8. Repeat this test on your gas water heater.

If you have a fireplace, start a fire in it. When the fire is well underway, check for backdrafting again at your furnace and gas water heater draft hoods. If it's present, you must install a duct to provide the fireplace with outside air.

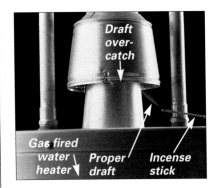

Draft over-catch. Gas fired water heater. Proper draft. Incense stick.

Carbon monoxide tester. No draft.

- Learn to recognize a properly adjusted gas flame. It should burn crisp and blue. If it's orange, it needs adjustment — call a professional to do it for you.

- Have a professional check all heating appliances every year.

- Have your chimney cleaned annually, before the start of the heating season and especially if you frequently use a fireplace or wood-burning stove.

- If you need a new furnace, choose a "sealed-combustion" model. These units draw air directly into the combustion chamber from the outside and vent the exhaust gases back out.

- Have your chimney checked every fall for such blockages as bird or squirrel nests.

- Have your family vehicles' mufflers and tailpipes checked and replaced if necessary.

- If you've recently remodeled your house for energy efficiency, have the carbon monoxide level checked by the utility company.

- Don't sit in a parked car with the engine running and the windows closed, or let the engine idle in a closed garage.

- Never use a charcoal grill indoors.

- Never use a kitchen stove or oven for heating purposes.

- Avoid extensive use of kerosene heaters. Better yet, don't use them at all.

- Don't put furnaces and water heaters in an enclosure unless you provide adequate ventilation, perhaps ducted in from outside. Your local utility can give you guidelines on what to do.

- Don't use liquid propane gas lamps, heaters, or gasoline lanterns indoors or in an RV, unless they are properly vented to the outside.

- Never use an unvented gas heater inside the house.

Detectors, the Best Defense

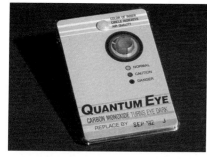

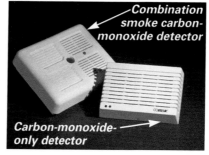

Least expensive but requiring regular monitoring are small chemical detectors (left and middle). These change color when exposed to a certain level of the gas. They must be replaced at least every year. Most important, you need to develop the habit of checking them regularly, looking for that telltale color change.

Electronic detectors (right) are more expensive, but you don't have to monitor them. Just like a smoke detector, the alarm will sound if a certain level of carbon monoxide is present. Some models are a combination smoke, carbon monoxide, and natural gas (methane) detector. They require a 120-volt power source.

Indoor Clues

- Persistently stuffy, stale, or smelly air.

- High humidity, often showing up as moisture on the surfaces of windows.

- Soot around the outside of the fireplace, furnace, or chimney.

- No draft in the chimney.

- A hot draft from the chimney into the house.

- The smell of exhaust fumes.

Work Better, Work Safer

Swing Easy

Keep the chains on a child's swing from causing an injury by covering them with foam pipe insulation. The insulation makes the chains easier and softer to hold and prevents chain links from pinching or cutting children's fingers.

Fireproof Shop

Don't buy flammable liquids in large quantities — buy just enough to do the job. Store flammable liquids such as paint, tung oil, varnish, or thinners in tightly sealed containers away from the furnace or heaters and out of children's reach. Keep a fire extinguisher in your shop area as a precaution against fire.

Keep flammables away from children

Burn Prevention

Each year, thousands of children are burned or scalded by tap water that is too hot for delicate skin. Turn down your water heater thermostat to 110 degrees F so small children cannot hurt themselves by turning on the hot water.

Power Tool Concerns

Leaving power tools out in the open, in the workshop, garage, or storage shed is an invitation to disaster for children. All power tools should be placed in a locked cabinet with the key in a location inaccessible to children. Going one step further and disabling gasoline-powered tools by removing their spark plugs is a minor inconvenience compared to the potential tragedy that can result from misuse.

Lacquer Thinner Dangers

The fumes from lacquer thinner are heavier than air. Because of this, they can collect along the floor and can hide in corners for as long as a few days. When this happens, even the smallest spark could ignite the fumes. The spark can originate from turning on a light switch or from the electric motor of your refrigerator starting up. Even someone coming into the room and lighting a cigarette could cause the fumes to ignite.

Any time you use a flammable solvent such as lacquer thinner, the work area must be well ventilated and away from any heat source, and you should always follow the manufacturer's instructions.

Disposing of Toxic Rags

While taking precautions when using solvents, paint strippers, and other chemicals is important, it's equally important to take the same precautions in disposal.

Rags soaked with combustible liquids can ignite spontaneously. All rags soaked with solvents (mineral spirits, denatured alcohol, paint thinner, etc.) or linseed oil should be spread out flat to dry (or hung on a clothesline) in a well-ventilated area, away from children, pets, and flames. Once they've dried, they can be thrown away with the rest of your garbage.

Rags soaked with furniture finish strippers can be disposed of the same way, as long as the paint stripped was not lead based. If it was, call your local health department to find out where the rags should be taken.

Environmental Hazards Guide

The Environmental Protection Agency and the Federal National Mortgage Association have produced a booklet about environmental hazards in the house. *A Home Buyer's Guide to Environmental Hazards* explains how radon, lead, asbestos, formaldehyde, ground water contaminants, and other hazards can affect your health. Testing for these substances is explained, and a listing of government offices that conduct tests or certify testing labs is included. Write to: Consumer Information Center, Dept. 427X, Pueblo, CO 81009. The cost of the guide is 50 cents.

Be Careful with Buckets

Those plastic 5-gallon pails that drywall compound and paint come in are very handy, but don't leave them around with water in them — they can kill! Dozens of young children have drowned from tipping over headfirst into 5-gallon buckets full of water, according to the U.S. Consumer Product Safety Commission. The children, generally under 2 years old, are top heavy and cannot right themselves after they fall in. So if you're using a 5-gallon bucket with liquid in it, keep it away from where kids gather.

Save Your Sight

Most home workshops do not have fresh, running water. Should a caustic chemical accidentally splash into your eyes, time is of the essence. Help is as close as two (one for each eye if necessary) prudently placed bottles of the preserved saline solution used for soft contact lenses. Keep the bottles in your shop — they might just save your sight someday. Use the solution according to standard procedure in situations where eye irrigation is indicated as first aid treatment. Seek medical care as soon as possible. Saline solution should not be exposed to temperature extremes, bottles should be stored with caps on tight, and you must obey the expiration date.

Tile Cleaners and Health

Specialty cleaning products often work wonders, but their very strength can make them dangerous unless you follow the directions carefully.

Tile cleaners often contain sodium hypochlorite (chlorine bleach) and must follow labeling guidelines set by the U.S. Consumer Product Safety Commission. Some companies add even more safety information.

Sodium hypochlorite is an irritant to mucous membranes. For those who have difficulty breathing due to respiratory ailments, inhaling the product may make it even more difficult to breathe. Breathing these fumes can also affect your heart rate and blood pressure, so these products should be avoided by those with heart problems.

Garage Fire Hazard?

Never, never, never replace an attic entrance hatch with a screen — doing so creates a major fire hazard, especially if the hatch is in an attached garage. The large volume of air that flows up into the attic acts like a chimney and, in the event of a fire, would draw the fire

up into the attic and spread it quickly throughout the house.

For houses with attached garages, most building codes require an unbroken fire barrier between the garage and the living area — including your attic. This fire barrier is usually ⅝-inch fire-retardant drywall on the entire wall between the garage and house. Local code may also require a metal or a fire-rated wood door with a self-closer.

Vinyl Ducts Can Catch Fire

Be careful if you're installing vinyl ducts instead of aluminum for a clothes dryer. Ducts that are longer than 20 feet can accumulate enough lint to become a fire hazard.

In a recent year, almost 14,000 such fires were identified, in which 20 people died. So play it safe — keep your vinyl dryer duct short or use aluminum.

Workshop Smoke Detector

If you need to replace your present smoke detectors, use multistation units and wire them all together. Then if one goes off, they all will. Multistation detectors are available from hardware stores and fire alarm dealers. They must be wired together with 12-3 or 14-3 cable in accordance with your local electrical code.

It's not a good idea, however, to put a smoke detector inside your shop or garage. The dust and fumes can make the smoke detector inoperable or set off a false alarm. Instead, put the alarm just outside the door to these areas.

If you're concerned about the possibility of a fire starting in the garage or shop, consider installing self-closing doors to those areas, either metal or wood that have a one-hour fire rating. Also make sure you have a working fire extinguisher handy that is rated for use on all types of fires.

Kitchen Safety

When cooking, turn pot handles in toward the center of the range top so they will not be bumped and spilled accidentally. Never use a chair for climbing; keep a step stool in the kitchen to reach the upper cabinets. And keep a fire extinguisher near the exit and equip the kitchen with a fire or smoke alarm.

Makeshift Hearing Protectors

Protect your ears in situations where you don't have hearing protectors handy by rolling up toilet paper, dampening it slightly, then sticking it in your ears. It really works!

Thinking Safely

There's bad news and good news for DIYers. The bad news is the U.S. Consumer Product Safety Commission estimates that every year more than a quarter of a million people require medical attention for injuries they suffer while using tools in the home.

The good news is that you can save your skin if you just keep your head on straight. Because most accidents happen inside your head before they ever

injure your body, start your personal safety campaign by deciding to follow a few basic rules described below.

First, wear the right clothing before working. Never wear loose clothing, which can get caught in power tools, and do wear eye protection. Then think through the consequences of every hand, arm, leg, and foot movement before you make it; literally predict the consequences of each movement. At first this will slow you down a lot, but in time you will become aware of these consequences instinctively, and work will go faster.

Don't wear loose clothing

Evaluate your mood. If you're feeling grumpy, angry, tired, impatient, or otherwise out of sorts, forget that project. Watch a ball game instead.

Generate a healthy fear of your power tools; if the day ever comes that you lose your last speck of fear, that may be the day you cut off your finger

— or worse. If you have to leave your tools, be sure to shut them off, unplug them, or remove any safety keys.

Remove safety keys from machinery

Some injuries can develop over a long period of time; use masks and respirators to protect your lungs and ear muffs or plugs to save your hearing.

Concentrate. Keep kids, pets, and other distractions out of your hair. If a friend or neighbor stops by to chat, stop your work. Think about what you're doing at that very moment, not about the next step in the project.

Make a personal commitment to do things the right way, even if this means taking more time than you want to. For example, forget about working with dull tools, blades, and bits; they'll only do you in. Take time to sharpen them. Don't force tools to get the job done faster; they'll just turn on you. Don't take shortcuts that put you on a shaky ladder, force you to hold a tool awkwardly, or place you in an off-balance

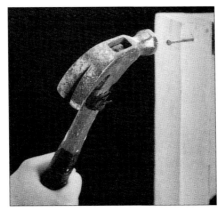

Don't use worn tools

position. Hurry is the major enemy of safety, as it is of good craftsmanship.

Treat electricity gingerly. Every year 600 people die of electrocution in and around their houses. It's the second-highest cause of accidental death, after falling. Use only double-insulated power tools; don't stand in water while working; wear rubber-soled shoes; don't poke tools or fingers into the unknown; and install ground-fault circuit interrupters on outlets (see page 90).

All of this may sound a bit morbid — and it is if the fear of death and dismemberment becomes a preoccupation. But by simply sharpening your sensitivity to everyday risks, you can enjoy knowing that you've tipped the odds against injury miles in your favor.

The Right Protective Mask
If you take a minute to think, you'll probably realize that in your basement, kitchen closet, workshop, or garage there are solvents and chemicals that

can kill you almost immediately or over a period of time.

There's no reason to panic, though. With common sense, caution, and a couple of inexpensive protective masks, you can avoid bad experiences with these materials.

Dust masks and respirators are much more readily available on hardware store and home center shelves than they were just a couple of years ago. There are two reasons for this. The variety of potentially hazardous materials most home owners use keeps growing, and consumers are growing increasingly aware of the risks. Some of the new synthetic compounds used in pesticides, cleaners, adhesives, and finishing materials, despite their warning labels, are too new for anyone to really know their long-term effects or how much of an exposure is safe. Second, manufacturers are now finally supplying the general public with a variety of efficient, low-cost protective devices.

There are two basic types of pollutant hazards you will encounter around the house: airborne solid particles, and airborne spray, vapor, or gases. Each type requires its own kind of protection.

Solid Particle Masks. Most solid-particle material in the air is visible and relatively easy to filter out; it's what your mother would call dust and it's usually not toxic. However, nontoxic doesn't mean harmless. Coal and silica dust and asbestos particles, for example, are known to cause serious lung damage when inhaled. (The most common

advice given for asbestos, the only one of the materials mentioned here that is likely to be encountered in the house, is to leave it alone if it is intact and not giving off particles; if it is not intact, have it removed professionally.)

Less harmful particles, such as sawdust, the stuff you sweep out of your garage, or the mold spores you breathe while raking leaves, can be a nuisance at best and a serious irritant to your upper respiratory tract at worst. Long-term or repeated exposure could give you chronic cough, a forever-running nose, or lung congestion. And dust can be either the vehicle or the cause of an allergic reaction if you are so prone.

Disposable *paper cup masks* are inexpensive and are fitted over the nose by means of a formable metal strip. They are good for cutting back on nuisance dust but, depending on the fit of the mask and the size and type of particles, can let through as much as 30 percent of the dust.

Paper cup masks

Considerably better filtering and a tighter face seal are provided by the self-shaping soft *rubber mask* and by the cloth and *plastic-edged mask* with replaceable filters. Both types have fiber/cloth filters that you can rinse out several times before having to discard them.

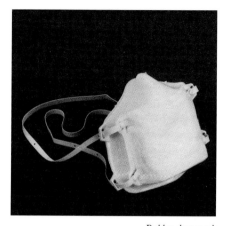

Rubber dust mask

Plastic edged mask

Respirators for Sprays and Pesticides. All three types of dust masks described here are largely ineffective against almost any spray, organic vapor, chemical substance in gas form, fumes from epoxies or adhesives, or any mist from paint, lacquer, varnish, or enamel. Many of these substances are highly toxic to humans, and coping with them is a more complex task than simply filtering out dust particles.

Your body knows how to deal with most nontoxic dust. Nasal hairs and mucous membranes trap it, and any small amount of dust that does get into the lungs is easily dissolved and eliminated from your body. But synthetic chemicals mystify the body. It can't trap or detoxify them and, unlike particles, gases and vapors are absorbed into the blood where they can cause toxic reactions in many organs, especially the liver and kidneys.

The *twin-cartridge half-mask respirator* shown (right) is the answer to this kind of pollutant. It's a grandchild of the World War I gas mask, except that it offers no eye protection. The pliable rubber mask body holds two cartridges that contain chemical-absorbing material. The standard organic vapor cartridges that usually come with the respirator, plus the cloth filters that go over them, will protect you from most, though not all, varieties of toxic fumes. Read the instructions carefully to determine just which toxins this standard cartridge will *not* filter out; if you have occasion to use these toxins, be sure to buy the appropriate cartridge.

Unlike dust filters, you can't tell just by looking when a chemical cartridge is used up, so it's especially important to follow the recommendations in the instructions and replace the cartridges if you detect any odors while wearing the respirator. Cartridges have from 4 to 16 hours of life, depending on the type and concentration of the substance being filtered.

Twin-cartridge half-mask respirator

Other Hints for Avoiding Self-pollution. Masks and respirators should really be thought of as a second line of defense. The first and best defense is to avoid using toxic materials wherever possible. But that's easier said than done. The ideal glue or the most effective herbicide or the most durable finish may also just happen to be the most toxic. Read labels with extreme care and pay attention to the warnings and precautions.

Another first-line defense is to ventilate your work area. Open windows, use fans, and keep air moving between your face and the source of the fumes even when wearing a respirator. If the weather is too cold to ventilate the area thoroughly, consider putting the job off until a warmer day.

Some toxins are absorbed through the skin, so cover up as much as you can. Keep your hands away from your mouth and food out of the work area. Wash your clothes and take a shower after using a toxic material.

Glossary

AC

Alternating current; standard household current, so called because it reverses direction at a regular frequency, usually 50 (in Europe) or 60 (in North America) times per second.

Alligatoring

Small cracks in the finish of a piece of furniture resembling alligator hide. It is caused by the finish expanding and contracting; it does not affect the wood under the finish.

Amp

Short for "ampere," the amount of current flowing past a point in an electrical circuit every second. Household circuits are rated by the number of amps (the volume of electric current) they can handle.

Asphalt

A waterproof substance that is found in nature and is also a by-product of petroleum refining. It saturates the backing mat and holds the mineral granules used to make asphalt shingles used on roofs (also called composition shingles). When mixed with gravel it is used for paving. Home owners can buy materials to patch small defects in asphalt paving; new paving must be done by a professional.

Barrel (hinge)

The hollow round portion of a hinge that connects the leaves and allows insertion of the hinge pin.

Bead

A continuous strip or length of caulk, glue, adhesive, or similar substance, often along a joint.

Beam

A length of lumber or metal used as a horizontal support in construction.

Bevel

An angled edge. Or, to cut the end of a piece of wood or other material or the edges of a hole at an angle.

Bonding agent

In tile, plaster, and masonry work, a chemical that helps one material, such as a plaster patch, adhere better to another material.

Butt hinge

A type of hinge with flat leaves that are mortised into the edges of the pieces being joined.

Cable

A bundle of wires twisted or woven together and covered by a layer of sheathing.

Canvas

To cover a plaster wall with a special heavy-duty fabric and adhesive to conceal fine cracks and blemishes and to provide a new surface for painting or hanging wallpaper.

Casement window

A window that is fastened in its frame with a hinge and that opens at one side, the top, or the bottom, often by means of a crank mechanism.

Caulk

A flexible waterproofing compound used to seal seams, such as those around windows, and joints, such as those between tiled surfaces.

Cement

A mineral powder used as an ingredient in concrete and mortar; also, any of a type of adhesive.

Chalking

Releasing a white powdery substance as a result of weathering; usually refers to paint and house siding.

Circuit breaker

A switch that automatically interrupts the flow of electricity in a circuit when the amount of current exceeds a particular amperage.

Concrete

A hard material made of cement, sand and/or gravel, and water; used for paving and construction.

Countersink

To drive a screw or a nail so the head lies just below the surface.

Cure

When used about adhesives and cement-based materials, to become completely hard as a result of chemical actions within the substance. Curing can take weeks, months, or even years after the substance feels dry or hard to the touch.

DC

Direct current; the type of current produced by a battery, so called because its flow is constant in one direction.

Double-glazed window

An energy-efficient window having inner and outer sets of glass panes, often sealed in the sash and separated by air or an inert gas such as argon. It is used to create a thermal barrier. A variant, the triple-glazed window, is sometimes used in regions with very cold climates.

Double-hung window

A window with two sashes, one above the other, in which both the top and bottom sashes can be slid in the frame.

Dowel

A usually short, thin, round stick of wood that is used to strengthen a wood joint, usually in furniture; the dowel is inserted into matching holes bored in adjacent pieces.

Drywall

A type of construction material that comes in large sheets and is used to make walls and ceilings; it consists of a core of gypsum that is sandwiched between layers of heavy paper and is available in a variety of sizes. Also called plasterboard, wallboard, and Sheetrock.

Drywall tape

A form of tape made of paper or fiberglass-mesh that is used to seal and conceal joints between pieces of drywall. May be self-adhesive.

Feather

To spread and thin the edges of a patching substance like plaster or joint compound in order to blend it with the surrounding surface.

Fill valve

The mechanism on a toilet that allows the tank to refill with water after the toilet has been flushed; shuts off water flow when the tank is full.

Flange

Any flat rim or rib in a plumbing fixture or pipe that allows it to be fastened into place.

Flapper valve

The flat rubber stopper at the bottom of a toilet tank that opens to allow water to flow from the tank to the bowl when the toilet is flushed and closes to allow the tank to refill.

Flashing

Sheet metal used to waterproof roof valleys and the joints between the roof and the chimney or other protrusions.

Float

Any of several tools used to work and smooth a surface. A grout float is rubber and is used to work grout into spaces between tiles. Wood and magnesium floats are used to smooth the surface of concrete after pouring and while it is still wet.

Float ball

A large hollow rubber or metal ball inside a toilet tank that is attached to the fill valve. It drops with the water level when the toilet is flushed to open the fill valve; it rises with the water level as the tank refills and shuts off the fill valve when the water reaches a certain level.

Flush

Even with an adjacent surface.

Flutes

Rounded parallel grooves, as on a dowel, allowing glue to flow freely.

Flux

A paste or liquid applied to clean metal surfaces before soldering, brazing, or welding.

Frame

In construction, the basic structure that gives shape, strength, and support

to a wall, window, or other opening; also refers to the underlying structure of a building.

Furring

Strips of thin wood or metal that are attached to joists, studs, or walls to create a level surface for attaching drywall or paneling.

Fuse

A safety device that protects an electrical circuit by interrupting the circuit when the current flow exceeds predetermined limits. Some appliances have their own fuses.

Galvanized

Coated with zinc to provide protection against rust.

Gang

To join one or more parts, such as electrical switches, so they can be operated simultaneously.

Glazing

Glasswork. Also, glass or any other transparent material used for making windows.

Glazing compound

A thick, waterproof caulk used to seal the joint between the glass and frame in a window.

Glazing point

A small metal clip used to hold glass in place in a sash.

Ground

Any wire or other object that provides an electrical current with a connection to the earth.

Ground wire

A wire that provides a safe, direct path to the earth for the current in an electrical device.

Grout

A cement-based mortar that is used to fill the spaces between floor, wall, or counter tiles to keep dirt and moisture out and to improve appearance.

Hinge pin

The long metal piece that slips into a hinge barrel to secure the hinge leaves together.

Insulation

A nonconducting material that is used to prevent the transfer of heat, sound, or electricity across a surface. Electrical wires are usually insulated with a plastic coating and house walls are insulated with substances such as fiberglass or foam.

Jamb

The pieces that form the visible framework of an opening such as that for a door or a window.

Joint

The place where two surfaces meet, as between a wall and floor, sections of pipe, or bricks.

Joint compound

A thick paste used in conjunction with drywall tape to seal and conceal joints between sheets of drywall. Also known as drywall compound.

Joist

Any one of a group of horizontal boards (often 2x6 or larger) set on edge and parallel to each other to support a floor or a ceiling.

Knockout

A thin round section of plastic or metal in an electrical box that can be punched out in order to make a hole through which wires or cable may be run.

Lacquer

A clear, durable, solvent-based, moisture-resistant wood finish. It is not as waterproof as varnish and is more resistant to heat and chemicals than shellac.

Laminate

Any material, including plywood, made up of two or more layers bonded with adhesive and compressed under heat. Usually stronger but more flexible than a like thickness of solid material alone.

Lath

Any of a set of thin narrow strips of wood or metal fastened to rafters, joists, or studs to form a support for plaster, slates, or tiles.

Leaf (hinge)

The flat surface of a hinge that is fastened to one side of the surfaces being hinged — for example, one leaf to the door and one to the jamb. Leaves are connected by the hinge barrel.

Ledger

A horizontal board that supports the ends of joists.

Level

Horizontal; perfectly parallel to the surface of the earth.

Lift chain

The chain inside the tank of a toilet that connects the flapper valve to the flush handle. It raises the flapper valve to allow water to flow from the toilet tank into the bowl when the handle is pressed down.

Live wire

The wire in a circuit that carries the current. Also called the hot wire.

Mastic

A pastelike, tarry substance used as an adhesive in some types of tile and masonry work.

Molding

Decorative strips or sections of wood, tile, plastic, or other material that are used primarily to conceal a joint, such as crown molding between a wall and ceiling or shoe molding between a wall and floor.

Mortar

A thick cement-based substance that hardens and is used to hold bricks and other forms of masonry in place.

Mortise

In furniture construction, a usually rectangular cavity cut into a piece of wood or other material to receive a tenon on another piece for forming a joint. Also, the action of cutting such a cavity.

NIOSH

National Institute of Occupational Safety and Health. A U.S. government agency setting safety and health standards for equipment, procedures, and materials in the construction and other industries.

Neutral wire

The wire in a circuit that is not electrically charged.

On center

A basis for measuring that starts at the center of one structural member and goes to the center of the next, such as with joists. In residential construction, joists are usually spaced 16 or 24 inches apart as measured from the center of the top edge of one joist to that point on the next. Stud spacing is also measured this way.

Piano hinge

A hinge with a thin barrel that extends the length of the parts to be moved.

Plumb

Vertically level; perfectly perpendicular to the surface of the earth.

Point

To remove and replace the mortar between bricks. Also called tuckpoint.

Polyurethane

A synthetic varnish that is clear, nonyellowing, hard, fast drying, and resistant to wear, water, and alcohol.

Primer

A substance, usually a special type of paint, that is used to prepare a surface such as metal or tile so that the final finish adheres properly.

Rafter

Any of the parallel members that support a building's roof.

Rail

A horizontal structural member of a door, cabinet, or table.

Sash

The framework of a window into which the panes of glass are set.

Screed

A long, straight board used to level the surface of sand, gravel, or poured concrete and to remove excess material.

Shank

The relatively long, straight part of a nail, pin, or screw.

Sheathing

In electrical work, the material covering a cable and holding its constituent wires together. In structural work, the first covering of boards or waterproof material on the outside walls of a frame house or on a roof.

Shellac

A natural clear wood finish made of insect secretions suspended in denatured alcohol and used for finishing fine furniture. It stains easily, is not waterproof, can be softened by alcohol, and has poor heat resistance.

Shim

A thin, often tapered piece of wood or other substance used to fill space for support, leveling, or fit.

Sill

A horizontal piece that forms the base of a structural frame.

Single-hung window

A window with two sashes, one above the other, in which only one sash (usually the lower) can be moved.

Soffit

The underside of a roof overhang, often covered with a soffit panel having small openings for venting.

Solder

An alloy of tin and lead used when melted to join metal surfaces such as pipes and plumbing fittings. Also, to join two pieces of metal using heat, flux, and this alloy.

Spackling compound

A pastelike substance used to fill and repair cracks and small holes in drywall before painting.

Spline

A long, thin, flexible strip of rubber, fiber, or other material used to wedge something in place. For example, rubber spline is used to hold a piece of screening in the frame of a window screen and fiber spline is used to hold a sheet of caning in place in the seat of a chair.

Square

Forming a perfect 90-degree angle.

Stile

A vertical member of a structure such as a door or cabinet.

Strike

To level and smooth a new mortar joint in masonry work after the mortar sets but before it hardens.

Stucco

A brittle, durable, cement-based material used to form a hard finish on exterior walls.

Stud

A vertical framing member to which sheathing, drywall, paneling, and other finish material may be attached.

Subfloor

A continuous sheet of plywood or other sturdy material that extends under all the walls of a frame house and onto which the underlayment and finish flooring are laid.

Template

A pattern or mold to guide the cutting or shaping of a workpiece.

Tenon

A protrusion cut into one part of a joint to fit a matching mortise in the second part of the joint .

Terminal screw

One of several screws, often color coded for safety, on an electrical device such as a switch or receptacle by which the wires are fastened.

Thread-joint sealant

A liquid or paste, or a type of self-adhesive tape used to seal and lubricate a threaded joint.

Trap

A loop of pipe in a plumbing fixture such as a sink or toilet that holds a small amount of water to form a seal that prevents sewer gas from escaping into the room.

Undercut

To cut back the sides of a hole slightly so that the mouth of the hole is narrower than the bottom, locking in a patch filling the hole.

Underlayment

A layer of plywood or other rough flooring installed over the subfloor after the walls of a frame house are built and to which the finish flooring (carpet, tile, hardwood, etc.) is attached.

Valley

The joint where two sloping sections of a roof meet.

Vapor barrier

A sheet of plastic or other nonporous material that retards the movement of water vapor through walls, floors, and ceilings.

Varnish

Any of a variety of tough, clear, durable wood finishes that resist water, heat, and alcohol. Most varnishes that are available today are synthetic.

Volt

The amount of force needed or used to push electricity through a wire.

Watt

The quantity of electricity being used at any given moment. The number of watts is determined by multiplying volts times amps.

Weather stripping

A long, thin, flexible length of waterproof material used to seal gaps around the edges of doors and windows to block out moisture and drafts.

Index

This book was produced by Redefinition, Inc.,
for The Reader's Digest Association, Inc.,
in cooperation with *The Family Handyman* magazine.

If you have any questions or comments, feel free to write us at:

The Family Handyman
7900 International Drive
Suite 950
Minneapolis, MN 55425

Measuring the Metric Way

Use these guides and tables to convert between English and metric measuring systems.

FASTENERS

Nails are sold by penny size or penny weight (expressed by the letter d). Length is designated by the penny size. Some common lengths are:

2d	(25 mm/1 in.)
6d	(51 mm/2 in.)
10d	(76 mm/3 in.)
20d	(102 mm/4 in.)
40d	(127 mm/5 in.)
60d	(152 mm/6 in.)

Below are metric and imperial equivalents of some common **bolts**:

10 mm	⅜ in.
12 mm	½ in.
16 mm	⅝ in.
20 mm	¾ in.
25 mm	1 in.
50 mm	2 in.
65 mm	2½ in.
70 mm	2¾ in.

CALCULATING CONCRETE REQUIREMENTS

Multiply length by width to get the slab area in square meters. Then read across, under whichever of three thicknesses you prefer, to see how many cubic meters of concrete you will need.

Area in square meters (m^2) (length x width)	Thickness in millimeters		
	100	130	150
	volume in cubic meters (m^3)		
5	0.50	0.65	0.75
10	1.00	1.30	1.50
20	2.00	2.60	3.00
30	3.00	3.90	4.50
40	4.00	5.20	6.00
50	5.00	6.50	7.50

If a greater volume of concrete is required, multiply by the appropriate number. To lay a 100-millimeter-thick patio in an area 6 meters wide and 10 meters long, for example, estimate as follows: 6 meters x 10 meters = 60 meters square = area. Using the chart above, simply double the concrete quantity for a 30-meter-square, 100-millimeter-thick slab (2 x 3 m^3 = 6 m^3) or add the quantities for 10 m^2 and 50 m^2 (1 m^3 + 5 m^3 = 6 m^3).